EEVeTeC

EEVeTeC

The McGregor Solution for Managing the Pains of Fitness

**Dr. Rob Roy McGregor
and Stephen E. Devereux**

Illustrated by Bill Hoest

HOUGHTON MIFFLIN COMPANY BOSTON   1982

Library of Congress Cataloging in Publication Data

McGregor, Rob Roy, date
   EEVeTeC.

   Bibliography: p.
   1. Sports — Safety measures.   2. Physical education
and training.   3. Sports — Accidents and injuries.
4. Sports — Physiological aspects.   I. Devereux, Stephen E.
II. Title.
GV344.M37   617′.1027   81-20197
ISBN 0-395-32042-9   AACR2

Printed in the United States of America

D 10 9 8 7 6 5 4 3 2 1

For Jennifer, Robbie, Gordon, and Molly McGregor —
and especially Barbara — who have given so freely of their
patience and support.

For all of the patients whose confidence and cooperation
have helped to inspire this book.

———————————

And for M.K.D. . . . "finis origine pendet."

Acknowledgments

OUR THANKS TO Kimball Prince, television commentator, recreational athlete, and bon vivant, for getting us together during the fall of 1978 and encouraging us to think about a book.

Thanks to M. Richard Robinson, Jr., president of Scholastic Magazines, Inc., for his encouragement and help during the early stages of this project.

Special thanks to Bill and Bunny Hoest. When we realized that we wanted something special in our illustrations, we had the great good fortune to be referred to a man who is not only one of the most talented cartoonists in the world today, but is also a warm, engaging, creative personality. An inspiration throughout the project, Bill Hoest has contributed more to the tone of *EEVeTeC* than we could ever have imagined.

Special thanks to Bruce Weber, editor of *Scholastic Coach Magazine,* who helped us write and rewrite sections of the text after our first draft was completed in 1979. Without Bruce Weber, *EEVeTeC* would not resemble the book that follows. We are grateful to him for his efforts, his patience, and his friendship.

Thanks and a tip of the hat to Grant Ujifusa of Random House who lured us, lulled us, and finally let us go — older but wiser!

Our profound thanks to Grace Heron, loyal secretary to Rob Roy McGregor Associates, Inc., since 1978, who has unstintingly provided accurate and efficient typing, filing, and a general sense of direction, stemming from her many years of doing the same thing for other authors.

Thanks to Dr. Stan Plagenhoef, who helped us immeasurably during the spring of 1979 with our understanding of biomechanics and the evolution of our "Anatomy of Activity."

The following researchers worked extensively to contact experts, accumulate information, and draft the "other sports" material that appears in chapter 8: Betsy Gillis; Susan Goodkin; Lester Greenman; Gordon Scannel; Becky Tung; Ellen Webber; Jay Weinstein; and especially Elaine Garofoli, without whom our initial months of research would not have been possible.

The following magazines kindly ran solicitations for us during the summer of 1979. As a result, we received hundreds of interesting and helpful letters from their readers: *Tennis Magazine, Runner's World, Golf Digest, Swimming World, Bike World, Bowling, National Racquetball,* and *Racquet.*

EEVeTeC has been through more than a dozen rewrites. Throughout it all, our typists have been extraordinarily patient. Thanks to Susan Clermont, who got us started. And special thanks to Dale Rinkel, who managed somehow to find the energy, patience, and discipline to keep going, even after we told her "one last time" so many times she must have thought us crazy.

To Ruth Hapgood, our editor, and Austin Olney, editor in chief of Houghton Mifflin, we owe more than the usual authors' thanks. We had begun to founder and started to doubt, when their confidence and enthusiasm gave us the energy to see this project through to its end.

Ours is the third book to be written by a staff member of Sports Medicine Resource, Inc. Always hard pressed by our growing patient load, both the professional and clerical staff provided help whenever solicited — and most important, when needed but unsolicited.

Finally, we have consulted with literally hundreds of doctors, athletes, and other experts during the past three years. No list could possibly be complete. In particular, we recognize that we owe special thanks to the dozens of people we've quoted in the following pages and whose stories we've told, despite the fact that their names are by and large not listed below.

FROM THE MEDICAL COMMUNITY: Dr. Tenley Albright, Dr.

Sidney Alexander, Dr. Joseph Arena, Dr. Robert B. Arnot, Dr. Arthur Bernhang, Dr. Arthur Boland, Dr. David Brody, Dr. Robert Buxbaum, Dr. William Clancy, Dr. Irving Dardick, Dr. Arthur Dickinson, Dr. Charles Dilman, Dr. John Donovan, Dr. James Forbes, Dr. James Glick, Dr. Harry Hlavac, Dr. Craig Hoyt, Dr. Stanley James, Dr. Howard Knuttgen, Donald Labourr (R.P.T., A.T.C.), Dr. Robert E. Leach, the late Dr. John L. Marshall, Dr. James O. Morse, Dr. Stanley Newell, Dr. Arthur Pappas, Dr. Howard Parker, Dr. Alan Richardson, Dr. Michael Robinson, Dr. Alan Ryan, Dr. Joel Sapperstein, Dr. Robert Scardina, Dr. Joseph Seder, Dr. William Shea, Dr. George Sheehan, Dr. David Simmons, Dr. George Snook, Dr. William Southmayd, Dr. Kenneth Sparks, Dr. Victor Spear, Dr. Marc Stess, Peter Stone (R.P.T.), Dr. Cornelius Stover, Dr. Ginger Weeks, Dr. Gordon Weiker.

FROM THE SPORTS WORLD (ATHLETES, COACHES, TRAINERS, EXPERTS): Ginny Akabane, Arthur Ashe, George Atkinson, Jack Barnaby, David A. Benjamin, Joe Bernal, Lenny Bernheimer, Asher Birnbaum, Dave Cowens, James "Doc" Counsilman, Tom Derderian, Rick Devereux, Dave Fish, Jim Fixx, Jerry Hilecher, Gul Kahn, Mo Kahn, Rob Kiesel, Bill Norris, Stan Smith, Roger Wetmore, Gary Wiren.

Contents

Acknowledgments   vii

Foreword by James F. Fixx   xiii

Introduction: At the Starting Line   xv

I. Managing the Pains of Fitness

1. Introducing the McGregor Solution   3
2. EEVeTeC Explained   19

II. Why EEVeTeC Works

3. The Anatomy of Activity   37
4. Getting into Shape   59
5. Picking Your Sport   80

III. EEVeTeC Applied

6. Tennis   95
7. Running   153
8. Other Sports   204

IV. When EEVeTeC Isn't the Answer

9. Sportache or Medical Problem?   241
10. Self-help for Inflammation   261
11. OK, Doctor, It's Your Turn   283

Afterword: It Hurts but You Don't Want to Quit   299

Foreword
by James F. Fixx

NOT LONG AFTER I had finished writing *The Complete Book of Running* a new development in the sport caught my attention. It was that whenever athletes became injured, in increasing numbers they were relying on specially trained foot doctors known as podiatrists. Wanting to discover whatever I could about this freshly ascendant breed of healer, I began asking questions: What, exactly, do podiatrists do? Which of them are most highly regarded? Repeatedly, I noticed as I pursued my inquiries, the same recommendations kept turning up, and before long I found myself in the office of an articulate, energetic, joyfully iconoclastic podiatrist with the story-book name of Rob Roy McGregor.

I spent part of a day with Dr. McGregor. I watched him treat, cajole, and encourage patients. I listened to his thoughts on sportsmedicine. ("If you don't hurt," he said, "I don't want to see you. You don't need me.") By the time I left his office I knew I had encountered something new and quite wonderful. Here, for the first time in my experience, was a doctor who would, it was apparent, rather not treat you if he could avoid it. Plainly, he was happiest if you could treat yourself — or, best of all, if you could somehow avoid treatment altogether.

This arresting viewpoint illuminates every page and paragraph of the present book. Unlike most sportsmedicine guides, *EEVeTeC* is not a mere pain-by-pain compendium but a thoroughgoing, practical work of sports philosophy that belongs in the library not just of every athlete but of every physician, of whatever sort, who has occasion to see athletes. It elucidates a method for (1) avoiding injury whenever possible and (2) dealing with unavoidable injury in a logical, proven manner that every athlete can devise for himself or herself as the occasion requires.

There is, in short, no book anywhere quite like it. I will not be surprised if it becomes a classic in its field.

Introduction:
At the Starting Line

WHEN STEVE DEVEREUX AND I had already completed more than six months of research for this book, it was the summer of 1979, and I was beginning to think seriously about running the Miami Marathon during January 1980. Throughout August and September I endured my share of aches and pains as I increased my weekly mileage. Steve, in turn, was teaching tennis on Long Island as he had during so many previous summers — with one important difference. For the first time in his life, Steve found himself teaching without being able to swing a racket. He was trying to rehabilitate a badly injured right elbow, which had finally developed into a classic case of "tennis elbow" after Steve had failed to use EEVeTeC himself during the previous months and years.

You'll learn all about the self-help system we call EEVeTeC in the following pages. During the summer of 1979, however, Steve and I were only beginning to comprehend the importance of what we were discovering. We knew we were on the right track, and that we had something important to say to a great number of recreational athletes. But we still had a long way to go to complete this book. Autumn turned into winter; race day finally came and I finished Miami; Steve eventually started hitting tennis balls again; we talked endlessly to athletes, doctors, and other experts; and finally the "McGregor Solution" was born.

During the past three years Steve and I have become all the more persuaded that EEVeTeC is the answer, no matter what your sport, no matter who you are. Recently, I saw an article in a medical journal about "Space Invader's wrist" — a condition that is apparently developing with alarming frequency among the enthusiasts of certain video games. Then there is "musher's knee," a complaint that dog sled drivers are now reporting in significant numbers. And, of course, there are the thousands of runners and other athletes who keep coming through my door at Longwood Podiatry Group, Inc., in Brookline, Massachusetts, many of them with chronic running and tennis problems that I know they could have avoided if they'd used EEVeTeC at the first sign of their aches.

Last September I gave a slide presentation entitled "Sport-aches" to the runners gathered at a clinic before the 1981 America's Marathon in Chicago — the first marathon I'd run since Miami in 1980. Before I dimmed the lights and showed various slides made from the illustrations Bill Hoest drew for this book, I asked a few questions of the 350 runners before me.

How many in the audience had ever experienced "runner's knee," Achilles' tendinitis, anterior compartment syndrome, or any of the other common medical problems that I routinely see in my sportsmedicine practice? A number of hands went up.

How many had experienced a twinge of knee, ankle, hip, or foot pain any time during either a race or a training run? Not surprisingly, virtually everyone raised a hand.

Finally, I asked how many in the audience had ever gone to a doctor because of sports-related pain. An overwhelming majority of hands were raised. When I asked how many felt their doctor had been of little or no help, a surprising number of hands stayed up.

"All of you, no doubt, experienced occasional aches while training for tomorrow's race," I remarked. "Many of you have been frustrated at the inability of doctors to help with these aches. Nevertheless, all of you have somehow managed to avoid developing acute or chronic pain, despite experiencing classic warning signals. That twinge of knee pain could have developed into runner's knee, but it didn't, or you wouldn't be here today. Your doctor probably didn't help, and you may not even know what made the difference. But I do. I know what you changed or adjusted, without even knowing where you ached or why.

"The answer is EEVeTeC," I explained. "That's what I'm here to talk about. I have a simple self-help system that you can use to identify your problems in the future, and to manage, if not avoid, recurrent pain. That's the subject of the following slide show, which I call 'Sportaches.' "

As I have learned to expect when I talk about EEVeTeC, many people came up to me after my presentation in Chicago to say that they had finally begun to understand what it was they had been doing all along to stay out of trouble as athletes.

·

EEVeTeC is a process, not a panacea. We don't pretend that we can work miracles, or that all of you will manage to avoid developing acute or chronic aches and pains. We only know that EEVeTeC works, at least if you give it a chance *before* you develop a medical condition such as tennis elbow, runner's knee, golfer's hip, or any of the many other complaints that people regularly bring to my office. EEVeTeC is also the key to rehabilitating your body after an injury.

While I was training last summer for America's Marathon, there were a number of days when I sensed I was about to get into trouble. On one occasion, about six weeks before the race, I started to develop some knee pain that really scared me — until I remembered EEVeTeC. I checked my shoes and found that I needed a new pair. I changed the course I'd been following during my training runs around my home in Concord, Massachusetts, to minimize running on roads and confronting hills. I started stretching an extra ten minutes before and after each run. And my knee pain disappeared entirely.

Every recreational athlete routinely makes similar adjustments to avoid aches, whether or not he or she understands why such efforts make any difference. That's the purpose of this book. We'll explain *why* EEVeTeC works at the same time we teach you once and for all *how* to manage the pains of fitness.

There are a few of you who should be extra careful — no one should use EEVeTeC for backache, for example, at least not without talking to a doctor first; likewise, if you have a history of surgery or previous injury, you would be wise to consult your doctor before attempting to manage the pains of fitness on your own — but most of you can profitably use what Steve and I have learned during the past three years of research and writing. Of that, I am completely certain.

•

I recall vividly how I felt while I was getting ready to go to Daley Plaza for the start of America's Marathon last September. I was more than a little nervous. Then I remembered that the difficult thing about running a marathon is getting ready to run it. In Chicago I felt better as soon as I remembered that I was already a "winner." To those of us who play sports for fun or recreation, to win is simply to be able to play.

There I was at the starting line, along with thousands of other runners who had gathered to see Chicago on foot. All of us had used EEVeTeC in some way to arrive at that moment. We were all "winners," even before the race began.

My hope, of course, is that you will use this book to ensure that you are ready to participate in your favorite sport whenever and wherever you want to. Good luck and Godspeed.

ROB ROY MCGREGOR

April 1982
Concord, Massachusetts

Part I

MANAGING THE PAINS OF FITNESS

Equipment

Environment

Velocity

Technique

Conditioning

1

Introducing the McGregor Solution

MOST BOOKS START with a premise. Not this one. We'll begin with a promise.

If you play sports — if you ever lace up a pair of running shoes or tennis sneakers; if you ever swing a racket, a bowling ball, or a golf club; if you ski, ride a bicycle, or jump rope; if you go for long walks or regular swims; if you do anything dynamic in an attempt to stay fit or achieve a more satisfactory quality of life — sooner or later you are going to need this book.

That's a promise, an unqualified guarantee. It's a guarantee we can offer without hesitation.

You're going to need this book if you play sports because sooner or later you're going to develop a nagging joint-related pain. It doesn't matter why or how much you play your sport. Sportaches happen in all sports and at every level of competition. And when it's your turn to be hampered or sidelined, you'll discover something a lot of athletes already know. Doctors often simply can't help.

How do I know? I'm a sportsmedicine doctor.

•

Until recently there was no such thing as sportsmedicine. There is still no degree in sportsmedicine and no such academic discipline. Doctors become sportsmedicine specialists because of an interest in sports and sports-related problems. Sportsmedicine doctors simply declare themselves.

It happened to me one September morning, a couple of days after Labor Day, 1973. A mountain of paperwork had brought me to my podiatric clinic early. In those days I spent most of my time tending to "high-risk" feet. People with high-risk feet have diseases that make them especially susceptible to sudden, serious infection, ulceration, and gangrene — sometimes even necessitating amputation. My patients were generally sick people, and I was a doctor who specialized in treating their foot problems.

As I sat in my chair, with my back to the door, completing all those exotic forms that turn doctors into accountants or data processers, I never dreamed that the course of my life was about to change.

Suddenly I sensed a presence in the room. I turned and saw a man about five feet ten inches tall, with the most intense eyes I'd ever seen. His was a beady-eyed, challenging stare, a look I have seen many times since — the hallmark of the injured long-distance runner.

"Hi, I'm Eric Groon," he said.

"Your appointment is at 9:00 A.M.," I replied. "You're an hour early. I'll be with you in a few minutes."

I went back to work, but Eric didn't move. After what seemed an endless silence, I spun around again in my chair.

"Dr. Hurwitz sent me," he said. I could sense the desperation in his voice. "He said you are a runner and know all about runners' problems. I'm a runner, I have a problem, and I need your help."

It was just that simple. For years I had been consumed with the problems of high-risk feet. Suddenly, I became a doctor concentrating on runners' aches. When Eric Groon started to explain his problem to me, I began to practice sportsmedicine. I went from specializing in high-risk feet to studying and treating something we never learned about in medical school — the "high-use" foot of an athlete.

My colleague, Ed Hurwitz, had really put me on the spot. Without any warning, he had sent me a patient, promising "miraculous" results. Of course, Ed Hurwitz's endorsement was very flattering. It was far from true, but it presented a challenge — something I've never backed away from. After all, I *was* a runner. At that time I actually ran a couple of miles now and then. And if my friend Ed Hurwitz thought I knew my stuff, well then I'd just have to know my stuff.

I got right down to business. "How much are you running?" I asked Eric Groon.

"I was doing seventy until I hurt myself three weeks ago. Since then I've had to cut way back."

"Seventy?" I thought to myself, "Seventy what — and where — and when?" I tried to keep my composure, but this problem had to be met head on.

"Seventy what?" I asked.

"Seventy miles a week," he replied. "What did you think?"

During the next hour my thinking was clarified considerably. Together, Eric and I explored his running history, his training pattern, and his problem. I conducted a complete examination, including a thorough look at all of his running shoes, which Eric had been bright enough to bring along with him.

Before long I'd confessed my relative lack of running experience. However, since I'd been caring for feet for twenty-two years, I told Eric that I thought I could help him. I knew I wanted to help, so Eric and I went at it.

Within a year I'd treated Eric and a few of his friends as well, like John Cedarholm (a recent United States fifty-kilometer record holder) and Jim Shapiro (who went on to write two books about marathoning), all quality athletes. Eric, John, and Jim eventually eliminated their aches. Each also improved considerably on his performance in previous Boston Marathons. And I ended up as one of the podiatrists tending to the runners at the finish line.

That was it. I was hooked. By the next year, I, too, was running five miles or more every day. I completed my first Boston Marathon in 1975. For better or worse, I had become an avid runner and a sportsmedicine doctor.

•

Today, most of my patients at Longwood Podiatry Group, Inc., in Brookline are either professional or recreational athletes. They are not just runners. The people I see during an average week complain of a variety of aches and ailments incurred on tracks, roads, slopes, rinks, courts, and golf courses.

Athletes need doctors. There isn't a single dynamic activity where a doctor isn't required at one time or another. However, at least half the people I see regularly in my practice have one thing in common. They shouldn't be in my office. I mean it. I wish they'd never come to see me. I'm the sportsmedicine doctor who's trying to keep patients out of his waiting room.

It's true. And it's not because I don't like people. Nor is it because people don't like me. There are actually two reasons why I try to discourage a number of patients from bringing their problems to me: (1) I don't want to be the doctor who frustrates and angers people when he can't help them, and (2) I don't want to be the doctor who is himself discouraged when there's nothing a doctor can do.

Les Van Pelt is a good example of someone who should never have wasted his time and money coming to see me. Unlike Eric Groon, John Cedarholm, and Jim Shapiro, all of whom are among the athletic elite, Les is just an average recreational athlete. He makes his living as an electrical engineer and runs as a hobby — and he cares a whole lot about running.

Like many other runners, Les is very bright and determined. His sessions with a doctor are incredible. Les asks more questions than a prosecuting attorney. He's determined to get to the bottom of everything and wants very badly to understand whatever a doctor is saying to him. Unfortunately, there's often not very much that any doctor, including myself, can say to a patient like Les.

The first time I met Les he was complaining of a vague pain in his ankle. He told me that his discomfort usually increased during his daily morning run and that his ankle often continued to bother him for three or four hours afterward. By the time we found each other, Les had developed a certain degree of inflammation. That presented no real difficulty. Doctors, of course, are trained to deal with inflammation. I knew I could help Les with his swelling and acute pain. However, he could just as easily have managed his inflammation without my help, as we'll explain in chapter 10. More important, since I had no idea what was causing Les's ache, I knew that we would be treating his symptoms and not his problem. Unless we could figure out why Les was hurting, I had to expect that he would experience occasional pain again as soon as he resumed running.

Les and I compiled a complete history. It revealed no significant accidents or previous problems. I was concerned to learn that Les's mother and father had both suffered from arthritis. But at age thirty-seven Les showed no signs of being arthritic. In fact, he was in superb health. His self-diagnosis indicated that his occasional joint aches — he had had problems with his hips and shoulders as well as with his ankle — were the natural result of a high level of activity. I concurred. Les told me that in addition to running he played tennis and did some cross-country skiing and hiking during the winter months.

My examination revealed that Les was "grossly normal" — a medical term meaning that he was as healthy as could be expected. X-rays indicated some signs of wear and tear in several of his ankle and foot joints. But in view of Les's athletic history, none of what I saw was unusual.

As is all too often the case with patients like Les, I was stuck. I had nothing very profound to offer in the way of treatment or advice. Since Les had explained that he generally ran first thing in the morning, I suggested that he might have fewer problems if he stretched a little more before each run. He certainly seemed to be a little tight. That was the best I could do. I felt guilty and inadequate, but I prescribed a specific series of stretching exercises and told Les to keep in touch.

Four weeks passed. I finally got a phone call.

"Doc," Les reported, "I did your exercises faithfully every day. No help. Then one day, as I drove to work with my ankle throbbing, I thought, 'Why don't I try running in the afternoon? Maybe the activities of the day might help loosen me up.' "

Les had solved his problem. He now runs every day without pain. Having experimented with a variety of solutions, he had finally found an answer on his own. For Les to do what he wanted to do, he had to do it when his body was relatively limber. The exercises I had prescribed for Les might have solved his problem. They weren't a bad guess. But that's all they were — just a guess. I couldn't be with Les during the intervening four weeks while he considered and tried lots of other adjustments in his running equipment and environment. Les had to solve his own problem. And I really couldn't help. He had to do it by himself.

Like Les, more than 50 percent of the patients I see aren't sick. Nor are they injured. They don't need a doctor. Of course they're hurting. But they don't have the kind of acute or chronic medical condition that requires my help. That's why I say that half the people I see every day should be treating themselves, taking care of their own ailments.

•

If you're an athlete who's hurting — and if you play sports, sooner or later you will be — you may think your only choices are to see a doctor or ignore your pain. Both choices may be very wrong.

The story of Les Van Pelt should help persuade you that the first option isn't always correct. If you're in a doctor's office when you shouldn't be, you're wasting the doctor's time as well as your own time and money. But playing in pain may not be any smarter. If you ignore a minor hurt, it may very well become a major hurt — and a major problem.

Perhaps you're asking yourself, "If doctors don't have all the answers and I can't play through my pain, what am I supposed to do?" Your ache may not require treatment by a doctor, but it obviously does require some sort of attention, since it just won't go away.

There is a solution. That's what this book is all about. You can manage your own aches and pains, especially if they aren't acute or haven't become chronic — and sometimes even if they have. You just need to follow a simple formula, making certain adjustments in the way you play and prepare to play your sport. It may sound complicated at first, but as you go through our formula step by step, you'll find that it's actually quite easy to do as Les Van Pelt did. You should be able to solve your own problem.

Let's say you're a runner who suffers from leg pain when you run. That's the problem Polly Shelly brought to my office a couple of years ago.

"I don't know if I really should be here," she explained. "When I first began to run, I had pains in both knees, but they went away. Now, however, my right leg has been bothering me more and more, and it seems to have kicked up some discomfort in my right hip. My husband says that if I gut it out, my pain will go away as I train. Will it?"

Or maybe you're a tennis player who dreads backhands because they hurt. Steve Devereux, my co-author, remembers seeing a better-than-average player at his club who had suddenly started running around his backhand at every opportunity. Six months before the same player had given Steve a good match, primarily because his topspin backhand was so effective.

"Why are you running around your backhand?" Steve asked him.

"I can't stand it anymore," the man responded. "Every time I hit a backhand, I get a sharp pain in my elbow. My forehand may not be as effective, but at least it doesn't hurt." Does that sound familiar?

Or perhaps you're a golfer whose front hip aches on the downswing. During a recent flight to Chicago the passenger sitting

next to me was a businessman in his early forties. He saw me reading a running magazine. ''I don't know how you can run,'' he said. ''I tried it, but it was just too bloody painful.'' Golf, it turned out, was his game. One reason he had taken up golf was because he figured it would be safe. At least he'd be free of those awful aches and pains his runner friends were always talking about. However, things had not worked out quite that way.

Although he seemed to be in pretty good shape, this particular golfer said he had started giving away more strokes than he should because of a recurrent pain in his left hip, which was causing him to compromise his swing. He told me he was beginning to feel that he'd be better off playing something a little less strenuous — like chess.

Or maybe you're a swimmer whose shoulder hurts whenever your arm enters the water. Swimmers have their own aches and pains, and occasional shoulder pain is particularly common. Olympic gold-medalist John Naber told me about his experience with ''swimmer's shoulder'' after we both had spoken at a pre-race clinic in Los Angeles. A swimmer addressing a group of runners? Why not? John pointed out to the rapt audience that swimmers could develop aches just like runners.

Or perhaps you're a bicyclist who suffers leg pain whenever you thrust against your bicycle pedal. My friend Mel Schwarz recently decided to give up running because of constant heel pain. Since he didn't want to become completely idle, Mel turned to bicycling. His heel pain disappeared, but Mel has now developed a knee problem, which has started to make even bicycling seem like too much bother.

If any of these case histories sounds like yours, this book is for you. *You* are the athlete I'm talking about.

Let's go a step further. Suppose you've had your pain for some time. You've neglected to do anything about it, and it's finally gone beyond the occasional stage. You now have a non-stop problem. Your aching joint hurts all the time, not just when you run or hit your backhand or pedal your bike.

A chronic ache means that you're out of options. Plan on weeks or months of rest and treatment. Only when your pain finally dissipates will you be ready to resume your favorite sport. But even after rest and medical treatment you may not be completely cured. Should you expect to remain pain-free if you go back to playing the same sport, in the same way, with the same equipment, and under the same conditions? Sad to say, the answer is usually no.

Pain is caused by a problem. When you hurt there's a reason. If you let an ache become acute or chronic, your pain can be treated by a doctor. However, when your ache finally dissipates, you'll still have your problem. You'll still need advice that most doctors won't be able to give you. This important lesson is one that I was fortunate enough to learn early in my sportsmedicine career. And I learned it in a memorable fashion.

I opened the door to our runners' clinic one afternoon and in walked Ian McCausland, backpack and all. He was quite a sight. In the process of taking his initial history, I routinely asked for Ian's address.

"Halifax," he replied.

"Halifax, Massachusetts," I said slowly as I wrote.

"No, sir," said Ian, "that's Halifax, Nova Scotia."

"And what brings you here?"

He looked me straight in the eye and answered, "I came here to see you."

"You must be joking," I said, shaking my head.

"No, sir," said Ian, "I'm trying to make my college track team and I have this heel pain. I got some pills from my doctor and, sure enough, the pain went away. But when I started to run again, my pain came back. Then the doctor gave me a shot that got rid of the pain again — temporarily. But when I started to run, there it was again. My doctor threw up his hands. He said he didn't know what to do next. So I wrote to Dr. George Sheehan. Dr. Sheehan suggested that you were the doctor who could solve my problem. So here I am."

Fortunately for both of us, Ian's problem wasn't new to me. His Canadian doctor had been treating the symptoms of a problem for which I'd already developed a system of management. I prescribed some specific changes in Ian's running equipment, technique, and conditioning. McCausland went back to Nova Scotia — and made the team.

If your case is like Ian McCausland's, this book is also for you. *You,* too, are the athlete I'm talking about.

•

If you have been suffering occasional pain while you play, you probably don't need a doctor. Likewise, if you've recovered from an acute or chronic hurt, most doctors won't know what

SPORTACHE

you need to do to avoid a relapse when you start to play your sport again. Why are most doctors so helpless? Because you don't have a medical problem. Your condition will not respond to medical treatment.

Nevertheless, *you can be cured*. You won't usually find the answer at your doctor's office, because there is no medical cure for your problem. You'll have to treat yourself, looking within the context of your sport for the answer and being ready to make adjustments in when, where, and how you play, as well as how you prepare to play.

You have a *sportache*. Sportaches are the pains of fitness. If you have a sportache, you are healthy, but you hurt. Sportaches are very different from the illnesses of the sick or the injuries of the disabled.

We'll give you a much more thorough answer to the question, Sportache or medical problem? in chapter 9. For now, just remember that the pain of a sportache usually stops when you stop your sport. Sportaches are a problem in every dynamic sport. Whether you play your sport to become fit, or work at your fitness to be able to play your sport, sportaches are the price you'll eventually have to pay for being an athlete.

The word *sportache* is a simple two-syllable compound word, combining *sport* and *ache*. If you have a sportache, you are not sick, and you are not injured. Therefore, traditional words like *injury* and *ailment* are inappropriate.

Remember Polly Shelly's leg pain as she ran? That was a sportache. Steve Devereux's friend's tennis elbow pain? That was a sportache. The traveling golfer's aching hip? Jim Naber's swimmer's shoulder? Mel Schwarz's bicycler's knee? Those were sportaches, too. Sportaches aren't the exclusive province of runners, tennis players, golfers, swimmers, or cyclists. Bowlers are also vulnerable, as are skiers, racquetball and squash players, and a variety of other recreational athletes.

Painful sportaches can be managed, if not avoided. But doctors usually can't help — at least not until your condition becomes acute or chronic. You have to help yourself. We call the answer the "McGregor Solution." It isn't complicated. You don't need a medical degree to understand it. And you won't get a bill at the end of the month either.

The McGregor Solution is designed to help you eliminate your own sportaches. It's based on common sense, as well as fundamental knowledge of how the human body works. An elaborate scientific explanation is unnecessary. After years of observation, we know that the solution works and we think we know why. We hope scientists will one day be able to show us precisely how it works, with carefully developed and statistically valid tables of results. For the time being, however, we know from experience that the McGregor Solution is effective. I am persuaded that it's the only answer for the various athletes who show up regularly in my office with a history of sports-related pain but without a currently acute or chronic medical problem. If you have a sportache, the McGregor Solution is the only way you can eliminate your ache and get on with your favorite activity.

If science always turned you off in school, don't despair. You are going to understand the McGregor Solution, despite the fact that we'll have to use a few seemingly scientific terms to explain how it works. We'll go through the solution several times, step by step, until every element becomes crystal clear.

·

The McGregor Solution began to evolve when I first realized that many of the patients I was seeing needed more than mere treatment for their pain and other symptoms. Early in my sports-medicine career it dawned on me that the majority of the people I was seeing also needed help with the problems that were causing their sports-related pain.

Eric Groon actually started pushing me toward the solution. As I've already confessed, when Eric first came to my office, I was only an occasional runner. I was jogging a couple of miles every few days, but I was by no means an expert about running. My desire to help Eric forced me to go out and learn more about everything runners were doing, starting with the shoes they were wearing. In particular, I had to become more knowledgeable about the kinds of special shoe inserts (orthotics) that runners were using. Runners like Eric were logging up to 120 miles a week, and as a result their needs were very different from those of the patients with high-risk feet I had previously been serving. Suddenly, I was seeing patients whose problems were more a matter of exceptionally high use.

Even as I expanded my own running horizons and became

increasingly knowledgeable about the runner's primary piece of equipment — the running shoe — I consulted a variety of sources to learn about the effects of concrete, hills, sand, and snow on the runner's body. I had to understand how the runner's environment affected the body, as well as how increasing or decreasing speed and adjusting stride length could make a difference during and after a run.

I also had to learn how to run. I remember saying during an early television interview that "running is the only sport that doesn't require lessons." I've since discovered that's not entirely true. In point of fact, you're a lot better off as a runner if you learn to run properly. To help patients like Eric Groon, I eventually concluded that I had to know about running technique and become an expert on the runner's equipment and environment as well.

Finally, I began to appreciate the importance of conditioning. After years of evaluating feet according to their appearance, I realized that the only important thing for a runner is what his or her feet are strong enough and flexible enough to do.

Johnny Kelley's feet are a good example of the fact that appearances can be deceiving when it comes to athletes' feet. Johnny was the Boston Marathon winner in 1935 and 1945 and an Olympian in his forties. Now well over seventy, he is still a marathon runner at an age when many folks are thrilled just to be able to get up in the morning.

One of the highlights of my life as a runner was doing six miles with Johnny on his seventieth birthday. We enjoyed our ramble through the peaceful woods and along the shore front surrounding his Cape Cod home. As we cooled off following our run, with feet up and beverage in hand, I asked Johnny if he'd ever had any physical problems.

"No," he said, shaking his head vigorously. "Not one."

"Nothing?" I said, almost disbelieving. "Feet, legs, knees, hips? Nothing?"

"Nothing," he replied firmly.

Then he took off his shoes and socks. I was shocked. I remembered all my textbook drawings and photos of bad feet; Johnny had all the classic problems. In fact, he might have been the model for all those photos and drawings. What a foot — bunions, hammertoes, low arches — the worst! And yet Johnny had never had a foot problem. Never an ache.

After I saw Johnny Kelley's feet, I realized something I've never forgotten since. It doesn't matter what an athlete's foot looks like: the important thing is how it functions. High-risk feet can be identified by appearance. However, the amount of use a foot can tolerate is more a function of conditioning than design. Conditioning, of course, can be equally decisive in other parts of an athlete's body, and we'll get to that in a later chapter.

•

Thus, the McGregor Solution began to take shape. When I had finally reasoned the whole thing out, I began to suspect that it would be applicable to all sports — not just running. Why couldn't it work for golfers and bowlers and tennis players? That's when Steve Devereux walked into my life — in pain.

My co-author first came to see me as a runner with knee pain. Eventually, we solved Steve's knee problem with orthotics, stretching exercises, and an adjustment in his running routine. We also discussed the fact that he had recently stepped up his running because of another bona fide sportache — elbow pain that had temporarily forced him to stop playing tennis.

An experienced tennis instructor and player, Steve explained that he had been having twinges of elbow pain for years. Then, suddenly, his ache had become acute. During one of our early meetings, I mentioned that I thought some of the things I had learned about managing runners' aches might be applicable to tennis players' problems as well. Steve was very interested. In fact, he quickly became a real advocate of what the two of us eventually decided to call the McGregor Solution. Steve found that the solution worked for the people he was instructing, as well as for his fellow pros and himself. At about the time he began hitting tennis balls again — with a new racket, a different backhand grip, and a new appreciation of the need to condition his forearm — Steve and I started working on this book.

•

What is the McGregor Solution? It's really nothing more than a formula by which you can adjust a series of variables, some of which determine the amount of stress your sport creates in key joints of your body, and others of which determine how much sport-related stress your body will be able to tolerate. The variables of the McGregor Solution are divided into five categories: equipment, environment, velocity, technique, and conditioning.

Steve and I spent many hours trying to come up with an easy way for you to remember the five elements of the McGregor Solution. Eventually, I remembered a friend in podiatric medical school who taught me the mnemonic, "*My Aunt Loves Periwinkles,*" to help me remember the letters *M, A, L,* and *P,* which stand for the four important types of bacteria: *M*onotrichous, *A*mphitrichous, *L*ophotrichous, and *P*eritrichous. It wasn't particularly artful, but it worked.

In thinking about a catchy phrase for the McGregor Solution, Steve and I eventually settled upon *Extra Endeavor Values True Courage,* and *Every Effort Very Truly Counts.* Neither one is quite as striking as my aunt and her periwinkles, but both phrases have the advantage of being very much in the spirit of the McGregor Solution. We also came up with a new word made of the first letters of *E*quipment, *E*nvironment, *V*elocity, *T*echnique, and *C*onditioning, or *E-E-Ve-Te-C.* We pronounce the word "evah-tech." As in, "If you're a rambling wreck, try EEVeTeC," or, "Make an easy check, with EEVeTeC." You'll be seeing the term *EEVeTeC* over and over throughout the remainder of this book.

Let's look at the elements of EEVeTeC one by one. Just to orient you, here is a quick description of each of the five components that constitute the McGregor Solution.

The first *E* is for *equipment*. Equipment includes the implements and accessories of your game, as well as your clothing and personal gear. If you're a golfer, equipment means your clubs, your bag, your balls, your tees, your gloves, your towel, your cap, your shoes, your sweater, your raingear, and so on. If you're a tennis player, equipment means your racket, your strings, your balls, your shorts, shirt, or skirt, your warm-up clothes, your sweatband(s), your sun visor. If you're a bowler, your equipment includes your ball, wrist guards, and shoes. And so forth. In other words, equipment means everything you use to play your favorite game, plus everything you wear before, during, and after play.

The second *E* is for *environment*. Environment covers a multitude of variables — including where you play, the surface you play on, when you play, against whom you play, and so on. Have you ever had trouble with the lighting when playing tennis indoors? Have you ever had to adjust your delivery on an overly slick bowling lane? Have you ever experienced unusual pain while running on flat concrete? These are environment problems.

Ve stands for *velocity*. Velocity is how fast or slow or hard you play your sport. If you're a tennis player, it's how hard you swing your racket. If you're a golfer, it's how fast you swing

your club. If you're a runner, it's how fast you try to run. If you're a swimmer, it's how hard you swim. And so forth.

Te stands for *technique*. How do you play your game? Do you have classic technique? The better your technique, the more chance you have to avoid developing sportaches. Technique is one of the five vital elements of the McGregor Solution. It means how you hit your backhand in tennis, how your foot strikes the ground as you run, how you start your downswing in golf, how your arm enters the water in swimming, and so on.

Finally, *C* is for *conditioning*. Conditioning is a concept most recreational athletes don't understand. It's a lot more comprehensive than many people think, and it plays a very important role in the prevention and management of sportaches. Conditioning includes your overall strength and flexibility, plus a proper warm-up and cool-down before and after play.

Once you know the five elements of EEVeTeC, the only remaining task is to know what to do about them. The key to the McGregor Solution is change. If you're having a problem — a sportache — you've got to make some basic changes in your equipment, environment, velocity, technique, or conditioning. Otherwise, your ache will continue to bother you and will probably get worse. How to use the McGregor Solution is the subject of the next chapter — ''EEVeTeC Explained.''

2
EEVeTeC Explained

No TWO BODIES are identical. Everyone knows, for example, that no two individuals have exactly the same fingerprints. Many recreational athletes fail to appreciate, however, that each of us also has a different tolerance for sport-related stress.

The McGregor Solution is a formula for managing the stress *your* sport places on *your* body. If you are experiencing pain when you play your favorite sport, one of two things must be happening.

1. The forces of your sport are too much for your body, meaning that you'll have to reduce those excessive sportforces if you want to continue playing.
2. Your tolerance for sportforces is less than it should be, usually because of poor technique or inadequate conditioning.

You can *eliminate sportaches* — manage stress — by adjusting your EEVeTeC to *reduce sportforces* or *increase your tolerance*. That's the basic principle behind the McGregor Solution.

This chapter will explain in detail how you can use EEVeTeC to avoid and manage your own sportaches, regardless of your sport. If you play tennis or run, you're in luck. There's a whole chapter in part III about each of those two very popular sports. If your sport is golf, racquetball, squash, bowling, bicycling, or swimming, there are specific tips for you in chapter 8, although in less detail. But even if we haven't talked in particular about your favorite activity in part III, the McGregor Solution will work for you. We're going to teach you how to use it in the following pages.

Reducing Forces

It's usually easier to reduce sportforces than it is to increase your body's tolerance for sports-related stress. The variables that you can adjust in your effort to reduce sportforces — *E*quipment, *E*nvironment, and *V*elocity — are generally easier to deal with than the variables that determine your body's tolerance for sportforces — *T*echnique and *C*onditioning. Most recreational athletes should therefore try to reduce sportforces as much as possible before they attempt to increase their tolerance for sports-related stress.

Imagine, for example, that you are a tennis player with elbow pain. If you are like most people, you will probably choose to buy a new racket, strung with gut at the proper tension, at least if your only other option is to take a series of expensive lessons on your backhand. Likewise, it probably sounds a lot easier to try to eliminate your ache by switching to regular pressurized balls and throwing away the more durable pressureless balls you have been using than it does to embark upon a six-month conditioning program to build up strength in your forearm.

This is your first line of defense when faced with an ache: Do everything you can to reduce the forces of your game. There's no mystery about how to reduce sportforces. You must adjust your *E*quipment, *E*nvironment, or *V*elocity.

Equipment

Whatever your sport, a few basic equipment adjustments are always possible. Moreover, the equipment and clothing you choose can be crucial in your effort to avoid and manage sportaches. If you're a runner with foot, ankle, or knee pain, for example, your first equipment consideration should obviously be whether you have the best possible running shoes for *your* feet and *your* running program. You need to become expert about the pros and cons of various shoes. The matter of whether or not you need orthotics can be slightly more subtle, as is the question of when your running shoes need to be replaced.

Some possible equipment adjustments are not obvious at all. If you're a tennis player with elbow pain, for example, you will certainly consider changing rackets — composition, grip size, string tension, balance, and so on — but would you also imagine that your troubles might be eased simply by wearing a hat (so you can see the ball and thereby minimize mis-hits) or by purchasing a wristband (to keep your grip drier and minimize the effort you have to exert to prevent your racket from twisting)?

Equipment variables are more numerous and diverse in your sport than you may think. Let your common sense and imagination guide you. Consider any and all possibilities. Be thorough. A small change in your equipment can result in a big difference in how you feel.

Environment

The number of variables you can adjust in your sport environment may also come as a surprise to you. A simple change in *where* you do your favorite sport or activity may make the difference between a chronic ache and months or years of pain-free sports participation. I am persuaded, for example, that tens of thousands of runners could eliminate their running-related sportaches by simply changing or varying their running surface. A

person who is not able to go a mile on asphalt, with its relatively high impact forces, may well find that running on a golf course, river bank, or cinder track is virtually pain-free.

When you do your sport can also be decisive. Hitting into a strong wind in tennis or golf, for example, may require just enough extra effort to cause you to develop an ache.

Likewise, at least in a sport where you have an opponent or partner, the question of *whom* you play against or with can be important. In tennis, for instance, the spin or pace that certain opponents add to their shots may be all it takes to trigger an ache in your elbow or wrist. The person you exercise with can make a similar difference in running, swimming, or bicycling. If exercising with a friend causes you to go faster or farther than usual, an ache can easily result.

Make your sport environment work for you as much as possible. Adjustments in environment sometimes reduce sport-forces to the point where it's possible to achieve pain-free participation without changing anything else.

Velocity

Velocity is a very straightforward variable. It's easy to adjust and can decisively reduce sportforces. Whatever your sport or activity, you should generally resolve to go about it as slowly as possible (within reason). Velocity relates to speed and as such is relative — too fast, too slow, or just right. Most of the time, however, you'll find that it helps to slow down your performance at the first sign of an ache.

There are three reasons why a slow, deliberate motion is usually preferable to a faster motion — regardless of your sport.

1. A fast motion generates higher forces. The faster your movement, the greater the forces generated when you play your game.
2. A fast motion is harder to control. If you insist on doing anything quickly, you are much less likely to be able to control precisely where key joints will be at the moment of peak force — see "Technique" below.
3. A fast motion may not be energy efficient. A tired muscle leads to an unprotected joint. If a muscle is too tired to absorb forces, they will be transmitted to your connective tissue. Fast motions

generally tire out your muscles more quickly. On the other hand, runners sometimes discover that it can be less stressful to speed up. More about this in chapter 7.

Among the reasons that it is usually better to be slow and deliberate than it is to be fast and loose, the most important is that if you reduce velocity you reduce sportforces. If your sport involves impact (tennis and golf, for instance), a fast motion increases both external and internal force loads. There are greater forces within your joints as you prepare for peak force and recover from it. Likewise, a fast swing in tennis and golf results in higher impact forces and generates significantly higher swing forces within the joints of your upper extremities.

You should find that deliberate, controlled movement helps you to avoid and manage sportaches. In addition, a slow, deliberate motion will enhance your performance in most sports. Tennis coaches, for example, are always trying to get their pupils to swing slowly — to accelerate gradually — rather than to take wild, uncontrolled, fast swings. The same thing is true of golf. If you learn to reduce the velocity of your game, you may not only reduce forces and help yourself to avoid and manage sportaches, you may also improve your overall sports performance and enjoyment.

If you've done everything you can to reduce forces but you still have an ache — or if you interpret your sportache as an indication that you need to increase your body's tolerance for sportforces — then consider your technique and conditioning.

Increasing Your Tolerance for Stress

Technique

Sports technique can be a very complex subject. There are, for example, hundreds of tennis instruction books. Considerable debate continues about the benefits of topspin and the desirability of various grips and strokes. In terms of avoiding and managing sportaches, however, the question of tennis technique is conceptually straightforward.

The joints of your limbs are much more stable in certain positions than in others. Your sports technique increases your

Relatively unstable.

Relatively stable.

Relatively unstable.

Relatively stable.

body's tolerance for sportforces to the extent that your technique places key joints of your body as close as possible to their most stable position at the moment they must absorb and transmit peak force loads.

If you're a tennis player with elbow problems, for example, you probably realize that the position of your wrist and forearm at the moment your racket strikes a tennis ball can be decisive. Your wrist should be fixed and straight — not bent. With an adjustment in your grip, swing, or timing, couldn't you manage to have your wrist and forearm more stable when you play? Such an adjustment could make the difference between a lifetime of elbow problems and years of pain-free tennis participation.

Certain motions in certain sports simply do not permit your joints to be stable at the moment of peak force. However, everything is relative. When you serve in tennis, for example, or when you do the crawl as a swimmer, your arm and shoulder are far from their most stable position at the moment when sportforces are their peak. However, if you develop shoulder problems in either sport, it should help to try to minimize the extent to which your shoulder is disadvantaged when it must absorb and transmit sportforces. Despite the fact that both tennis and swimming often require you to raise an arm over your head, there are ways to adjust your tennis and swimming technique so that shoulder stress is lessened.

Adjustments in your sports technique are often simple to make. A coach or friend may be able to help you make a key change in your game literally overnight. Runners, for example, often find it relatively easy to change their stride or their running posture once someone explains to them what they need to do.

I myself discovered recently how easy it can be to adjust technique. During March 1980 I gave a clinic on fitness at the Taos Ski Valley. My audience included recreational skiers, ski instructors, and professional ski patrollers. The small Taos audience was ideal. They sat in rapt attention while I discussed sportforces and talked about the McGregor Solution. By the time I had finished several people were even calling out perfect answers before I could finish asking my questions. It was a superb class. The audience left buzzing. Suddenly, a particularly striking man appeared before me. He was short, lean, obviously an athlete.

"Sorry, Dr. McGregor," he began. "I was late. I missed the first part of your presentation. But I did catch something about what you call the stable position. I was very interested in how you related it to skiing. Believe it or not, I've been trying to refine and teach a similar concept for years. You're one of the few people I've ever heard who is actually talking about something I'm convinced is true for skiing. People ski better *and* have fewer aches after skiing if they can learn to ski with their hips, knees, and ankles in a relatively stable position."

For one of the few times in my life, I was temporarily speechless. Fortunately, I recovered in a few moments and began asking questions myself. I learned that the man's name was Dadu Mayer. Eventually I discovered that Dadu is an outstanding skier, as well as a ski instructor extraordinaire — a pro with whom skiers come from all over the world to work.

Dadu and I instantly plunged into an animated conversation about the McGregor Solution. Before long I had confessed that one of my greatest desires had always been to ski with a pro who could help me test the solution on the ski slopes. Dadu beamed with pride. "Today's your lucky day," he declared. "I'm your man. Meet me at the base of the mountain some day soon and I'll show you what it is to keep your knees stable as a downhill skier."

A few days later I had the lesson of my life. Two things happened simultaneously. First, Dadu quickly identified certain flaws in my skiing technique. He suggested changes he promised would allow me to ski with control under virtually any conditions. Second, I realized that Dadu's tips were going to improve my health. As soon as I followed his advice and adjusted my technique, an ache in my right thigh that I'd noticed for years whenever I skied seemed to disappear. I'd always attributed the discomfort I experienced on the slopes to poor conditioning. Dadu's lesson proved that my problem had actually been poor technique. My upper leg had bothered me when I skied because my knees were almost always bent too much, even on relatively flat terrain. In other words, I discovered that I am fit enough to ski without pain as long as I ski properly. However, I am not well enough conditioned to ski incorrectly.

·

Despite how easy it was for me to make important adjustments in my skiing technique, I recognize that a change in sports technique may prove a difficult and frustrating proposition. If you've hit your backhand or your long woods a certain way during years of tennis or golf, for example, it may be very difficult for you to change. Also, you may wonder if all the bother and expense are really worth the effort. Perhaps you would be willing to do virtually anything to manage your sportaches, if only you could avoid having to change your technique. Since few instruction books or coaches talk in terms of your body's stable position, you may even wonder how to adjust your technique to enhance joint stability.

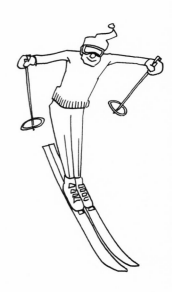

Don't despair. In most sports classic style or technique is the same as healthy or safe technique. When you improve your performance by getting as close as possible to the classic technique of your sport, you also improve your health — and vice versa. I like to emphasize this important phenomenon by explaining that "good technique is good medicine." In virtually every sport you'll find that an element of the classic technique you'll learn in any good instruction book or from any competent coach is to keep key joints in your arms and legs in as straight or stable a position as possible at moments of stress. We'll explain why, in detail, in the next chapter.

The infamous "poke" backhand in tennis, for example, which is generally believed to be at least partially responsible for millions of cases of "tennis elbow," is also a very ineffective stroke. If you hit your backhand by leaning back, dropping your

racket head, pronating your forearm, and poking at the ball as
you straighten your arm at the elbow, you will eventually develop elbow pain because your elbow is too bent at impact.
You'll also never have a very effective backhand. Any coach or
pro can suggest basic improvements in your stroke. The result
should be both a better backhand *and* a healthier arm.

Conditioning

Your conditioning is the other major variable that determines
the amount of stress your body will be able to tolerate when you
play your favorite sport. Only adequate strength and flexibility
enable you to achieve and hold your stable position. Conditioning makes proper technique possible.

We'll be talking about conditioning in greater detail in chapter
4. Meanwhile, however, let me assure you that conditioning
does not necessarily mean an elaborate program to build
strength, flexibility, speed, and endurance. Granted, "getting
into shape" is what football players do in training camp, and
what baseball teams concentrate on in Florida in March. Such
extensive preseason conditioning is now an important part of
professional sports. Rigorous training no doubt helps professional athletes to avoid injuries and sportaches. However, conditioning for the recreational athlete does not have to be as
extensive or onerous as you may think. Your general conditioning may be adequate without much more than regular participation in your favorite sport or activity in conjunction with an
active lifestyle.

In fact, in many ways — at least in terms of EEVeTeC —
general conditioning is not as important as three other conditioning habits: limbering up, warming up, and warming down. When
you are applying the McGregor Solution to your sportache, you
need to think not only about your general conditioning but also
about these three other separate conditioning areas.

GENERAL CONDITIONING

Make no mistake about it — if you are willing to embark upon an extensive general conditioning program, you may well be able to achieve pain-free sports participation in your favorite recreational sport without making any great effort to reduce forces or to improve your technique. General conditioning can be a sort of all-purpose insurance.

LIMBERING UP

Limbering up is conceptually very easy. Before you start your sport or activity, try to do ten minutes of calisthenics or stretching. Remember, always stretch slowly — do not do bouncing or jerky stretches. When you bounce or jerk your muscles lock, preventing constructive stretching. Try to get loose and warm before you begin your run, tennis game, golf game, swim, bike ride, or whatever. When you are limber your connective tissue is less vulnerable than it is when you are stiff and cold.

WARMING UP

In addition to a brief limbering-up period, which should take place before you begin your sport or activity, you should also warm up during the first ten or fifteen minutes of play. *Start slowly*. As a runner, for example, you might want to get in the habit of beginning your regular run very gradually. Don't be afraid to start and stop a few times before you work up to your normal training pace.

If you're a tennis player or runner, you'll find tips for an enjoyable warm-up period at the end of chapters 6 and 7. If your favorite sport isn't among those we have discussed in detail, you can easily devise your own warm-up routine. Make it fun. Nothing is more important than to develop the habit of doing some basic limbering up and warming up before you start generating the real peak forces of your game. Literally millions of sport-aches result every year from the fact that recreational athletes plunge into their favorite sports or activities without being sufficiently limber or warm. Forces your body could tolerate if it were warm and loose may simply be too much for your connective tissue when you are cold and tight.

WARMING DOWN

After you finish your sport or activity, you cannot afford to sit around in wet clothes. You should immediately put on a dry shirt, as well as a sweater or warm-up jacket. Do a few minutes of stretching and then shower.

Many recreational athletes are stiff and sore after they exercise simply because they do not understand how much their bodies need to wind down after exertion. You should ideally spend ten or fifteen minutes warming down after you play your favorite sport. At the end of any running event in a track meet, the contestants go slowly around the track once or twice. Likewise, you may have noticed that the horses don't simply stop when they cross the finish line at the Kentucky Derby. Take an "extra lap" when you do your favorite sport or activity. You'll develop far fewer aches as a result.

•

So there it is: EEVeTeC explained. It's really quite easy to eliminate sportaches with the McGregor Solution. If you're a recreational athlete, you'll probably want to adjust the variables in order: equipment, environment, velocity, technique, and conditioning. If you are a tennis player experiencing slight twinges of elbow pain, you might consider changing the type of racket you use, your string tension, or grip size. Those are equipment changes. If you're still in pain, you might then try a different opponent or a different playing surface. That's environment. Or you might change the pace of your game by playing doubles

instead of singles or by hitting two half-speed serves instead of a cannonball followed by a blooper. That's a velocity adjustment.

In adjusting your equipment, environment, and velocity, the first three elements of the McGregor Solution, you will be reducing the sportforces of your tennis game.

If you still hurt, you may consider trying to improve your technique. You could ask your pro how to hit your backhand properly — if that's the stroke that seems to be causing your elbow pain. Proper technique and pain-free play go hand in hand. Finally, you should think about conditioning. A strength and flexibility program along with a proper warm-up and warm-down might be all you need to alleviate your ache. In adjusting your technique and conditioning, the final two elements of the McGregor Solution, you'll be increasing your ability to withstand sportforces.

That's it. It's that simple. If you experience occasional twinges of pain when you play your favorite sport — sportaches — you have three choices: (1) You can reduce sportforces by adjusting your Equipment, Environment, and Velocity. (2) You can increase your body's ability to withstand sportforces by improving your Technique and Conditioning. (3) You can play in pain.

There's another choice, of course. If you've played in pain in the past, you've probably considered it. It's the most common single piece of advice given by frustrated doctors to equally frustrated patients. You can quit. Quitting is a legitimate option if you've tried everything else first. And sometimes it's the only appropriate choice. However, you shouldn't quit your favorite sport until you've tried the McGregor Solution. Moreover, your

doctor shouldn't let you quit until he or she is certain you have tried EEVeTeC. There's almost always a way to play without pain.

It is true that some people cannot participate in certain sports without developing aches. I frequently see patients who could never become long-distance runners, for example. Certain bodies simply were not designed to spend hour after hour running. No adjustment in equipment, environment, velocity, technique, or conditioning can change that fact.

One of my patients, Frank DeNardi, is a good case in point. A high school and college sprinter, Frank once confessed to me that he always dreaded the long miles he was required to cover while training for his events. The continuous pounding of his feet on the local roads made his knees, ankles, and feet ache. After college Frank abandoned running, turning instead to tennis for fitness and fun. But when running boomed in popularity during the 1970s, Frank's wife talked him into taking it up again. She had already run her first Bonne Bell ten-kilometer race, and she thought training with her husband would be great.

It didn't take long for Frank to get his wind back. He was still in good shape. But once he got above six miles a day, he started getting those old college aches again. At two or three miles he was comfortable. But the ten-mile runs just about destroyed him.

Frank came to see me, more for confirmation than for original diagnosis. He'd already figured out that his body was designed to sprint, not run distances. My exam showed that he had a high-impact foot, the type that doesn't absorb shock well. As a result, his body was taking too much cumulative stress when he ran long distances.

Frank will never win the Boston Marathon, although he can certainly continue to enjoy tennis and skiing. He'll always have his memories of his college sprinting days. However, he's just not cut out to be a long-distance runner.

Fortunately, Frank DeNardi is the exception and not the rule. Most of us can participate in most sports without developing "runner's knee," "tennis elbow," "golfer's hip," "swimmer's shoulder," or the other common pains of fitness.

The McGregor Solution is the key to pain-free sports participation. With EEVeTeC you can prevent an ache caused by your favorite sport or activity from getting worse. Often you can even make it disappear entirely. There's no pill, no injection, no surgical procedure that will eliminate your sportaches. But you *can* help yourself. First, you must reduce sportforces as much as possible. Second, you must increase your body's ability to withstand stress.

The McGregor Solution is very simple. And it works. Prove it to yourself, if you like. Turn to part III. We guarantee that you'll relieve existing aches, as well as avoid new pains. On the other hand, if you want a more complete understanding of why the McGregor Solution works, read on. Chapter 3 discusses sportforces and joint design — the anatomy of activity.

Part II

WHY EEVeTeC WORKS

3
The Anatomy of Activity

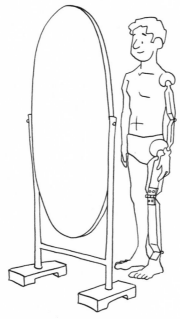

To UNDERSTAND THE FORCES you have to contend with when you play your favorite sport — as well as where you are likely to hurt and why — all you need to appreciate are a few basic facts about your sport and your body. Once you understand sportforces and joint design, you'll begin to understand why EEVeTeC works.

Sportaches are the pains of fitness. If you have a sportache, you've been more active in your pursuit of fitness than your body was ready or able to be. To understand why you have your pain, as well as what you'll have to do to eliminate your problem, you simply need to understand what I call the anatomy of activity.

The anatomy of activity isn't the same as the anatomy we all learned in biology class. It also isn't the same anatomy I was taught in podiatric medical school. What doctors mean when they talk about anatomy is a firsthand familiarity with the inside of your body. A doctor can't treat you for disease or injury without knowing what a normal body looks like on the inside. For obvious reasons, no doctor ever forgets his or her first experience using a scalpel on a human body. But you don't learn about the anatomy of activity by cutting into human flesh.

If you're sick or injured, be grateful that your doctor spent months in medical school dissecting human cadavers and examining different body parts. However, if you have a sportache, you don't have a medical problem. A doctor usually can't help. If your knee hurts when you run, for example, you don't generally need someone who has dissected a human leg to diagnose and treat your problem. Likewise, you don't need to study

books and look at pictures that explain how your knee is constructed — which tendon attaches which muscle to which bone, etcetera. You and your doctor rather need to become acquainted with a whole new type of "anatomy." Medical students don't learn about it in their books or in the dissection lab because EEVeTeC doesn't require an understanding of conventional anatomy any more than sportaches require medical attention.

When I first began to tend to the "high-use" problems of athletes like Eric Groon, John Cedarholm, and Jim Shapiro, I realized that what I had learned about anatomy in school wasn't going to be of much help. I quickly concluded that I needed to know more about sports than medicine. Knowing what a particular muscle, tendon, or joint looked like in a textbook or under a microscope didn't tell me much about how it functioned or what was happening when an athlete asked his or her body to do more than it was ready or able to do. Eventually I realized

that the anatomy I needed to know about was the anatomy of
activity.

Your body is a fantastic structure. Each part — every bone,
muscle, artery, organ, every cell — is a marvel. However, if
you're an athlete with an ache, the most important thing is not
what your body is, but what it does. The anatomy of activity is
the study of what your body can do, as well as what your sport
does to it.

•

If you hurt when you play your favorite sport, chances are that
you have pain in or around a joint. Otherwise, you hurt in a
muscle that is straining to move or stabilize a joint. Sportaches
are joint-related pains.

In the pages that follow we'll be focusing exclusively on the
joints of your arms and legs. That's where the aches you can
deal with on your own generally occur. Sure, the "hip bone's
connected to the backbone" as the song says, but this book isn't
going to minister to your aching back. For back diagnosis, back
repair, and back exercises, see your doctor first!

Sports — like all other dynamic activities — require joint
movement. And joint movement is made possible by various
muscles. Your muscles move your bones. Therefore, even if
your sportache begins in a muscle, it is joint related in the sense
that the work that has resulted in an ache was performed to
enable one or more of your joints to move. Also, muscle pain
that arises during sports participation often ends up in a joint.
If, for example, your forearm muscles begin to ache after ten
minutes of hitting backhands, continued play will generally result in an aching elbow or wrist.

When a muscle or muscle group doesn't have sufficient
strength or flexibility to meet the demands of your sport, the
joints of your arms and legs are subjected to considerable stress.
And stress — which we defined in chapter 1 as the amount of
force actually affecting your joints — is a function of two things:
(1) the size of the forces of your sport, and (2) the stability of
your joints when they must absorb and transmit peak sportforces.

If you want to eliminate sportaches, you must first recognize
and appreciate sportforces — the sources of the stresses that
result in sportaches. Then, and only then, will you be able to

appreciate the importance of understanding how the principal joints of your arms and legs were designed to work and the necessity of making every effort to keep key joints as stable as possible when sportforces are at their peak.

Sportforces

There's no doubt that the word *force* conjures up all sorts of scientific visions. In fact, certain scientists known as biomechanists spend all of their time measuring and discussing the forces inherent in movement and producing sophisticated motion analysis. Their findings are of considerable assistance to coaches, trainers, and professional athletes. I have worked closely with biomechanist Peter Cavanaugh at Penn State University, and he helped immensely with the design of a revolutionary golf shoe that I developed for Etonic during the late 1970s. In addition, Stan Plagenhoef, one of the most highly respected biomechanists in the world, was of invaluable assistance when Steve and I were brainstorming before writing this book. Nevertheless, I am persuaded that the concerns of the biomechanist are not, by and large, the concerns of the recreational athlete.

You don't need a degree in biomechanics to understand how EEVeTeC works any more than you need a medical degree. All you need is a basic conceptual framework that enables you to identify and deal with the forces of your sport. An uncomplicated overview of sportforces will help you understand how it's possible to minimize and manage your sportaches with EEVeTeC.

•

The dynamic sports we are concerned with in this book — the ones that cause sportaches — all require motion. If your sport requires or encourages you to make movements your joints weren't designed to perform, or if your sport requires a joint to absorb or transmit forces in an unstable position, you're likely to develop a sportache.

Think about your knees, for example. As we'll discuss in detail in the next section, your knees are safest when they're only slightly bent. They are less secure and more vulnerable when they're fully flexed — out of their stable position. Moreover, even the slightest repetitive twisting can cause your knees

to ache. Do you play your sport with your knees constantly bent or twisted? If so, you're likely to develop an ache.

Don't confuse aches with breaks or wear with tear. A broken bone or dislocated joint isn't a sportache. Sportaches arise gradually. They result from overuse, not trauma. A tennis player might develop tennis elbow after weeks or months of hitting backhands improperly. However, elbow pain that is the result of crashing full tilt into the back fence is definitely not a sportache.

If you develop tennis elbow, your forearm muscles have simply been unable to cope with the cumulative stress of hitting

tennis balls. You may have been jarring your arm with virtually every shot. When your elbow begins to ache, you know that the forces generated on the tennis court have exceeded your body's tolerance for stress.

Muscle strength and flexibility are required for you to absorb sportforces. Likewise, both strength and flexibility are required if you expect to achieve and hold the stable position of any joint. If your muscles aren't up to the task, stress is created in your connective tissue.

Despite the fact that all sports require motion — and thereby generate stress — every sport has its own unique movements. Jogging, for example, obviously requires you to move your body in a way that is different from the way you have to move on the tennis court or golf course. Likewise, swimmers and racquetball players use their bodies in sharply contrasting manners. Various activities place varying degrees of stress on the joints of your arms and legs. However, although every sport generates its own forces, all sportforces follow a common pattern.

•

Regardless of your sport, sportforces occur in a cycle. *Preparatory forces* are followed by forces generated at the moment you actually do what you've set out to do, *peak forces*, which are followed finally by *recovery forces*.

To identify the moment when your cycle of sportforces culminates — when preparation ends and recovery begins — you need only ask yourself what you are trying to do when you play your favorite sport.

All sports have their moment of truth. What is the objective of your sport? Do you hit or throw a ball? Do you have to push or pull against resistance? You should be able to identify a moment that is the focus of your effort. That moment is also the moment when the cycle of sportforces you must tolerate in your activity reaches a turning point.

We call the moment of truth in sports the instant of *peak force*. Peak force is *not* necessarily the same thing as maximum force. For example, a basketball player taking a jump shot encounters a moment of maximum force when he or she pushes off the ground. The moment of peak force comes at the instant when the basketball is released. Usually, however, sportforces are at their highest level at the moment of peak force.

Every sport has its own unique movements.

For Björn Borg, whose primary objective is to hit a ball with his tennis racket, peak force occurs at the moment of impact between his racket and the ball. For Bill Rodgers, whose objective is to move over twenty-six miles of ground at approximately five minutes per mile, peak force occurs every time each of his feet hits the ground. For Mark Roth, whose objective is to propel a sixteen-pound bowling ball into the pins sixty feet away, peak force occurs every time he releases the ball. For John Naber, whose objective is to move quickly through the water from one end of a swimming pool to the other, peak force occurs every time he thrusts with his arms and legs.

In addition to recognizing the moment of peak force in your sport, you must also appreciate the fact that sportforces come in two different varieties — *external forces* and *internal forces.*

External forces flow into your body from the outside and travel up your limbs — from hand to wrist to elbow to shoulder, for example. In contrast, internal forces are generated within your joints and travel down your extremities — from your shoulder to your elbow to your wrist to your hand. Whether they are flowing into or out of your body, sportforces affect the least stable joint of the limb along which they are traveling.

Not all sports expose you to external sportforces. However, if you play a sport that does involve external forces, the moment of peak force is particularly significant. At that moment external forces flowing into your body from the outside combine with internal forces generated within your joints, exposing your body to maximum stress. In other sports external forces are not a factor, although there is nevertheless a distinct moment of maximum effort or peak force.

•

Recreational sports can be divided into three categories: *impact, resistance,* and *release.*

Tennis and golf, obviously, are impact sports. Your primary goal is to hit a ball. There are dozens of other similar sports, including racquetball and squash. Running is also an impact sport. Your feet impact the ground with every step, a minimum of 800 times per mile per foot.

Swimming and bicycling, on the other hand, are resistance sports. You are thrusting against resistance in both cases. You don't hit anything and nothing hits you.

Finally, any sport in which you throw an object is a release sport. Included are sports from bowling to shot-put to Frisbee. If yours is a release sport, there is neither impact nor resistance at your moment of peak force. However, you can generate considerable internal forces as you wind up for your delivery as well as when you follow through after release.

Whether yours is an impact, resistance, or release sport, or some combination, like baseball — where you impact (hit the ball) and also release (throw the ball) — various external considerations affect the amount of force you must tolerate when you play.

Running on concrete generates greater stress than running on grass. If you're a tennis player, returning Roscoe Tanner's serve will be harder on your arm than hitting back your little daughter's blooper. Third gear on your bicycle is tougher on your legs than first gear. A sixteen-pound bowling ball creates more stress in your bowling arm than a thirteen-pound ball.

However, although external considerations are a factor in all sports, only the impact sports actually require you to deal with both internal and external sportforces. When you hit a ball (whether with a racket, club, bat, or some other implement) or when your feet hit the ground, a measurable force actually flows into your body in addition to the internal forces generated within your joints as you prepare for and recover from impact. In contrast, if your sport involves resistance or release rather than impact, external forces are not a consideration, despite the fact that external considerations may determine the size of the internal forces you'll have to be able to withstand.

The McGregor Solution doesn't just apply in situations where there are external forces. That would limit its effectiveness to impact sports only, which is by no means the case. EEVeTeC also applies to sports like bicycling. Cyclists can use the McGregor Solution to reduce the amount of work they have to do when they pedal, as well as to increase their ability to keep their joints as stable as possible at the moment of peak force. It's true there are only minimal external forces in bicycling and other nonimpact sports. But there are external considerations — including the gear the cyclist has chosen, whether he or she is riding uphill or against the wind, and so on.

If your favorite activity involves impact and you're worried

about an ache, you need to think about reducing both external and internal sportforces. On the other hand, if there is no impact involved in your sport, you still have to work to keep internal forces to a tolerable level when you play.

Study the accompanying illustrations of the tennis player and the bicyclist. The tennis player is going to have to deal with both incoming (external) and outgoing (internal) forces. As it happens, both sets of forces are going to have to be absorbed in her elbow. In contrast, the cyclist is gritting her teeth as she thrusts against the pedal. Sportforces are flowing one way, out of her body, through her bent knee, the pedal, the bicycle wheel, and beyond.

All sports have internal sportforces. As your body moves to and from the moment of peak force in your sport, stress is created within your arms and legs. Impact sports also have external sportforces. When you hit a tennis ball or golf ball, for example, internal forces are generated within your shoulders, elbows, and wrists as you wind up and swing. Stress is created within these joints because muscles, tendons, and ligaments are put to work, moving your skeleton and pulling, pushing, and grinding against each other in the process. Peak force occurs at impact, when your body must also be able to tolerate the significant external forces that come flowing into it through your racket or club. Finally, additional internal forces are generated as you strain to follow through and recover after each shot.

•

Every sport has its own cycle of sportforces. If you're a runner, moving each foot from its farthest-back position to the moment when it contacts the ground is the *preparatory phase*. Then comes the *moment of peak force,* when your foot is flat on the ground. Finally comes the *recovery phase,* from the instant your toes leave the ground until your foot is again in its most backward position.

If you swim, the preparatory phase involves the downward movement of your arms into the water. The moment of peak force comes when your hands pull through the water. Finally comes the recovery phase, when your arms sweep out, up, and away from the water, followed immediately, of course, by the preparatory phase for your next stroke and the next moment of

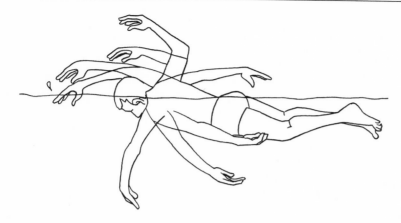

peak force. Your legs, incidentally, are going through their own force cycles as you kick.

For a quarterback throwing a football, movement of the arm toward the release point constitutes the preparatory phase. Then, following the moment of release (peak force), the arm continues downward and across the body. That's the recovery phase.

No matter what your sport, if you want to use EEVeTeC to avoid aches, you have to identify the movements you must make to get your body set to encounter each moment of peak force as well as to withstand and recover from that moment. Each movement, each phase in the cycle of sportforces, requires your body structures to move in a variety of ways to stabilize your joints. Work generates force, resulting in stress.

Sportforces are the key to sportaches. If you can learn to recognize and reduce forces, you can avoid or manage many aches.

Joint Design

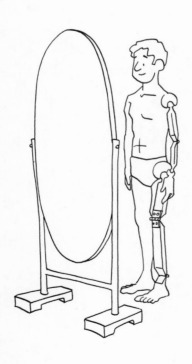

Take a look at yourself in a full-length mirror, arms and legs bare. Relax. Study your body, first from the front, then from the side.

How are you standing? Chances are your feet are almost parallel, with your legs a few inches apart, your knees slightly bent, your arms hanging easily at your sides, and your head erect.

In this relaxed but erect posture the joints in both your arms and legs are in their strongest, most stable position. The key to understanding joint design is to perceive that your joints are more stable in some positions than others. The stance you've instinctively assumed in front of the mirror is what we call your *stable position*. You won't find the term *stable position* in any medical textbook. It's a phrase that we use to help you understand the anatomy of activity.

Anatomists refer to the "anatomic position," a precise description of the bone-to-bone and joint-to-joint relationships of the various segments of your body. Kinesiologists and biomechanists talk about the "neutral position," an even more precise description of your body's geometrically related angles. What we call your stable position, however, is not precisely the same as the basic body position described by either the anatomist or the kinesiologist. Your stable position is simply the position you adopt instinctively when you stand at ease. It is also *the position in which the joints of your arms and legs can best deal with stress.*

Look at yourself again in the mirror. With your feet almost parallel, take a closer look at your knees and elbows. They should be slightly bent, not rigid or locked. Your wrists should also be relaxed, with your palms turned toward your hips.

Right now, of course, you're standing still. Sports require movement, which is possible only because of the joints that allow your arms and legs to extend, flex, and rotate. However, you may not appreciate exactly how the range of motion of these key joints is limited.

All of the joints in your upper and lower extremities have

precise limitations on how far they can go from their stable position without pain. Have you ever noticed how difficult it is to scratch an itch in the middle of your back? That's the result of a limited range of motion in your shoulder, elbow, and wrist. Likewise, if you've ever sprained or twisted an ankle, you know that your ankles have a sharply limited range of motion. Have your friends told you that you often put your foot in your mouth? Try it. It isn't easy — because of a limited range of motion in your hip, knee, ankle, and foot.

You don't have to be able to put your foot in your mouth to finish a marathon or win the club doubles championship. However, most sports do require movements that take the joints of your arms and legs well away from their stable position. Sometimes you are even encouraged or obliged to attempt movements that exceed the range of motion of key joints. When you try to exceed the normal range of motion of a joint, your body may well hurt. Likewise, when you ask your joints to absorb or transmit forces in an unstable position, you can expect pain.

•

The human skeleton is a model of design efficiency. The bones that make up your joints have an intrinsic stability. That stability is guaranteed by the precise architectural relationship of one bone to another and reinforced by ligaments and capsules, which hold your bones together, as well as by muscles and tendons, which both move and stabilize your joints. When you think about your body, do you imagine the skeleton you used to see hanging in the biology classroom at school? Remember, that was just a collection of dead bones, strung together with wires and screws. Under your skin are various vital structures that actually hold your live bones together — your ligaments, muscles, tendons, capsules, bursae, and other connective tissue. Those structures are stressed when you ask your body to do more than it was designed to do.

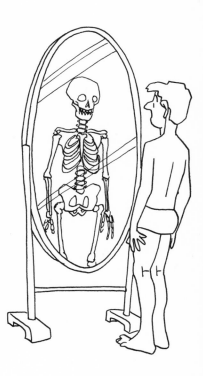

The structures that move, stabilize, and protect your joints can withstand the stresses of your sport *only if* (1) your joints are used as they were designed to be used (in other words, if you don't try to exceed your normal range of motion) and (2) those same joints are as close as possible to their stable position when they have to absorb or transmit sportforces.

When you are standing still, the only forces with which you

must deal are the forces of gravity. When you play sports, on the other hand, you are rarely stationary and your body is constantly being buffeted by sportforces. In fact, some sports oblige you to absorb and transmit sizable force loads in a consistently unstable position. Your shoulder is unstable when you hit a tennis serve. Skiers don't always ski very well with their knees in the stable position. If you're a golfer, how far do you think you could hit your tee shots if you kept your hips stable?

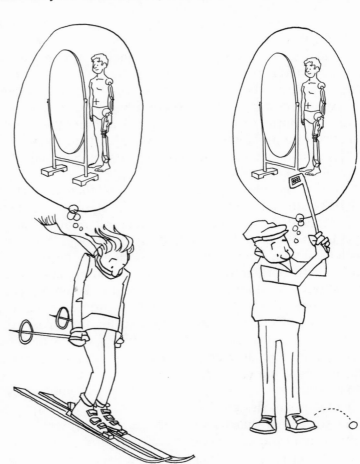

Make the various motions of your sport, now, while you are still in front of your mirror. Are there moments when certain joints are away from their stable position simply because of the demands of your sport? If so, you'll either have to minimize sportforces or increase your tolerance for stress. Otherwise, you'll eventually have to pick another sport or learn to live with perpetual aches. Minimizing sportforces requires careful consideration of your equipment, environment, and velocity. If your technique is good, increasing your tolerance for stress is a matter of conditioning.

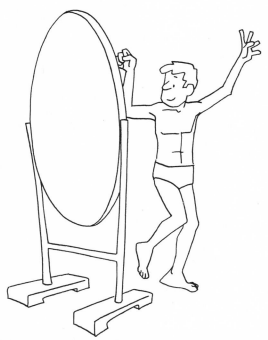

On the other hand, if you think your technique may be at fault, remember that if you can improve your technique you'll not only get key joints closer to their stable position and thereby eliminate aches, but you should also improve your performance.

•

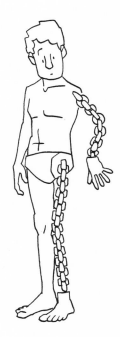

The joints of your upper and lower extremities are part of what biomechanists call a *kinetic chain*. Kinetic means motion. And a chain has a series of links. In a kinetic chain motion is exerted, extended, and absorbed within the links. In addition, as with any chain, a kinetic chain is only as strong as its weakest link.

In the human body there are two basic kinetic chains. In your lower extremities your hips are linked to your knees, which in turn are linked to your ankles and then to your feet. In your upper extremities your shoulders and hands are linked by your elbows and your wrists.

Various superb athletes have had their careers shortened or destroyed by a single weak link in the kinetic chain of their upper or lower extremities. Billie Jean King, for example, might have won even more than her twenty Wimbledon titles if she had not been severely hampered by knee problems. Joe Namath ended a brilliant football career early because his weak knees eventually made him an ''all-arm'' quarterback, susceptible to all-too-frequent interception. And how about Bobby Orr, one of the greatest hockey defensemen of all time? How far might he have gone without his weak knees? Why did Sandy Koufax quit baseball? His elbow, right? Do you know why Rod Laver finally quit pro tennis? Same problem.

Conditioning can supply an important measure of protection, especially for a weak link in any one of your four kinetic chains. But some joints are simply more vulnerable than others, a fact that it is important for you to appreciate.

There is an important correlation between the versatility and the vulnerability of certain parts of your body. The less versatile a joint, the more vulnerable it is to both injuries and sportaches. Have you ever wondered why both recreational athletes and pros experience by far the greatest number of problems with their knees and elbows? Because those two joints are the *least versatile* in the human body. They're functional hinges — period. In comparison, your more versatile hips, shoulders, and wrists are much less vulnerable to the pains of fitness. Let's consider your key joints, one by one.

Knee

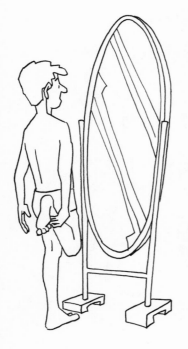

Look at yourself again in your full-length mirror, standing in the stable position. Stay relaxed. Without moving your hip or thigh, bend your right knee to bring your foot up behind you. This bending action is called *flexion*. Simply put, flexion means bringing two parts of your body closer together.

Now straighten your leg and return your foot to the ground. This is called *extension*. It's the opposite of flexion. You are now moving two parts of your body away from each other.

Can your knee do anything besides flex and extend your lower leg? Can you move your lower leg in the other direction — toe up — by bending at the knee? Of course not. Certainly you can execute a kicking motion. But your knee won't bend beyond the point where your lower and upper legs are aligned. When you swing your leg up in front of you, the kicking motion comes from your hip.

Your knee functions basically as a hinge. It opens and closes — flexes and extends — very well. And that's about it. It doesn't open beyond roughly 180°, and there is practically no twisting or rotating when you stand in your stable position. A slight degree of rotation does take place as your knee straightens. Nevertheless, your knee is *not* a versatile joint. That's why it's highly susceptible to sportaches.

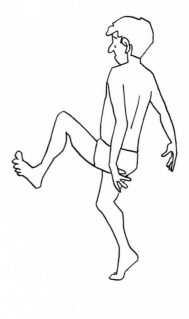

Elbow

Your elbow is the "knee" of your arm. In terms of flexion and extension it works much the same way. Go back to the mirror. Start with your right arm in its most stable position, hanging at your side with your palm toward your hip. Now flex your elbow. You can bring your hand almost up to your shoulder.

Next return your lower arm to its stable position. Will it go beyond the point where your arm is hanging at your side? A little, if you are loose jointed. Otherwise, no.

Like your knee, your elbow functions as a hinge. It opens and shuts. It does so naturally and without pain. Your elbow also allows limited rotation of your forearm. Before human beings evolved into standing animals, elbows and knees served similar functions. Now, your elbows are slightly less vulnerable than your knees because your forearm can rotate. Also, because you don't walk on your hands, your elbows don't have to bear your weight in addition to absorbing and transmitting other forces. However, your elbows are still quite susceptible to other stresses.

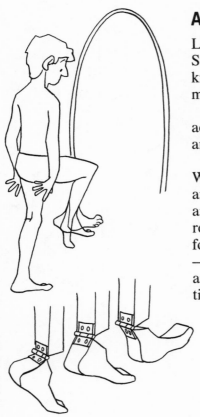

Ankle

Like your knees and elbows, your ankles are also hinge joints. Stand in your stable position. Raise your right foot and flex your knee. Then point your toes down toward the ground. The movement takes place in your ankle hinge.

Many people believe that the rolling in and out of the ankle actually takes place in the ankle, but it does not. In the strictest and most scientific sense, your foot actually does the rolling.

Think about the phenomenon we call a "sprained ankle." What serious athlete, recreational or pro, hasn't sprained an ankle? The pain and disability is in your ankle joint, but your ankle has not actually caused the problem. It's your foot. What really happens when you sprain or twist an ankle is that your foot rolls — usually to the outside, occasionally to the inside — beyond its normal range of motion. This places stress on your ankle joint and causes a separation or tear in the connecting tissue that holds your anklebones together.

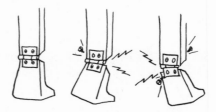

Do you know anyone who has given up skating because of "weak ankles"? Chances are that's not their problem at all. They probably have weak feet. Because your ankles were not designed to permit your feet to roll very far in either direction, they lack an important versatility that they frequently need — especially in sports.

Hips and Shoulders

Your hips and shoulders are much more versatile — and therefore much less vulnerable to sportaches — than your knees, elbows, and ankles. They can move in a variety of directions. Thanks to your hips, your legs can rotate and swing forward, backward, and to the side. Because of the design of your shoulders, your arms can move through almost a complete circle as well as extending easily to your side and overhead.

Even though they permit hingelike motion, your hips and shoulders are not hinges. They're ball-and-socket joints, designed for easy, painless rotation. It's possible, of course, to push a ball-and-socket joint beyond its limits. Tennis players

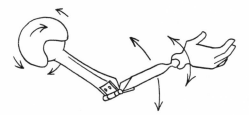

and swimmers know all about shoulder problems. Golfers frequently complain of hip pain. But compared to your elbows, knees, and ankles, your hips and shoulders are far more versatile. If the rotating stresses that sometimes cause shoulder and hip sportaches occurred in your hinge joints, they would literally tear them apart.

Feet, Wrists, and Hands

Your most versatile and least vulnerable joints are at the ends of your limbs. That is as it should be if you're an athlete, because these are the joints that must deal directly with the track surface, bicycle pedals, water, racket, golf club, and so on. I refer, of course, to your feet, wrists, and hands.

Let's start with the foot. Perhaps you're saying, "Time out! Up till now you've been talking about joints, like ankles, knees, and hips. Now, all of a sudden, you're introducing an anatomic *part* — the foot. Why the inconsistency?"

Actually, there's no real inconsistency, since the subject we're addressing in this chapter is the anatomy of activity, or what your body *does*. Because your feet are obviously key to much of your movement — at least when you're standing up — there is no way to understand the anatomy of activity without first knowing what your feet are designed to do.

Also, although the human foot is not actually a single joint like the ankle, knee, or hip, it does function as a joint when you are active. Therefore, it seems appropriate to treat it as a joint for the purpose of the present discussion.

The human foot is a remarkable body part. It's really three things rolled into one: a mobile adapter, a support mechanism, and a rigid propulsive lever. To accomplish all three tasks, your foot needs twenty-six bones and eighty-six separate joints. In fact, half of the bones in your entire body are in your feet.

Your feet have a unique ability to adapt to the ground. Their

That's pronation.   **That's supination.**

mobile-adapter function is what enables your feet to roll in (pronate), or out (supinate) easily. Pronation and supination are found in the hand also. Your hands, like your feet, are composed of a number of bones and joints, which function like a single joint when you play sports. Imagine hitting a forehand with exaggerated topspin. You do it by rolling your racket over the ball. If you're a tennis player, take a practice swing now. Notice that your hand is rolling in, toward your thumb side. That's pronation. Now shift to your backhand and again try to hit a topspin shot. This time you're rolling your hand to the outside. That's supination.

The ability of your feet to roll in and out easily is what provides the kind of stability you need in sports. Picture a skateboarder or surfer keeping balance by rolling at the feet. Imagine a broken-field runner in football, planting a foot and cutting away. Picture a golfer as she addresses her ball, which is lying on the side of a hill. What if the mobile adaptability of her feet didn't allow a stance with one foot up and the other down?

Your foot also serves as a support mechanism. Standing, even standing still, requires your feet and the joints of your feet to be locked. Otherwise, your feet would break down or cave in under the weight of your body. That's why, when you must stand for an extended period, you tend to roll your feet to the outside. The outside area of your foot is the load-bearing part. Like a bridge, it's uniquely designed to bear weight.

The third function of your foot is to enable you to lift your body off the ground. It acts as a propulsive lever. To accomplish this, the foot must be able to lock all its loose joints under the arch. This happens when your foot moves from pronation to supination. Your body is lifted off the ground through the hinge-like joints at the ball of your foot and at your toes.

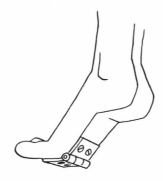

Running provides an excellent example of the many things your feet can and must do when you play certain sports. Within milliseconds your foot lands, rolls in, adapts to the running surface, rolls out, locks to become a propulsive lever, and lifts off through your toe joints.

One of the most significant recent discoveries in sportsmedicine is that the main reason runners have so many knee, ankle, and hip problems is that a foot isn't doing its job properly. In other words, if your feet fail you, you may not know it. You may not feel *foot* pain. Your feet may transmit the forces of your sport to other, less versatile joints in your lower extremi-

ties, in particular, your knees. Does that mean your feet won't ever feel the stresses of activity? Of course not. But the versatility of your feet makes them relatively ache-free.

At the wrist we find the greatest joint versatility in the human skeleton. Just picture the magician's "sleight of hand." Your wrist permits virtually 360° motion. Like your feet, because of their versatility, your wrists often transmit stress to less stable joints. Excessive wrist motion is a prime cause of elbow pain for tennis, racquetball, and squash players.

Your hands, like your feet, are really a series of bones and joints. Each hand functions as a claw. Like your feet, your hands are very versatile and relatively ache-free.

•

Remember, if you have either a current ache or a history of joint problems, reducing sportforces and increasing your ability to withstand stress can save you considerable pain and frustration. That's the foundation of the McGregor Solution.

You should be better able to understand how EEVeTeC works now that you understand the two parts of the anatomy of activity. *Sportforces* are obviously key, as they are the source of the stress that results in sportaches. If you understand sportforces, you can grasp the importance of reducing forces at the first sign of an ache. Likewise, an understanding of *joint design* and *stable position* should help you to accept the need to position and condition key joints to increase your tolerance for stress. Now, to complete your understanding of how EEVeTeC works, you need to know more about getting into shape and picking your sport — the subjects of the next two chapters.

4

Getting into Shape

MOST OF US PREFER to have things done for us. We'd rather not be told that we have to do something for ourselves. It's always easier to work at something when there are immediate, tangible results. Therefore, I suppose it shouldn't be surprising or disappointing to me to have patients look discouraged when I tell them that there isn't a pill, shot, or mechanical device that will eliminate their sportaches. But it always is. As a doctor I'd like to be able to perform some magic on each and every patient who comes through my door. But, of course, I can't. EEVeTeC always requires *you* to do something to eliminate *your* ache. And there are no guarantees that any one adjustment in your equipment, environment, velocity, technique, or conditioning will do the trick. EEVeTeC is a process, not a panacea.

Now that you understand the anatomy of activity a little better, perhaps you have begun to wonder why conditioning is at the end of the EEVeTeC equation and not the beginning. Possibly it has occurred to you that if you had enough strength and flexibility in key muscles, you might not have to worry much about the other four elements in the EEVeTeC equation. It's true. Conditioning can be an all-purpose insurance against sportaches. It can even function as a sort of cure-all after an ache has begun. So why do we even bother with the other elements of the equation? Why not simply tell people to "get into shape" if they want to avoid aches? The answer is simple. Although conditioning can be an all-purpose solution, it never seems as easy to "get into shape" as it is to buy new equipment, adjust your environment, or even improve your technique. The biggest frowns are always on the faces of the patients who leave my office with nothing more than a prescription for conditioning and a description of the exercises they ought to do. Conditioning, after all, is the ultimate example of something *you* must do *yourself,* something that usually has no immediate effect whatsoever.

Nevertheless, conditioning is something every recreational athlete must understand and appreciate. It doesn't have to be as difficult or distasteful as many people believe, and it can be remarkably effective. For one thing, conditioning is *not* an absolute: 150 sit-ups, 100 push-ups, a six-minute mile. You simply have to be in good enough shape to do what you want to do without debilitating pain, whether your goal is to walk, swim, ride a bike, play golf, play tennis, run, or whatever. Conditioning is relative. Your needs are your measure.

This chapter will provide an understanding of the whys and hows of general conditioning. To understand the importance of conditioning, you first need to be aware of the particular sportforces inherent in your sport. Next, you have to understand the particular stresses on your body as the result of who you are (man or woman, fat or thin, old or young, and so on) as well as the level of performance you are trying to attain. The pros figured that out long ago, and all of us should learn from their example.

The majority of professional tennis players experience elbow pain sometime during their playing careers. Moreover, a pro like Stan Smith — whose right elbow bothered him off and on for years during the 1970s and finally drove him to submit to surgery during November 1981 — has exactly the same options as you and I when it comes to managing his ache. Notwithstanding, he is likely to approach EEVeTeC in the reverse order — starting with conditioning, rather than saving it as a last resort. Why? There are at least two reasons.

For one thing, a professional often does not have as many easy ways to reduce sportforces as the average recreational ath-

Conditioning doesn't have to be difficult . . .

lete. It's not so simple for Stan Smith to change his environment or velocity and still play at a world-class level. Obviously, he can adjust his equipment, and he should also be able to make minor adjustments in his technique, despite the fact that a player like Smith already has virtually perfect strokes. But conditioning is really his only good option. That's because of who Stan Smith is and the level at which he's playing his game.

Second, and equally important, professional athletes are simply more ready, willing, and able than you and I to undertake a conditioning program. Conditioning usually becomes a habit for the pros — one that they often continue even after their professional playing careers are finished.

Steve Devereux's friend, Charlie Gogolak, is a good example of what can happen when conditioning becomes a habit. If Charlie's name sounds familiar, it's probably because you're a football fan. Charlie was an outstanding college place kicker at Princeton before going on to star with the Washington Redskins and the New England Patriots. Charlie's brother, Pete, another kicking star, will go down in National Football League history. His jump from the AFL Buffalo Bills to the NFL New York Giants precipitated the NFL-AFL merger.

. . . or distasteful.

Athletes like Stan Smith and Charlie Gogolak make their living with their bodies. Therefore, they aren't reluctant to subject themselves to a rigorous training program to function and play at peak efficiency. As professionals they are prepared to do a number of things that you and I might not be willing to do. They have the time and the motivation to work hard at getting into shape — at least if that's what it's going to take to eliminate a sportache.

When Charlie Gogolak began to experience frustrating elbow pain on the tennis court, he didn't react the way most recreational tennis players would have reacted. Although he was no longer playing pro football, Charlie nevertheless reacted as a professional athlete. He immediately thought of conditioning as the solution to his problem.

There are, of course, a variety of ways to condition key muscles once you suspect that the sportforces of your sport are going to cause you problems in a specific joint. Some people prefer to improvise their own conditioning program, utilizing paint cans, sandbags, and homemade weights. At the other end of the spectrum are the people who prefer the discipline and structure of an exercise center. If you are trying to rehabilitate an injured limb, I'd strongly suggest exercising under supervision. However, as long as your concern is to avoid aches and enhance performance, less structured and less costly conditioning can be every bit as effective and just as safe. It's your choice.

In Charlie Gogolak's case, fancy machinery was not required. He launched a self-designed, six-month training program designed to build up strength in his forearm. He started by doing wrist curls with five-pound weights. At the end of his program he was lifting sixty to eighty pounds, utilizing the same types of exercises that strength-training experts routinely recommend for athletes suffering from tennis elbow. It worked, and Charlie hasn't had elbow pain for more than three years.

Not everyone has the temperament of Charlie Gogolak. And, of course, your ache may not be in a joint that is as easy to exercise at home as your elbow.

Patti Catalano is an example of someone for whom conditioning at home wasn't the answer. When she came to see me in 1978, Patti was suffering from persistent hip pain. She was on the verge of emerging as the world-class runner she has since become, but Patti was in real trouble. After I had examined her and we had talked at length, I explained that I thought she ought to try to build up strength in her lower extremities on the Nautilus machines we have downstairs at Sports Medicine Resource, Inc., in addition to shortening her stride length and cutting back temporarily on a grueling training schedule. The conditioning exercises she had already been doing at home were obviously not sufficient to get Patti's body ready to perform at the elite level she was trying to reach. More important, I sensed that Patti had the right temperament and attitude to adjust to a rigorous, long-term Nautilus program. I'm happy to say I was correct. Patti managed her pain, improved her conditioning, and made her mark as a quality marathoner.

For most recreational athletes neither a long-term weight program nor a rigorous Nautilus program is realistic or required. General conditioning doesn't have to be all that difficult to provide you with an important measure of protection against sport-aches.

Every day — in my office, at clinics, in classes, on talk

shows — I find myself repeating the most important single piece of advice any doctor can give to an athlete: "If you stretch and strengthen, you'll probably never develop a sportache." A sweeping overstatement? Not really. As a sportsmedicine doctor, I have learned that the human body can perform if properly challenged. However, the challenge every athlete must meet is more than just getting out of bed and running three miles every morning or finding the time to play an hour of tennis every afternoon after work. The real challenge is to condition all your muscles, bones, and joints — to prepare them for what they are designed to do.

If you're an athlete with an ache, the key to conditioning is to concentrate on preparing specific muscles in *your* body for the specific sportforces of *your* sport. Before we get to our discussion of specific conditioning, let me remind you that the *C* of EEVeTeC also includes the need to start each sports season sensibly, as well as learning to limber up, warm up, and warm down every time you play your favorite sport.

Every March those of us who love baseball witness an example of the importance that the professional athlete attaches to starting the sports season sensibly. To baseball people — players and fans — the coming of spring is hailed not by a date on the calendar or by the sighting of some friendly bird. If you love baseball, it's only spring when you hear the first crack of bat and thump of leather. Spring starts when baseball players begin "spring training."

Recreational athletes often miss the point of baseball's vernal exercise. They don't doubt that baseball players need special training. "They have to get into condition. They're athletes. It's their business." Yet these same part-time, just-for-fun athletes frequently push and punish their own bodies beyond limits they would consider foolhardy for a baseball player. "Pitch nine innings in February? Ridiculous," they would surely say. Yet that's what they are really doing every day, without spring training. You've heard of a glass-armed pitcher. But did you ever see an athlete with four glass limbs? Just look as the majority of joggers, tennis players, and golfers anytime — particularly in early spring.

If you're going to play sports, learn to do what the pros do. Get in shape and stay in shape for what you're going to do. After

all, the only difference between a recreational athlete and a pro is one of degree.

"That's no big deal," you say. And you're right. Described this way, it sounds pretty simple. It certainly doesn't take a doctor to figure it out. However, if you *are* a doctor, it's all the more important to appreciate the significance of conditioning — as I learned early in my sportsmedicine career.

When I first began to practice podiatry, my average patient, suffering from aching legs as the result of going up and down stairs, would eventually opt for elevators and escalators. Having given in to his or her ache and stopped exercising, such a patient eventually wound up in my office. "Ah, weak foot," I'd say. "An orthotic will help." And one more soldier would join the growing army of foot sufferers!

But athletes changed all that. They said to me as they say all the time nowadays to other sportsmedicine doctors: "Baloney! Why should my legs ache? Damned if I'll take the elevator. I want to walk the stairs. Other people do. Fix me up."

Athletes used to drive many doctors to distraction. They refused to quit participating in activities that were causing stress when we knew that minimizing stress was a sure-fire way to keep various joints from aching. But they persevered and some doctors persevered and we all learned.

Today I might say to someone complaining of routine sore feet or tired legs: "Of course your legs ache. Your shoes aren't doing your feet and legs much good. You're out of shape. You're too heavy. Most important, you need to start exercising. Try some toe raises. Do some walking. Get into shape instead of coming to me for a crutch. One more soldier discharged!"

The Challenge: that's what conditioning is all about. You must not betray your body by asking it to do something it's not prepared to do. You need to "get into shape" to do whatever you're going to do — whether your goal is to walk, play tennis, or run a marathon.

•

There's no doubt that many sportaches are caused in part by insufficient conditioning. Fortunately, there's good news. You *can* do something about poor conditioning. The bad news is that you *must* do something. That's one reason why the *C* for conditioning is the last component of EEVeTeC. By the time you get to *C* in your application of EEVeTeC, you are out of options. You've already checked your equipment and your environment. You've adjusted your velocity. You've worked so hard on your technique that you could give lessons. What's left, short of quitting, is conditioning.

Your general conditioning is crucial to you as an athlete for one fundamental reason. Your chances of developing a sportache increase dramatically if key joints are unstable when they must absorb and transmit sports-related stress. Achieving and holding your stable position requires both strength and flexibility in the muscles that move, stabilize, and protect key joints, as well as a proper limbering-up and warm-up period before you start to play all-out.

If you realize an ache is coming and you suspect that the other four elements of EEVeTeC won't work or have already tried them and discovered they won't work, there is only one answer. You need to find a way to condition the joint that is bothering you against the particular sportforces generated when you play your favorite sport. You have a range of options from Nautilus centers with elaborate machinery and trained advisers to at-home exercise programs you can devise yourself without buying a single piece of equipment. The most important thing, however, is that you understand your conditioning goals. Before you begin

a conditioning program take a minute to survey your own needs. Ask yourself how much and what kind of strength and flexibility *you'll* need to be able to get and hold *your* joints in as stable a position as possible while you deal with the forces of *your* sport.

The *C* in EEVeTeC begins at the moment when your knee hurts, or your shoulder hurts, or you're having trouble with some other joint and you realize you'll have to strengthen or stretch something to be able to continue to play your favorite sport at the level you've now reached. You need to condition a particular joint against a particular sportforce. As a function of your genetics and your age and your background, there is, of course, a limit to how much conditioning you should expect to be able to do. However, unless you're a professional athlete in superb shape, there is certainly a long way to go before you reach that limit. You probably need to work on both strength and flexibility.

Strength

It takes a certain degree of strength to play sports without developing sportaches. For the most part you won't need the kind of brute strength required in weightlifting, for example. Recreational sports usually require endurance instead of brute strength.

The difference between muscle strength and endurance is one of degree. Strength means the maximum effort a muscle can make in a single contraction. Endurance means how well or how much it can work over a sustained period. Experts agree that most dynamic sports require both muscle strength and endurance. There is some reason to differentiate, since certain sports require more strength (golf, for instance), while other sports place an obvious emphasis on endurance (running). However, it seems sensible on balance to lump the two interrelated qualities together under the single umbrella of "strength." That's what we'll do from now on.

There are essentially two body tissues involved when we talk about strength — bone and muscle.

Bone

Too many people consider bone a hard, dead tissue. In fact, your bones are very much alive.

Like other tissues in your body, your bones are nourished by your blood stream. They are heavily bathed in mineral salts, such as calcium and phosphorus, all of which help give them strength. However, the fact that your bones are alive and require regular nourishment can lead to problems. Remember watching the astronauts exercising in their space capsule? Did you think they were keeping their muscles fit? Actually, they were keeping their bones fit. NASA doctors had determined that the astronauts might lose the mineral salts in their bones at a dangerously rapid pace while in the special environment of space. This condition is called osteoporosis. Exercise was prescribed to prevent osteoporosis from occurring during extended space travel.

Osteoporosis can also be a problem for healthy people after they're put in a cast for a fracture. When the cast is removed, X-rays often show spotty areas of mineral deficiency. Resumption of activity usually restores the missing minerals. To prevent unnecessary demineralization from occurring in the first place some experts have now begun to advocate a procedure called dynamic immobilization. Dynamic immobilization is a program of exercise for your injured body part during any period of immobilization. If you're faced with the need to have a cast, by all means discuss dynamic immobilization with your doctor.

Your bones can actually grow larger as well as stronger with exercise. This phenomenon is often found among baseball pitchers and tennis players. X-rays frequently reveal that the bones of their dominant arms are larger than those of their nondominant arms.

Can healthier, stronger bones help prevent fractures? That question has never been fully answered. The high percentage of young, healthy, well-nourished, highly trained competitive runners with stress fractures would seem to suggest that there are no guarantees. However, it's also possible that the stress of running may simply be too great for some people, even if they have otherwise healthy bones. Whether or not you are a runner, it makes good sense to condition your bones with regular exercise.

How do you strengthen bone? With total body conditioning. Don't exclude any body segment, regardless of which sport you play.

Muscle

To understand muscle conditioning, every recreational athlete needs to have a minimal working knowledge of muscle physiology.

Your muscles receive electrical impulses from your brain. They work by contracting. The specialized muscle tissue that enables your muscles to contract consists of dark, fast-twitch fibers as well as light, slow-twitch fibers. Recently, investigators have theorized that your muscles also have a number of intermediate fibers that can be recruited to serve as either fast or slow fibers, depending on demand.

Fast-twitch fibers provide strength and speed. Slow-twitch fibers provide endurance. The distribution between fast-twitch fibers and slow-twitch fibers in the muscles of your body is largely a fixed and inherited trait. The only accurate way to determine that distribution with any real precision is to do a muscle biopsy, by which a piece of muscle is removed surgically and carefully analyzed. However, it seems clear that regardless of the inherited balance between fast-twitch and slow-twitch fibers in your muscles, it is possible to enhance or change that balance through conditioning.

It is interesting that muscle physiologists have begun to prove that many of the theories and tests that coaches and trainers have been using for years really work. A good example of this is the traditional and respected vertical jump test. Standing next to a wall, an athlete first reaches as high as possible, making a mark with prechalked fingers. Then the athlete jumps and touches the same wall. The difference between an athlete's standing height and jumping height is the measure of the athlete's vertical jump. As a general rule, the springier, the stronger, the more explosive the athlete, the more fast-twitch fibers he or she has. However, an athlete can improve his or her vertical jump by training.

•

We've already mentioned that your muscles work by contracting. One type of contraction occurs when two bones are moved apart. This is called an *eccentric* contraction. Think of a push-up. As you raise yourself, the muscles in your upper arm contract eccentrically. The second type of muscular contraction occurs when the same two bones are going toward each other. When you lower yourself after a push-up, for example, those same muscles are still contracting. This is called a *concentric* contraction.

In the case of a push-up both your concentric and eccentric contractions are called *isotonic* contractions, because your muscles are working against resistance. There's a second basic kind of muscle contraction. It's *isometric* contraction, a contraction of muscle without any movement. Isometric contraction can take place at *any* joint angle. Flexing or ''showing your muscle'' is an example of an isometric exercise. You contract your biceps while holding your arm firmly at any angle you choose.

We know you can strengthen and enlarge your bones with exercise. The same holds true for your muscles. You can develop muscle bulk by stressing a muscle with essentially nondynamic work such as lifting weights. Dynamic work, emphasizing speed in a dynamic setting (sit-ups, for instance), tends to develop strength without bulk. Athletes who want to develop either sheer strength or endurance without losing their svelte look need only rely on dynamic workouts to avoid developing muscle bulk.

•

Your muscles are attached to your bones by specialized tissue called tendons. In some muscle-tendon units the muscle is relatively short and the tendon relatively long. In others the opposite is true. We're not sure exactly why, but the relative length of each of your tendons has something to do with the special function of each muscle.

Your tendons are made of a fibrous tissue that isn't well nourished by your blood stream. Also, your tendons are devoid of elasticity. They are vulnerable to problems for two basic reasons:

1. Your tendons are usually smaller than the muscles to which they attach. Stress is therefore concentrated in a smaller mass.
2. Your tendons are often exposed to the pressure of bones, since they frequently pass over several joints.

Nature has tried to make up for the fact that your tendons are relatively vulnerable to injury as a result of their inelasticity and location. Most tendons have two protective cushioning mechanisms: (1) bursae, pillowlike sacs placed at points of potential irritation, where tendon meets bone and tendon meets tendon; and (2) special sheaths that cover each tendon and secrete a lubricating fluid so that they can glide, not grab. Nevertheless, you can still reduce the chance of injuring a tendon by conditioning each entire muscle-tendon unit.

It appears that muscles weaken and tendons shorten with inadequate activity. However, the same kind of general strength conditioning helps both. Therefore, when we talk about strengthening your muscles, we are talking at the same time about promoting the health of your tendons.

Flexibility

On the other side of the conditioning balance scale is flexibility. If you doubt that both strength *and* flexibility are important, ask the coach or trainer of any college or professional team. Flexibility has been determined to be a key factor both in accident prevention and improved performance. Many teams are hiring special flexibility coaches to design individualized programs for their athletes.

Bob Anderson, author of the widely read book entitled *Stretching,* and consultant to various teams and athletic groups, has devoted much of his life to the study of flexibility. A fine college athlete, Bob thereafter let his body go to seed. He gained a significant amount of weight and got terribly out of shape.

Then Bob caught the stretching bug, lost dozens of excess pounds, and improved his sport performance. Now he lectures all over the country, making stretching and fitness look almost too easy. I know I've learned a lot by listening to Bob Anderson and studying his books.

Why the concern about flexibility? A great number of sport-aches occur in your hinge joints (knees, ankles, elbows, wrists). These joints in particular require the fullest range of motion possible, something that can be inhibited either by faulty joint design or faulty mechanics. In a significant number of cases, inflexibility is at fault.

Faulty design means that your bones cannot go through their full range of motion, either because of an inherited or an acquired defect. Faulty design is *not* a matter of inadequate flexibility. In an otherwise normal joint, your bones can nevertheless be somehow abnormal, usually as a result of a defect, an accident, or an operation. Despite your best efforts, you may simply be unable to perform the motions of your sport. A bowlegged skier, for example, will find it difficult to bend his or her knees and hold an edge across the slope. Even if you're not bow-legged, a bony overgrowth in the front of your ankle, caused by wear and tear or the result of an alteration from injury, can create a similar type of problem. In such cases stretching usually won't do any good.

Faulty mechanics, on the other hand, are often the result of a correctable inflexibility or weakness. If you have a sportache, the muscles that enable a given joint to move may be either too weak or too tight. Remember, your muscles do not have to get tighter as they get stronger, as least not if you stretch. Muscles can be tight but weak, and flexible but strong. More often than not aches that result from faulty mechanics are the result of an overly tight muscle or muscle group. Possibly, you are simply tight by nature. Or perhaps you've been exercising without making any particular effort to stay flexible. In either case, stretching can correct faulty mechanics and thereby eliminate aches. That's why flexibility is so important.

•

When it comes to measuring strength and flexibility, we're all different. There's not even any standard, universal, self-applied test of strength. The only accurate strength tests currently available require sophisticated equipment and must be administered by trained personnel.

It is not only difficult to measure strength, it's also very difficult to interpret the results obtained when muscle strength is measured. This is because your absolute strength is meaningless until you make it clear what exactly you want to do, for how long, and how often. Also, strength is meaningless without detailed information about muscle balance.

I was talking recently with Dr. Howard Knuttgen, a former president of the American College of Sports Medicine, editor of its prestigious *Medicine and Science in Sports,* professor of exercise physiology at Boston University, and author of *Complete Conditioning: The No-Nonsense Guide to Fitness and Health.* I asked Dr. Knuttgen what the exercise physiologists feel is the most important unanswered question in the area of athletic performance and health. He replied: "Rob, I think what we really need to do is get a better sense of balance between muscles. We don't have a good understanding, and we need to document it better than we have." That certainly conforms to my experience as a sportsmedicine doctor. When athletes ask how strong they need to be in a given set of muscles, I never know what to say except "strong enough." Pain, of course, is an important indication of weakness.

At Sports Medicine Resource, Inc., my colleagues and I used to count on our ability to test a patient's strength manually. We'd ask the patient to put a certain anatomical part, such as a knee, through ranges of motion against our resistance. Obviously this was a highly subjective evaluation at best. On the basis of such an evaluation we would then prescribe some system of exercises.

Our lives became easier at SMR and our patients were helped more when we acquired a sophisticated machine called a Cybex, which is designed to measure muscle activity around a given joint in a very precise and scientifically reproducible manner. If we want to test the muscles acting on your knee, we simply strap your leg to a lever arm attached to the machine. The operator can then operate a dial that determines the amount of resistance against which you'll have to work. The result is transferred to a moving piece of paper. The graph may remind you of the chart you get when your heart is tested — a not inappropriate comparison, incidentally.

If we decide to test your strength on the Cybex, we'll be looking at three things: (1) absolute strength, (2) strength at speed, and (3) strength at endurance. Your Cybex graph, when interpreted, will provide several important pieces of information. For one thing, we'll be able to tell exactly where any muscle weakness lies. We'll also be able to identify relative strength and weakness in opposing muscle groups. Finally, we'll be able to run subsequent checks to see if you are getting stronger as the result of the exercises we prescribe.

When it comes to flexibility, however, you should be able to evaluate your own relative tightness. In the process you should also discover a number of exercises you can do to promote flexibility if you decide that key muscles are overly tight. Get Bob Anderson's book, *Stretching*. Have a look at Hyman Jampol's useful paperback *The Weekend Athlete's Way to a Pain-Free Monday*, in which he describes a test you can take to determine your "flexibility profile." Ask other athletes or a trainer for the stretching exercises you should do to become more flexible in the muscles that stabilize and move the joint that is bothering you. However you decide to proceed, remember that the "test" is the exercise you need to keep doing if you fail.

When people ask me if they are "flexible enough," I like to follow the old New England tradition of answering a question with a question. I usually respond by asking, "Who are you?" It's my way of saying that there is no single answer or standard of flexibility. Different people have different problems and requirements when it comes to flexibility.

Jim Racklin is an illustration of one extreme. Jim first cornered me after a talk I gave at a medical symposium in Buffalo. He confessed that he had been having some knee and hip problems and wondered what suggestions I might have. Jim explained that he had been an athlete during high school and college but had confined himself pretty much to golf during his adult years. At the height of the running boom, however, he'd decided he'd like to take up jogging.

The more Jim Racklin ran, the more knee and hip problems he developed. When he and I first talked I suggested that it might be a good idea for him to consult an orthopedist in his area. I explained to Jim that although his aches were probably the result of simple muscle imbalance, he might also have an internal knee problem, especially in view of his past history as an athlete.

The following spring, at a meeting in Cincinnati, Jim cornered me again.

"How'd it go, Jim?"

"Well, Rob, I did see the orthopedist you referred me to."

"I trust everything is OK. How are the knee and hip?"

"A lot better. I've stopped running."

"What did the doctor say, Jim?"

"He said, 'Jim, you've got tight muscles. That's all there is to it.' "

"What does that do to your golf swing, Jim?"

"I just have to flatten it out."

"Are you running at all?"

"Well, it turns out there is no way I'm going to stretch enough to meet the demands I put on my body running, so I'm settling for bike riding and swimming, some tennis, and, of course, golf."

How do you know if you're like Jim Racklin? The fact is that most people who are naturally tight — especially adults — know that they're relatively inflexible, because they have always been tight. They recognize that they're the ones who never could touch their toes, who really can't bend over or do all the things that other people do. If they've tried sports that require flexibility, these same people also know that they can't do much about their congenital tightness. A person who is naturally very tight can never be transformed into a very flexible person.

At the other end of the flexibility spectrum, there are people like Molly, the youngest of the four children in our family. Back when Molly was three years old, she called to me one day, "Come and see what I'm doing, Dad!" I went and found Molly at the top of an open doorway. She had walked herself up by pressing both hands and both feet on the edges of the door casing, and working her way up to the top. Molly is indeed very flexible, a characteristic she inherits to a degree from both her mother and father.

People like Jim Racklin and Molly McGregor are the exceptions, however, and not the rule. Most of us — including many of the people who regularly populate the offices of many sports-medicine doctors — fall into the middle of the flexibility spectrum. There is no question that if you do not stretch key muscles, they become contracted. You can become tight just because you're not doing anything to stay loose. That's what happens to most people. They become what I call "Homo sapiens sedentarius." Even if they do exercise, many people don't stretch. Either way, whether you're tight because you've been too sedentary or whether you're tight because you've been exercising without stretching, correctable inflexibility can lead to trouble.

Your range of motion is basically a function of the flexibility of the muscles that move and stabilize key joints. Unless you are congenitally tight, you can increase your range of motion by stretching.

•

Aside from the flexibility of key muscles, another factor influences joint motion. Some people have a limited range of motion because of the character of a joint itself. Do your bones *permit* adequate motion? They may not, either because of an abnormal architectural relationship or because of previous injuries.

If you have a limited range of motion, it's important to be able to tell whether your problem is caused by muscles that are too tight or by bones that simply don't permit certain motions. You should be able to tell what is going on by trying (gently) to increase your range of motion. If you merely have tight muscles, when you reach the end of your range and keep pressing, you should be able to feel just the slightest give without pain. A hard end feel, on the other hand, is aptly named, because at the end of your range of motion you'll get a hard feeling. You should sense that there is no more motion to be found. The hard feeling is just that — bone on bone.

How do you know which person you are — and thus find out how flexible you are? If you really don't know, the best way to find out is to do any one or combination of the exercises given in a book such as Bob Anderson's *Stretching* (Shelter Publications, 1980). If you find various classic stretching exercises easy, you're flexible enough. You don't need to do anything more than you are doing. Perhaps you were simply born flexible, or maybe you've been stretching all along. If you can't pass a basic stretch test because you're like Jim Racklin, or you have a bony block, you're stuck. If you can't pass because you're a Homo sapiens sedentarius, then keep taking your test until you do pass it. If you're too tight because you've done nothing to stay loose, each test becomes the exercise you need to do to develop adequate flexibility. And remember, if you're stiff and sore after you stretch, your muscles are weak as well as inflexible.

Dr. George Sheehan, perhaps the best-known runners' guru, is fond of pointing out that we are all experiments of one. I learned this lesson recently at the New England Memorial Hospital. I had been asked to join an all-star group at a ribbon-cutting ceremony for their new Parcourse. I was very proud to be there. First, I thought it was wonderful that the hospital was making a strong and positive statement for health. "Use this and stay out," they were saying. "Use this and get out sooner." That's downright unbusinesslike for a hospital. Second, the assembled group was full of heavy hitters. There was Dave McGillivray, a young, superbly trained runner and one of my heroes. Dave won my respect and admiration when he ran across the United States to raise money for the Jimmy Fund. There was Mike Calhoun, executive director of Parcourse Ltd., creator of the course. And there was Bob Scheu, marketing director for Perrier, donor of the equipment. After a few introductory remarks, the four of us led most of the guests around the course. Along the way we demonstrated and discussed the values and virtues of each exercise. Then we had a friendly six-mile run.

For the next week I felt the effects of my Parcourse experience. I hadn't realized I had so many dormant muscles. As fit as I think I am because of my running, I wasn't up to the Parcourse. It's great, but tough. Anyone who has any doubts about his or her strength and flexibility should give Parcourse a try. If you can't go around the course without undue stress (as I couldn't) you may want to consider using it regularly as a conditioning tool.

The Parcourse is a super conditioning alternative. Rabbi Barry Silberg of Milwaukee is the champion of another good alternative exercise. He was the hit of the 1979 American Medical Joggers Association Boston Marathon meeting, not because he was a rabbi, not even because he's a running rabbi. Rabbi Silberg simply gave the most dynamic demonstration I've ever witnessed of an alternative complementary running tool: rope skipping. The rabbi had all those marathoning doctors on the edges of their chairs as he demonstrated the virtues of an exercise system that (1) can fit in your back pocket, (2) doesn't require much room, (3) eliminates all concern about the weather, and (4) can provide as much aerobic conditioning as running. Also, if you jump on both feet at the same time, you can train for running by skipping rope while at the same time minimizing musculo-skeletal stress.

Is the fact that rope skipping generates relatively little stress so important? Well, it certainly can be. Take my friend Bob Halligan, for example. Although neither he nor I can figure out exactly why, Bob had a triple arthrodesis performed on both feet ten years ago, when he was twenty-five. The operation fused certain bones in Bob's feet, leaving him with the ability to move each foot and ankle up and down, but making it impossible for him to roll his feet in and out. Bob's feet and ankles can function but are incapable of withstanding the kind of stress he would encounter if he ran day after day. Why is Bob Halligan so special? Because he has completed two Boston Marathons without any problems, and without running a single step in training! How? Sure, by skipping rope.

Another good alternative conditioning tool, at least for runners, is cross-country skiing. John Dimmock, Olympic trial qualifier in the marathon in both 1976 and 1980, and winner of the 1979 Mardi Gras Marathon, is a native Vermonter. So is Bill Koch, America's top cross-country skier. In fact, John and Bill grew up together. John often wonders what would have happened if each had started in the other's sport. "I'm sure Bill would have been a world-class marathoner," he says, "but I'm not sure I would have become a world-class cross-country skier." The point is that there are great tradeoffs in training — not absolute equivalents. John described with precision how he uses cross-country skiing in his overall training program in the December 1979 issue of *Runner's World*.

No one will ever know how many runners have been lost to cross-country skiing — that is, how many runners who started cross-country skiing as a complementary training tool eventually enjoyed it so much that they now run only to complement their skiing. Dr. John Hart, one of the winners in the Masters Division of the Trans Canada Ski Marathon in 1979, is a good example. A former marathoner, he still trains on the Boston Marathon course in the Newton hills. But he does it on roller skis.

Jess Bell, president of Bonne Bell, is an inveterate runner, skier, and race promoter. Jess started both the Nastar skiing program and the Bonne Bell ten-kilometer runs. During March 1979 at Jackson, New Hampshire, Jess and I staged the first Bonne Bell Run/Ski. We began wearing our cross-country clothes and running shoes. Our cross-country skis and boots were left at the side of the road. We ran two three-kilometer road loops, ending up at the "start." Then we put on our skis and boots and did a ten-kilometer ski loop. How did I do? It's just as George Sheehan says. Despite having run a creditable marathon only three weeks earlier, my thigh muscles still weren't sufficiently conditioned for the Run/Ski. I hope the Run/ Skis grow in popularity; they provide great experience. And next time I'll be ready.

Bicycle riding is another good alternative conditioning tool. As long as you maintain the same pulse rate riding a bicycle as running, the workout is equivalent. Cycling can also provide superb musculo-skeletal conditioning for key lower-extremity muscles, especially your quadriceps. Swimming, of course, is the ultimate non-weight-bearing aerobic fitness alternative.

A Few Books on Conditioning

Hundreds of books and articles have been written about how to get into shape. In particular, I can recommend the following books, among others. They are authoritative, well written, and easily understandable.

> *The Weekend Athlete's Way to a Pain-Free Monday* by Hyman Jampol (Houghton Mifflin Company, J. P. Tarcher, Inc., 1978).
>
> *Health and Fitness through Physical Activity* by Michael L. Pollack, Jack H. Wilmore, and Samuel M. Fox (John Wiley & Sons, 1978), in the American College of Sports Medicine Series.
>
> *Physiology of Fitness* by Brian J. Sharkey (Human Kinetics Publishers, 1979).
>
> *The Fit Athlete* by Roy Shephard (Oxford University Press, 1978).
>
> *Complete Conditioning: The No-Nonsense Guide to Fitness and Health* by David Shepro and Howard G. Knuttgen (Addison-Wesley Publishing Company, 1975).

No matter how you decide to do your general conditioning — whether you decide you are strong enough and flexible enough to avoid aches without anything more than regular participation in your favorite sport or activity, or whether you choose to use a Parcourse, take up some alternative sport(s), sign up for a Nautilus program, or buy a skip rope — the most important thing is that you make conditioning a lifelong habit. Remember, your bones and muscles will weaken without constant challenge. Moreover, your muscles will gradually become very tight if you don't do anything to keep them loose. That's what "getting into shape" is all about. Once you're in "great shape," you'll have to keep working to stay fit. The alternative is a sportache. In addition to finding a few minutes a day for general conditioning, you'll have to pick a sport or sports that are right *for you*. That's what the next chapter is all about.

5
Picking Your Sport

EEVeTeC WORKS. But even EEVeTeC may not be enough in certain cases. It's only common sense to realize that not every recreational activity is appropriate for every enthusiast. Some bodies simply aren't suited for certain activities. Picking a sport that is right *for you* is an important first step toward pain-free sports participation.

I'm a good example myself of the fact that some people are more suited for certain sports than for others. I enjoy a number of different activities. I ski, play tennis, golf, and skate. But I'm not destined to be a competitive tennis player, golfer, or skater. I don't have the coordination, agility, or sense of balance required to excel at those sports. More important, in the sports that I don't do well, I also tend to develop aches. For instance, when I hit too many tennis balls, not only do I watch an awful lot of them sail into the net or over the base line, but also my right shoulder starts to throb, because I rarely hit the ball correctly. Apparently, I hit the ball late on my backhand and my arm is too straight on my serve. I'm just not well enough conditioned to play for long the way I play.

First and foremost, I'm a runner. For the past seven years I've averaged thirty-five miles per week on roads, river banks, golf courses, beaches, cross-country trails, and tracks. I've participated in dozens of road races and marathons. I look forward to my daily run. Any time I miss it, I feel uneasy, restless, and unfulfilled. As long as I can manage to put one foot in front of the other, I'll be carrying my running shoes, looking for a free moment and some open space. Running is part of my life.

As a runner I'm convinced that anyone who doesn't run is missing something special. However, as a sportsmedicine doctor, I know that running isn't for everyone. I treat hundreds of runners and their aches every year. A surprising number of the runners I see regularly as patients simply weren't built to run. Others can do some long-distance running without undue pain, but they must absolutely avoid going "too far, too fast, too often." And it's incredible how many people who are otherwise sensible nevertheless succumb to the temptation to overindulge when they take up running.

Dr. George Sheehan, a living legend among contemporary runners, likes to talk about somatotyping — the science of body typing. George argues that only thin, shy, introverted people are cut out to be top runners. He often remarks that the average winner of the Boston Marathon is five feet eight inches tall and weighs 122 pounds. Does that mean that a six-foot six-inch, 270-pound specimen can never compete in marathons? Not necessarily. But it's very unlikely that someone with a such a build would enjoy running — just about as likely as my being picked to start at defensive end for the Green Bay Packers. According to somatotyping, the ideal runner — an "ectomorph" — will be a happier, more successful runner than either the barrel-chested competitive athlete (the "mesomorph") or the big-bellied, sedentary type (the "endomorph").

It certainly seems to be true that running appeals more to certain personalities and body types. But when I say that running isn't for everyone, I'm thinking of neither personality nor body type. My concern is your health. Some people simply can't become long-distance runners because their bodies won't tolerate the repetitive stresses of running. Some people can't run because if they do, they will develop chronic aches.

If you're not suited for a particular activity, you shouldn't be frustrated or ashamed. Instead of forcing your body to do something for which it wasn't designed, learn to accept your limitations. If your body wasn't designed to run long distances, why not pick another sport? You're in excellent company. Many pros who excel in other sports could never make it as distance runners.

Dave Cowens, the pro basketball star, was a patient of mine for several years before he finally retired from the Boston Celtics in October 1980. Dave has what I call "high-impact feet." His feet just don't absorb shock very well. You may remember that Dave finally decided to quit the Celtics because his aching feet and ankles would no longer permit him to play at the level he felt his fans expected of him.

Because of his feet Dave could never have become a distance runner, no matter how much he might have been willing to work at reducing forces, perfecting technique, or refining conditioning. As a basketball player, Dave knew that he could expect occasional aches, although his problems were manageable for a number of years before his retirement. When he swims or rides a bicycle, Dave has no foot pain whatsoever, because there is no impact. However, as a runner, he wouldn't stand a chance.

Dave Cowens is a marvelous athlete. An unusually dedicated pro, he always worked hard at his conditioning. He was particularly disciplined about stretching, which he did regularly as a Celtic. A common sight just before a game was to see Dave sitting on the floor, stretching. He found that he had to maintain a high degree of flexibility to play basketball without aches, and he was willing to pay the price of hours of stretching each week. But Dave could never have become a runner.

Millions of people have feet like Dave Cowens's without also having his patience and dedication. Perhaps you, too, have high-impact feet. If a dedicated athlete like Dave Cowens could never realistically expect to be a runner, how can you? Running is very stressful. Obviously, it's much more common to find that someone can't run without developing aches than it is to encounter an athlete who has been forced to quit tennis, golf, swimming, or bicycling because of chronic pain. But most bodies are more suited to one sport than another.

•

Picking your sport is an important part of avoiding and managing routine aches. How should you do it? Whether you're choosing your first sport or substituting for one that has caused you trouble, you should begin by recognizing your limitations. Then you need to understand the particular stresses inherent in various activities.

For years sport scientists have been working on developing sophisticated tools to determine athletic potential. Thanks to this research, it has become easier and easier for coaches to identify young people with the potential to become world-class performers. Soon it may even be possible to pick potentially outstanding high school and junior high school athletes.

Does this extensive and sophisticated research hold promise for those of us who only want to finish a four-hour marathon, win the club mixed doubles championship, or break ninety for eighteen holes of golf? Perhaps.

For the time being, however, there are no easy tests to determine which recreational activity is best for you. Therefore, the best and surest way to discover which sport you are most suited to play is to experiment. Try various activities. Since you're not planning to spend the next ten years training for the Olympics, you simply need to pick a sport you can enjoy without undue risk of acute or chronic pain. Your body will let you know soon enough if the activity you've selected is too stressful for you.

Possibly you'll find the trial and error method (sampling various sports) too time-consuming, too expensive, or a complete turnoff. Don't despair. The following three common sense guidelines can make it easier for you to choose an ideal activity.

1. You should pick a sport with sportforces within your body's range of tolerance. Remember that sportaches occur when sportforces exceed your body's tolerance for stress, and the most important thing to consider is the peak force. There are three basic types of sports: *impact* (for instance, running, tennis, and golf), *release* (bowling and throwing are examples), and *resistance* (swimming and cycling, to name two). Of the three, impact sports are the most stressful. If your sport involves impact, your body must be able to tolerate both internal and external sportforces. Therefore, if you're looking for a sport with a minimal chance of causing you a chronic ache, don't choose an impact sport.

2. Recreational sports can also be generally classified as either weight-bearing (running, tennis, golf) or non-weight-bearing (swimming or cycling). If you're concerned about developing lower-extremity sportaches, a non-weight-bearing sport makes obvious sense. (Note to the overweight: this tip is especially important to you. You're perfectly correct to believe that if you play sports regularly, you will probably lose weight. However, you must be careful to choose a non-weight-bearing or moderate weight-bearing sport in your effort to slim down. Otherwise, sports participation may bring on chronic aches as fast as it takes off excess pounds.)

3. We've said it before, but let's say it again. Sportaches generally result from repetitive stress rather than from a single instance of overload or overuse. Thus, sports with a built-in recovery period don't result in sportaches nearly as often as sports where force loads are constant and unremitting. If you're a runner, there's virtually no time for your lower-extremity muscles to rest between strides. If you play tennis, on the other hand, your body can rest and recover between shots, points, and games. Likewise, in swimming and cycling, there's always a healthy recovery period between peak force loads, at least if you're not paddling or pedaling all out. Better still, golf consists of about 5 percent play and 95 percent recovery time. If your endurance is at all questionable, you'll be better off with an activity that has a built-in recovery period. Pick your sport accordingly.

•

How will you know if you've made the wrong choice of sports? What if the sport you pick is more than your body can handle? It won't take long for you to figure that out. Your body will let you know. You'll develop an ache.

If you do develop an ache, by now you know what to do. Use EEVeTeC to reduce sportforces and prepare your body for the stress of sports participation. However, if your ache persists even after you apply the McGregor Solution — and it may — perhaps you simply weren't cut out for your present sport. You may actually have to quit your present sport entirely. Before you quit, however, you should consider two other options.

First, you may be able to continue with your present activity — if you can accept your limitations. Maybe you can't run a marathon. But you can still enjoy running for recreation. Likewise, it isn't necessary to run five or six times a week to call yourself a runner. Once a week — with other exercise two or three days — is better than nothing. The same common sense rules apply to tennis. You don't necessarily need to play an hour of vigorous singles five days a week. A set or two of leisurely doubles every few days may be all your elbow, wrist, or shoulder can stand. After all, it's still tennis.

Second, instead of quitting your present activity altogether, you may be able to eliminate your ache by simply learning to

balance activities. What this means is simple. As a rule, no athlete should rely exclusively on any one sport. Let's say you take up jogging. Once you build up to fifteen or twenty miles a week, you'll probably be hooked — both on running and on regular exercise. You'll feel good. You'll lose weight, you'll probably sleep better, and you'll feel calmer. Eventually, you'll probably also develop an acute or chronic lower-extremity ache. Using EEVeTeC, you'll presumably do everything you can to reduce and meet the sportforces of running. Possibly, however, nothing will work.

If you're the runner I've just described, don't panic. It's not at all unusual to discover that a chronic ache returns every time you approach your maximum weekly mileage. The prospect of exercising only once or twice a week may be alarming, and you may not like the option of running only a mile a day either. But you don't need to quit running altogether.

What can you do? Why not try one or two additional sports with different kinds of stress? Swimming and bicycling, for example, are both excellent conditioning activities. Neither activity, however, requires you to absorb repetitive impact force loads in your lower extremities. In other words, you may be able to continue running three to five miles once or twice a week if you balance your running with forty-five minutes of swimming or cycling on alternate days. Your level of fitness should stay the same — or, perhaps, improve. But the cumulative weekly stress to your lower extremities will be substantially reduced, and perhaps you will be able to continue your favorite activity (running) without pain.

Dr. Art Pappas, one of my partners at Sports Medicine Resource, Inc., and team physician for the Boston Red Sox, believes that the current trend toward participation in a single recreational sport or activity is ultimately destructive. Dr. Pappas believes that if you participate in just one activity long enough, you become a prime candidate for the kinds of aches that result from muscular imbalance. Certainly there's no doubt that your heart and lungs will benefit from regular exercise. But from a musculo-skeletal point of view, you may not really be healthy. I agree with Art entirely. If you're concerned about avoiding and managing sportaches, specialization isn't a good idea. The well-rounded athlete has a significant advantage over the person who runs or plays tennis every day and never does anything else.

George Atkinson, professor of recreation and leisure studies at Boston's Northeastern University, is another who opposes specialization. "For years," he remarked to me one day recently, "athletes have become increasingly specialized. Yes, performance has improved. But at what cost? We can now ruin an athlete's knees in only two years. Terrific! It's like the cows in Vermont. We've tripled their milk production. But we've cut their lifespan in half."

•

To have the best chance of using the McGregor Solution to eliminate sportaches, you must begin by choosing your sport or sports with care. Can you eliminate risk? Probably not. If you play sports, sooner or later you're likely to hurt. Your connective tissue — tendons, ligaments, and bursae — will start to complain. The forces generated in your sport will become more than your body can tolerate. You'll hurt — at least temporarily — as the result of the simple fact that you will inadvertently ask your body to do more than it can without pain.

No matter how carefully you pick your sport and regardless of how accurately you predict your sportaches, chances are that eventually you'll need the McGregor Solution. In the chapters that follow you'll see how we apply the solution to tennis, running, and six other popular recreational activities. If we haven't actually discussed your favorite sport, you can, of course, still use EEVeTeC. How should you go about it? It's really a three-step process.

First, ask yourself: What are the sportforces I must be able to tolerate when I play my sport? Think about your activity. What are you trying to do? Movement is the key to stress. What movements are required in your sport? In running, for instance, your goal is to move across the ground. The emphasis is on your legs, but running also requires arm movement. In comparison, as a tennis player you're trying to move the ball with your racket. Your arm(s) do most of the work, but you have to run around the court as well.

Thinking about the goal of your game should help you identify the moment of peak force you'll have to tolerate when you play. Remember, there are three basic types of peak force: impact,

release, and resistance. Where does your sport fit in? What kind of peak force must you be able to tolerate when you play? Do you hit a ball, pound the ground, or strike some other object? That's impact. Do you throw a ball or anything else? That's release. Do you thrust or push against something? That's resistance.

Once you've identified the moment of peak force in your sport, you need to analyze what your body does to prepare for and recover from that moment of peak force. Sportforces are cyclical. In an impact sport, like tennis or golf, there are special preparatory forces generated as you draw your racket or club back and begin your swing. After impact (peak force), additional forces are generated as you follow through or recover. In running these "internal forces" occur before and after every step.

As your body moves to and from the moment of peak force in your sport, stress is created within the joints of your arms and legs. These internal forces are secondary to the sportforces that your body must tolerate at the moment of peak force. However, they still play a definite role in the development of sportaches. Even if your sport doesn't involve impact, there are nevertheless preparatory and recovery forces, as well as peak forces, with which you must be able to deal.

Second, ask yourself: What sportaches are common to my sport? Don't worry about medical terminology unless you've developed acute or chronic inflammation or have suffered a direct injury. If you hurt occasionally when you play your sport, you have a simple sportache. It doesn't take years of medical training to figure out that elbow pain is elbow pain, knee pain is knee pain, and a sore shoulder is a sore shoulder — and nothing more. Leave the six-syllable, diagnostic words to the doctors. They'll use them when and if you show up with acute or chronic inflammation or a direct injury.

Once you understand sportforces, common sense alone should be enough to help you identify the most common aches in your sport. In tennis, for example, the moment of peak force involves impact between your racket and the ball. What happens at impact is more likely to lead to problems in your wrist or elbow than it is to cause problems in any other joint. That's just common sense. Ball impact forces must pass through your wrist and elbow before they can affect any other part of your body.

In contrast, every tennis player knows that there is also considerable shoulder motion in tennis, especially during preparation and recovery on the serve and smash. Since the forces you generate as you wind up and follow through for your serve and overhead are internal forces, it should come as no surprise that those forces primarily affect your shoulder. They come to rest in and around your shoulder before they can flow out to your elbow or wrist.

There's also considerable running, jumping, twisting, and sliding as you move around a tennis court. All of these movements expose your lower extremities to a variety of potential problems. Your knees, for example, are often pointing one way while your feet are heading another way. Remember what we told you in chapter 3 about knee rotation? Is it any surprise that tennis players develop their share of knee sportaches?

For the purpose of avoiding and managing sportaches — preventing acute or chronic aches from recurring as well as ensuring that they do not develop in the first place — the most important thing for you to understand is how and why the forces of your game result in stress to a given part of your body. Once you

understand that your knee pain as a runner is primarily the result of the fact that repetitive forces are generated each time your foot hits the ground and that the stress has become more than your knee can tolerate, it should be easy to grasp the importance of finding ways to reduce forces and increase tolerance.

Now that you've analyzed the sportforces of your favorite sport and identified the sportaches you are likely to develop, you're ready for the final, most important step in your application of the McGregor Solution.

Third, ask yourself: What solution is available to me as a recreational athlete with a simple sportache? The answer, of course, is EEVeTeC.

•

So much for how EEVeTeC works in theory. Now we come to its specific application to your sport. The McGregor Solution works for just about any dynamic activity. We convinced our writer friend, Bruce Weber, of this recently, despite the fact that Bruce is not an athlete. Working late one night at his typewriter, Bruce suddenly noticed that the outside of his left wrist had begun to ache every time he hit the keys. Earlier that day he had been hearing all about EEVeTeC from Steve, so Bruce thought he'd analyze his ache in light of the five variables — just for fun.

He listed the elements of the solution one by one. First, equipment. As he thought about it, Bruce realized that his ancient manual typewriter had started to offer unusual resistance. Likewise, a worn-out typewriter ribbon was making it necessary for him to murder the keys to get the images onto paper. In addition, Bruce suddenly realized that the chair he was sitting on, not his usual desk chair, was probably too low for his desk. He watched himself type for a moment and realized that the height of his chair *was* causing him to type with his wrist in a relatively unstable position.

"I suddenly knew I was going to be able to eliminate my ache," Bruce told us excitedly the next day. "I felt like a cross between Sherlock Holmes and Albert Einstein. It was very exhilarating."

Environment considerations were easy. "I had no business typing until two in the morning," Bruce later explained. "My fatigue was obviously contributing to my ache. And I should have replaced the burned-out bulb in my overhead light fixture.

Straining to see was making me generally tense, in my arms as well as elsewhere.''

Ace typist Bruce next realized that a morning deadline had panicked him into pushing particularly hard. Speed might be admirable for production, but trying to type as fast as he had been that particular evening didn't really seem advisable for continued good health. That's velocity. Technique and conditioning considerations also soon became obvious, although Bruce already suspected that he was going to be able to eliminate his ache by reducing forces with adjustments in his equipment, environment, and velocity.

Does the McGregor Solution work? It sure does — for tennis players, runners, golfers, bowlers, swimmers, cyclists, and everyone who is engaged in any dynamic activity. Read on. You deserve to have some fun using EEVeTeC to find a solution to your own aches. Good luck.

Part III

EEVeTeC APPLIED

6
Tennis

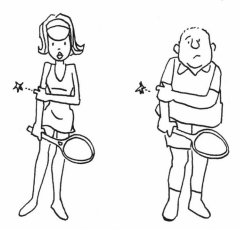

IF YOU'RE A TENNIS PLAYER with joint-related pain, you're in good company. The majority of tennis players over age thirty-five suffer from elbow pain sometime during their playing careers. That makes tennis elbow the world's most common sportache. With an estimated 30 million players in the United States alone, thousands of new cases spring up every day.

Of the most popular recreational sports, tennis and running are easily the most stressful. Among tennis players just about every joint is vulnerable, whether you're a beginner or a pro. If you play tennis, chances are that eventually you're going to hurt.

Fortunately, there are a number of solutions to tennis-related sportaches. That's one of the great differences between tennis and running. In tennis there are countless answers to a few reasonably well-defined problems. In running there are lots of problems with relatively fewer potential solutions.

Unfortunately, no single solution is guaranteed to relieve every tennis player's problems. But no matter what your ailment, you'll probably find a solution that will work *for you* in this chapter. You won't necessarily need a doctor or trainer, but you probably will want to consult a teaching pro or knowledge-able tennis equipment salesperson.

As with sportaches in any athletic activity, the first step toward managing tennis sportaches is to understand and appreciate sportforces. Next you'll want to identify your aches. Those two steps will facilitate your application of the McGregor Solution. In fact, once you start to apply EEVeTeC, you'll probably be surprised to discover how much you can do to reduce tennis sportforces as well as to increase your body's ability to withstand the inevitable stresses generated when you play.

Tennis Sportforces

Your primary goal as a tennis player is to propel the ball with your racket. Everything you do on the court — your ready position, your racketwork, your footwork — is designed to help you hit your shots solidly and with control. The moment when your racket collides with the tennis ball is the focus of your performance on a tennis court. It's also the moment when the sportforces of tennis are at their peak.

Tennis is an impact sport, meaning that every time you hit the ball, your body must be able to absorb and transmit not only the considerable internal forces you generate as you run to the ball, wind up, and swing, but also the external forces that flow into your body at the moment of impact. Every tennis player realizes that something happens at ball impact — the external force you have to absorb can give your arm and body quite a jolt. But don't forget that it also requires considerable muscle to get your racket and body moving (preparation) as well as to decelerate (recover) after impact. When you use your muscles, you generate forces within your joints. These internal forces contribute to the cumulative stress of the game.

Tennis sportforces — like the forces of every other sport — are cyclical. Compared to the forces generated during most other sports, the sportforces of tennis are relatively numerous, complicated, and stressful, which is why so many tennis players complain of sportaches.

Let's analyze the cycle of tennis sportforces from beginning to end.

Preparation

The joints of your hitting arm — arms if you hit with two hands on one (or both) sides — must be able to tolerate the considerable internal or "swing" forces generated each time you take your racket back and swing. It requires a certain amount of work to accelerate your tennis racket toward an oncoming ball. Work, of course, contributes to stress.

Racketwork in tennis shouldn't be as fast as racketwork in such sports as squash or racquetball. In fact, your tennis strokes should be relatively slow, smooth, and controlled. That would be ideal. But many of us don't have classic strokes. We tend to generate overly large swing forces through frequent attempts to hit too hard or with too much spin.

If you insist on trying to hit the ball as hard as Jimmy Connors or Martina Navratilova, or trying to apply top spin à la Guillermo Vilas, there will be a dramatic increase in the swing forces you generate as you wind up for your shots.

Your serve can cause problems even if you don't try to imitate Roscoe Tanner. Inherently, the service motion in tennis generates high swing forces. Because you cannot capitalize on pace supplied by your opponent, you tend to swing a lot faster than you swing on your other shots. Remember, the faster your motion, the higher the swing forces, and the greater the resultant impact force.

Moment of Peak Force

Researchers have told us two interesting things about what happens at the moment when a tennis racket and a tennis ball collide. First, if you hit the ball precisely in the "sweet spot" of the racket, minimum impact force is transmitted into your body. Your racket frame and strings absorb virtually all the impact force of a perfect hit. Considerable impact force may be generated, but there is minimal stress to your arm. Second (and now for the bad news), no one, not even a pro, hits a perfect shot very often.

Every time you hit a tennis ball off center, you expose your body to more of the external force generated at impact. Why? Whenever you mis-hit, your racket tends to twist or rotate in your hand(s). That tendency to twist is called *torque,* a word you're going to hear repeatedly in this chapter.

To resist torque, your forearm muscles have to do extra work, straining as you grip your racket to try to prevent it from twisting. You can't let your racket twist, after all, because then you would lose control over the direction of your shots. The greater the force that's twisting your racket, the sooner your forearm muscles will tire. And when your muscles give out, stress shifts to the connecting tissue that holds your joints together. The common result is a sportache.

The farther from the center of your racket you hit a tennis ball, the greater the torque. Every fraction of an inch makes a measurable difference in the force load transmitted to your body. When you get to the solution section of this chapter, you'll see that a number of our suggestions are designed to help you hit more of your shots closer to the center of your racket. You have to minimize torque to avoid tennis sportaches.

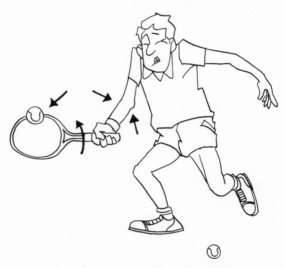

Torque also increases as a function of leverage. Your tennis racket is a relatively long lever arm. That explains why the impact force loads in tennis seem so much greater than they do in racquetball, for instance, which is played with a shorter racket. Two things — the amount of the impact force load and the degree to which you hit off center — determine the amount of impact force transmitted to your body every time you hit the ball.

Recovery

Next comes the recovery phase. Your muscles have to work to decelerate your racket while you are trying to control your follow-through. There can be considerable stress during decelera-tion, depending on how far out of your stable position you were at the moment of peak force. Let's say that you've stretched wide for a backhand. Your opponent's shot has gotten behind you, and you find yourself trying to flick the ball back over the net from an almost impossible position. You won't hit many shots like this without noticing that your follow-through (recov-ery) is painful.

•

The sportforces of tennis are not confined to your upper extrem-ities, despite the fact that the vast majority of tennis sportaches occur in your elbow, wrist, and shoulder. Tennis requires you to move around the court to get into position for your shots. In the process you also generate significant sportforces within the joints of your lower extremities. The resulting stress can create its own set of aches, particularly in your knees, legs, ankles, and feet.

Don't try to compare the running in tennis with long-distance running or jogging. A runner is exposed to steady, consistent, and predictable force loads in one, constant direction. In con-trast, when you play tennis, your running is designed to bring you to the ball, the course of which is anything but predictable. The lower-extremity sportforces of tennis are more of twisting and side-to-side motion, whereas jogging involves to-and-fro motion. Also, lower-extremity stress in tennis is far less than in running and jogging, thanks in large measure to the recovery period built into tennis. Because your running on a tennis court is not continuous, cumulative stress to your lower extremities is reduced.

Nevertheless, tennis frequently requires both your knees and your ankles to be away from their stable position when you run, as well as while you crouch in your ready position. As a result, considerable stress can be felt in these joints. The side-to-side twisting action of tennis often requires your muscles to struggle to get key joints in your lower extremities to their stable posi-tion. If this is impossible, your body must then transmit sport-forces in directions that can dramatically increase stress both to your bones and to the tendons, ligaments and bursae, which stabilize your joints. If your feet are in other than their stable (parallel) position at any time when you are running for a ball — and such an unstable position is the rule rather than the exception for a tennis player — forces are transmitted across (and not through) the hinge joints of your ankles and knees.

There are two moments of peak force in tennis. Upper-extremity peak force occurs as the ball hits your racket. Lower-extremity peak force occurs as each of your feet hits the ground. These two peak sportforces normally work independently. But if both your lower and upper extremities are out of their stable position at the moment of peak force, stress to your lower extremities can be increased. In addition, lower-extremity force loads increase substantially on hard or irregular playing surfaces.

Tennis Sportaches

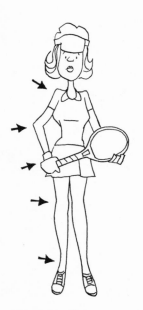

Tennis sportaches can occur in virtually any joint of your arms or legs.

Tennis sportaches can occur in virtually any joint of your arms or legs. Elbow pain is the most common complaint of recreational players, but wrist and shoulder aches also occur frequently, and ankle and knee problems are on the rise, both for weekend players and pros.

Although some top pros and a growing number of junior players have two-handed backhands, most tennis players still hit all of their shots with one hand. Thus, tennis sportaches usually occur in the elbow, wrist, and shoulder of your racket arm.

The primary tennis sportforce is ball impact force, which must travel through your wrist and elbow before it can reach any other part of your body. In fact, impact force rarely makes it past your elbow. Similarly, the swing forces (internal forces) that are generated as you accelerate and decelerate your racket also tend to stress your elbow, particularly if you try to rotate your forearm or use excessive wrist during any part of your tennis game.

Since your elbow is the first joint to feel stress whenever your arm is subjected to torque, whether from external or internal forces, it should come as no surprise that tennis elbow is the most common tennis sportache. The location of your elbow in the middle of your arm makes that almost inevitable. Think about what happens when you twist a towel at both ends. That's right. It knots up in the middle. Well, your elbow is in the middle of your arm. Like a towel that is being twisted, your elbow is stressed by dual forces on the tennis court, forces seeking to twist your arm before, during, and after ball impact.

If the stress of playing tennis doesn't produce elbow pain, you

may end up with a sore wrist. That's the second most common tennis ache.

Next comes shoulder pain. Although impact sportforces can only affect your shoulder after they've passed through your forearm (unlikely), the swing forces you generate during preparation and recovery produce shoulder pain as often as elbow or wrist problems because they flow from the core of your body outward and therefore pass through your shoulder first. Shoulder ailments are quite common among tennis pros, presumably because of the high swing forces generated when a pro serves or smashes an overhead, shots that require significant shoulder rotation and have to be hit with considerable pace at the professional level. Among recreational players, however, shoulder sportaches are much less common than elbow or wrist pain.

Footwork is important in tennis. You can't hit a ball if you don't get to it, and a tennis court is relatively large. You can expect to take hundreds, even thousands, of steps during a typical two-out-of-three set match. However, the sportforces affecting your lower extremities in tennis aren't nearly as significant as the impact and swing forces that affect your hitting arm. Tennis players incur more than their fair share of lower-extremity accidents and injuries, but sportaches are relatively rare, despite the fact that a variety of knee, ankle, and foot problems do crop up.

Elbow Sportaches

If your elbow and wrist are in a relatively stable position before, during, and after ball impact and if you manage to keep the forces of your tennis game to a level your body can tolerate, you can minimize elbow stress. Unfortunately, most of us hit the majority of our shots incorrectly. Moreover, we generally make no real effort to minimize sportforces when we play. The result is often tennis elbow.

Many different aches and pains go under the general heading of "tennis elbow." People who've never played the game complain of exactly the same symptoms as veteran players. Golfers, bowlers, cross-country skiers, racquetball and squash players, baseball pitchers, and football quarterbacks are all vulnerable. Tennis elbow can also result from carpentry, plumbing, gardening, typing, Frisbee, luggage handling, writing, and — attention, politicians — hand shaking. One doctor has even certified a case of "tennis elbow" for a woman who shot craps in a Las Vegas casino for six hours!

Tennis elbow has been the subject of medical attention and discussion for more than one hundred years. Although the debate continues concerning its precise medical cause, orthopedic surgeons nowadays feel that tennis elbow generally results from a strain or tear in one of the tendons attaching your forearm muscles to the bones of your elbow.

You don't need a medical degree to understand the basic pathology of tennis elbow. All you need to know is that the muscles that flex and extend your wrist, as well as the muscles that permit you to rotate your forearm, are attached to your elbow joint by tendons that are not particularly strong nor particularly well protected. When the muscles in your forearm are unable to withstand the stress of your tennis game — unable to work as hard as they must to absorb and transmit ball impact forces as well as swing forces — these tendons can easily be strained. The result is tennis elbow, which can produce either localized or general inflammation in or around your elbow joint, and which frequently involves long-term pain and incapacitation.

There are two main types of tennis elbow. Here's how to differentiate between them. Hold your arm straight out in front of you with your palm down. In this position, the top of your elbow is called the lateral, or outside, part. If that's where your elbow hurts, you have the classic symptoms of tennis elbow. In contrast, if your pain is on the inside (bottom) of your elbow joint, on or near your "funny bone," your problem is uncommon among tennis players, but quite common among "throwers" — baseball pitchers, football quarterbacks, and others.

Your doctor may diagnose outside elbow pain as lateral epicondylitis — inflammation of the area immediately around the lateral epicondyle, which is the bony projection you can feel just beneath the skin on the top of your elbow as you hold your arm out in front of you. Conversely, inside elbow pain is often diagnosed as medial epicondylitis. The medial epicondyle is your funny bone. However, as you know, there's nothing funny about tennis elbow.

Many doctors prefer to use the term *tennis elbow* only when they are talking about lateral epicondylitis. In fact, more than 80 percent of all tennis players with elbow problems have traditionally complained of pain on the outside of their elbows. Nowadays, however, recreational players are developing "thrower's elbow" in increasing numbers. This is presumably because they're trying to imitate the topspin forehands and twist serves they see the pros use on TV. While experts generally agree that lateral epicondylitis is more often than not a function of how you hit your backhand, medial epicondylitis is thought to be an outgrowth of forehands and serves. Either way, whether your pain is on the outside or the inside of your elbow, if your problem is tennis related, as far as the McGregor Solution is concerned, you have tennis elbow.

If you're suffering from medial elbow pain, you should know that your thrower's elbow can also produce ulnar nerve irritation. The ulnar nerve runs down the inside of your arm to your hand. That's the nerve that is compressed when you strike your funny bone. If you develop inflammation on the medial side of your elbow or if your racket handle presses too much on the base of the palm of your hand, the painful tingling you feel when you hit your funny bone can become chronic.

When you complain of tennis elbow and then describe the symptoms of medial epicondylitis, you may temporarily confuse your doctor. However, as a tennis player, you are correct to insist that your problem should be labeled tennis elbow. Either way, the ultimate solution to your elbow pain will come from tennis, not medicine.

Acute tennis elbow can practically incapacitate you. It will be extremely painful merely to straighten your forearm — with or without closing your hand or rotating your wrist. Routine activities, such as shifting gears in your car, brushing your teeth, shaking hands, or gripping a pen will become a nightmare. Hitting a tennis ball will probably be the last thing you'll want to do. In fact, it may be some time before you'll be able to play tennis again without pain. Your symptoms may persist for years, despite every effort at treatment and management.

Tennis elbow has begun when you feel a twinge of pain in or near your elbow as you hit a particular stroke. As with any sportache, if you're fortunate enough to have your elbow problem come on gradually — and smart enough to heed your body's early warning — you can prevent your pain from becoming acute or chronic.

Sometimes the symptoms of tennis elbow appear suddenly. Arthur Ashe knows. "I woke up one morning after a Davis Cup match and my arm hurt," he recalls. "It didn't hurt the day before, but it sure did then." Ashe's experience, however, was exceptional. Most of the time your body will give you a lengthy period of warning before you develop an acute or chronic ache.

Remember — and this point cannot be repeated too often — you have tennis elbow from the moment you begin to experience recurring elbow pain on the tennis court. You can wait, as many players do, to see if your pain will become incapacitating. Chances are that it will. Then you'll have to stop playing entirely and spend time and money treating your acute inflammation before eventually using EEVeTeC to avoid a relapse. Your alternative, of course, is to use the McGregor Solution right away — at the first sign of tennis elbow — and save yourself lots of pain, frustration, and money. It's your choice.

Wrist Sportaches

Every time you hit a tennis ball, both external and internal forces must pass through your wrist. If your wrist is in a stable position at the moment of ball impact (peak force), and if you don't use excessive wrist motion in any of your strokes, you may avoid developing an aching wrist.

However, if your game involves a lot of wrist movement or if the muscles you need to keep your wrist in its stable position are underconditioned, you run the risk of developing a tennis-related wrist problem. Worse yet, excessive wrist motion can also lead to elbow pain. Remember, the forearm muscles used to move your wrist are attached to the bones of your elbow joint.

Are you headed for wrist or elbow problems as a tennis player? Maybe. Do you chop your forehand, underspin your backhand, or roll your wrist over during your follow-through on either side? Do you punch your volleys with a firm wrist or do you slap at them? Do you use excessive wrist snap on your serve? Any of these stroking habits may start you on the road to trouble.

Any of these stroking habits may start you on the road to trouble.

If you finally need to see a doctor, your tennis-related wrist problems will probably be diagnosed as either tendinitis or a muscle stretch ailment. Your pain will usually be localized. However, if you use excessive wrist motion during your tennis game, you can develop synovitis, an inflammation of the entire wrist joint. And if your grip places direct pressure on the base of your palm, you can develop a tingling feeling in your little and ring fingers — the symptoms of ulnar nerve irritation or compression.

Shoulder Sportaches

Unlike elbow and wrist sportaches, tennis-related shoulder problems aren't so much a function of what happens at the moment of ball impact as they are a result of the stress to which your shoulder is subjected when you wind up or follow through, particularly on your serve and overhead. When you serve or hit a smash, ball impact forces are relatively low, as the ball is barely moving before you strike it. However, swing forces can be considerable.

Many teaching pros suggest "scratching your back" when you wind up for your serve, to make certain that you understand the importance of dropping your racket head and snapping your wrist. Try it, even if it isn't part of your normal service motion. You'll notice stress or pull in the front of your shoulder.

Where does your racket end up after you serve? If you sweep it down and across your body as most players do, you'll feel a slight strain in the back of your shoulder. Excessive backswing or follow-through on your ground strokes can also produce shoulder stress.

The most common tennis-related shoulder sportaches occur in the front of your shoulder. Your pain will usually be localized. If you eventually visit a doctor with acute or chronic discomfort, there are a number of diagnostic possibilities: tendinitis, bursitis, or a muscle stretch ailment are the most common.

Knee Sportaches

Tennis pros, like ski instructors, are constantly exhorting their students to "bend your knees!" Watch the pros as they prepare to receive a serve: knees and back bent, head low, eyes forward. Imitate their ready position the next time you play. You'll find that it's extremely tiring and can place a considerable strain on your knees, even if it does keep you low to the ground and thereby facilitate a good return.

Most good players not only bend their knees as they wait for each shot, they also stay low as they hit the ball. In addition, tennis is full of quick starts, jumps, and changes of direction, all of which create stress within your knees.

Torque is also a consideration, as it is in any sport where you move about on your feet. Remember the towel example we used to describe the effects of torque on your elbow. It's the same for your knees. Torque affects the middle link in any kinetic chain that is being twisted.

Doctors frequently diagnose tennis-related knee problems as patellar tendinitis or "jumper's knee." (Your patella is your kneecap.) Repeated jumps and improper landings as you move about the tennis court can cause fatigue and eventual irritation of the tendon connecting your kneecap to the quadriceps muscles in the front of your thigh. The usual symptom of jumper's knee is pain just above or below the kneecap, in the center of the knee joint.

There's more. If your entire knee feels swollen and inflamed, your doctor may diagnose your condition as "water on the knee." And "runner's knee" — chondromalacia to the medically oriented — isn't the exclusive preserve of runners. Tennis players, particularly women and those who tend to be slightly knock-kneed, may develop it too. Your pain will tend to be confined to one side of your kneecap. In addition, you may hear a clicking or grating sound when you extend your knee. You may also sense that your kneecap is no longer moving smoothly up and down as you walk or run.

Ankle Sportaches

Not uncommon in tennis, ankle problems are usually caused by an insufficient range of motion. That means your lower leg cannot flex or bend far enough toward your foot, usually because the muscle-tendon unit in the back of your leg is too tight or because a bony block in the front of your ankle is limiting your flexibility.

Tennis-related ankle problems are generally manifested as an ache either at or just above the point where your Achilles' tendon attaches to your heel. If your pain becomes acute or chronic and you go to a doctor, you may be told you have Achilles' tendinitis. Alternatively, you may develop an ache in one or several of the tendons that pass in front of your ankle.

Foot Sportaches

One of the major tennis-related foot problems is something often called *shoe-foot incompatibility*. An ill-fitting shoe — or an improperly positioned foot in an otherwise proper shoe — can result in a painful irritation on the back of your heel bone where the bone rubs against the counter of your shoe. Tennis players, like runners, often suffer heel pain, usually because their shoes provide insufficient protection for their heels. Sometimes the layer of fat that protects your heels somehow becomes packed down or is otherwise deficient. You can determine if this is your problem by pressing your thumb on the bottom center of your heel. If you feel bone close to the surface — and if it hurts — you need extra protection.

The stress generated as your foot pounds the tennis court over and over can also produce pain anywhere along the bottom of your foot. Think of your foot as a bow, with the muscles, tendons, and fascia underneath it as the bowstrings. You can probably imagine how constant or undue stress on the bow can pull the bowstrings either at their point of attachment or somewhere along their length. This problem is often called plantar (bottom of the foot) fasciitis.

Heel spurs can be a problem for tennis players as well as for other athletes. Often they are approached with either a sense of doom ("It's not a heel spur, is it?") or anticipation ("It's a heel spur, isn't it?"). Either way, the sufferer is looking to put a label on the ailment. There seems to be something romantic about a heel spur, perhaps because so many famous athletes have suffered from them. Surgery has helped some, like basketball's JoJo White and tennis's Arthur Ashe. For others, like basketball player Dave Cowens, surgery hasn't been necessary.

If you have a nagging pain in your heel, your doctor may tell you that it's a heel spur. In fact, X-rays of your feet and ankles may reveal heel spurs that you never knew you had and that have never caused you pain. Until your heel hurts, don't worry. If and when you do develop pain, EEVeTeC is your best bet for relief.

In addition to heel pain, tennis players often develop an ache around the ball of the foot. If your toes are cocked back or up on your foot — either because your sneakers don't fit you properly or because that's simply the way your feet are built — there is a significantly greater stress on the ball of your foot each time it hits the ground when you run around a tennis court. Your discomfort may be minimal at first, but a foot ache may eventually incapacitate you. Just as the mighty elephant can be humbled by a tiny thorn, you too will find yourself hobbling at courtside if you permit occasional foot aches to become acute or chronic.

Accidents and Injuries

Unlike sportaches, which can often be avoided and which you should usually try to manage on your own, there are a number of common tennis injuries that often cannot be prevented and should always be treated by an expert, especially if the problem seems severe.

Perhaps the most serious tennis injuries involve the eye. That's ironic. Your tennis instructor has no doubt told you to "keep your eye on the ball." Nevertheless, tennis players seem to be hit in the eye regularly, especially at the net. If a ball is hit right at your face and you're unprepared, you may be in trouble. Keep your racket up in front of you at the net and stay alert. Watch the ball carefully to minimize the possibility of the ball hitting the side of your racket and ricocheting into your eye, or hitting you in the eye directly. And if you wear glasses, make absolutely certain they're shatterproof.

Your lower leg is another part of your body that can easily be injured while you are playing tennis. In fact, just a decade after the invention of lawn tennis during the 1870s, a British physician published an article about "lawn tennis leg." The injury he described is still fairly common among tennis players and other athletes.

You may have experienced "tennis leg." After a quick movement on the court — let's say you have to jump for a volley or lunge to get your racket on a particularly hard serve — you suddenly feel intense pain on the inside of your calf. It feels as if someone has kicked you or hit you with a racket. In most games, however, that's unlikely. You probably haven't been shot from the sidelines either. Actually, tennis leg is a slight tear or rupture of a calf muscle. It is usually the result of a sudden weight shift — for example, when you lift off from the ball of your foot, swing your weight forward with your knee straight, and land directly on your heel.

If you decide to rush net after your serve, or poach when your partner hits a good first serve in doubles, you are particularly vulnerable to tennis leg. However, it can happen anytime, anywhere on the court. You can also pop an Achilles' tendon, tear a hamstring muscle, or strain a muscle in your groin. These are all common tennis injuries. When they happen, you need a doctor, and fast.

Probably the most common injury incurred on a tennis court is a twisted or sprained ankle. A sudden change of direction or an uneven landing after a lunge or jump for the ball can result in searing pain and immediate swelling on either side of an ankle.

Never treat an ankle sprain casually; it can disable you permanently. However, unlike many injuries that are basically unavoidable, your ankle problems can be minimized, especially if you know you have unstable ankles. Wear a bandage or ankle wrap around your ankle and foot when you play. In addition, you should make an effort to strengthen the muscles that may contribute to your ankle instability. If you play only occasionally, or if you're coming off an injury or protracted layoff, it's only sensible to take precautions against ankle sprains.

If you're careless with your follow-through when you serve, you can easily smash yourself in the shin with your racket. Any tennis player who has suffered this particular injury knows that it's no laughing matter, although your opponent(s) may find it amusing to watch you jumping up and down, clutching your lower leg and grimacing in pain.

Is this list of tennis aches and injuries complete? Of course not. There are all sorts of bizarre ways of doing damage to yourself on a tennis court, as one competitor in a recent U.S. Open discovered. The player in question, a relative unknown, had upset a seeded player in an early round. As his final passing shot landed just inside the baseline, he broke into a broad smile, let out a joyous whoop, threw his racket straight up into the air, and ran to jump over the net to shake his rival's hand. As he was literally in midair, his racket came down, conked him squarely on the head, and knocked him unconscious. He recovered, but promptly lost in the next round.

Tennis Solutions

Tennis sportaches, especially tennis elbow, can be eliminated with the McGregor Solution. The easiest way to manage the pains of fitness as a tennis player is to reduce the forces of your game. This may be as simple as making a basic adjustment in your equipment, changing your environment, or reducing the velocity of your racketwork and your footwork. If reduction of tennis sportforces isn't enough to eliminate your tennis sportache, you'll want to consider increasing your body's ability to withstand tennis-related stress by adjusting either your technique or your conditioning.

Remember, sportaches are the result of overuse — doing "too much, too often, too soon." To decide where to start in your effort to employ the McGregor Solution, you need to begin with a personal sports history.

If you're presently suffering from a tennis-related ache, try to determine whether you've done anything lately that might account for your problem. Have you bought a new racket? Perhaps you just had your old racket restrung? Have you recently switched from clay to hard courts? Are you playing regularly against a new opponent? Are you playing more often now than in the past? Have you been hitting your first serve harder than before? Have you made any recent changes in your strokes? If it's winter, are you finding that you don't have time to warm up with only an hour of indoor court time? Think carefully. Any of these seemingly unimportant facts, and others like them, can be at the root of your difficulty.

If you can pinpoint the origin of your present problem, you may well have also found its solution. If, for example, you remember that you bought a new racket just before your current elbow pain really started to bother you, you don't have to be a genius to decide what you ought to try first in your effort to eliminate your ache.

However, even after you get a racket that is easier on your arm, you may still have to make other adjustments in your tennis EEVeTeC. You may have to stop playing so often, try hitting your shots more softly, avoid excessive wrist motion on your backhand, and warm up thoroughly before you begin to play points. In fact, you may have to make a variety of other adjustments as well to rid yourself entirely of your pain. Let's begin at the beginning — with the reduction of tennis sportforces.

In tennis, ball impact forces are your primary concern. Therefore, reduction of tennis sportforces is largely a matter of keeping the two types of ball impact force to a minimum.

Reducing Forces

First, there's *absolute impact force*. Playing against bullet-serving Roscoe Tanner, you'll encounter far greater absolute impact force each time the ball meets your racket than when you play against your ten-year-old child. Similarly, a tightly strung racket generates more absolute impact force than a racket with loose strings. Further, if you're playing against the wind, you'll encounter greater absolute impact force than if you have the wind at your back.

Absolute impact force we define as the amount of force generated when your racket collides with a tennis ball — regardless of how much of that force actually reaches your arm. Obviously, the greater the absolute impact force, the greater the potential stress to your elbow, wrist, and shoulder. There are a variety of adjustments you can make in your tennis equipment, environment, and velocity to reduce absolute ball impact forces. At the same time, you'll be reducing stress.

Second, there's *effective impact force*. Remember, if you hit a tennis ball in the "sweet spot" of your racket, very little impact force reaches your arm. Therefore, effective ball impact force depends on how often and how far off center you hit your shots. Effective impact force is simply the amount of impact force that actually travels through your racket into your upper extremity.

You can reduce effective ball impact forces on the tennis court in a variety of ways. Since bad bounces often result in mis-hits, for example, a good hard court generates less effective impact force than a poorly maintained clay court. Likewise, if you can't see the ball, you'll surely mis-hit it. Therefore, you reduce effective impact forces if you wear your glasses when you play, and a hat may also help. Is the grip on your racket too small for your hand? If so, the effects of a mis-hit will be exaggerated — effective impact force will be increased. The answer: Build up your grip.

A number of the tips that follow are designed to help you reduce effective ball impact forces. The key is to adjust your equipment and your environment to minimize the number of times you mis-hit your shots. If you do everything you can to ensure that you're hitting most of your shots close to the center of your strings, you'll be OK even if absolute impact forces are relatively substantial — as they will be, for example, if you must return a hard serve or play downwind.

Finally, reduction of tennis sportforces also means minimizing the swing forces of your wind-up and recovery as well as the ground reactive forces generated when your feet impact the court. Swing forces are a function of velocity. The faster you swing your racket, the greater the internal forces generated within the joints of your upper extremity. (Note: A fast swing also results in greater absolute ball impact forces, so you reduce two kinds of tennis sportforces when you slow down your swing.) Quick abrupt movements also produce maximum sportforces within your leg and foot joints, and foot impact force is affected by both equipment (footwear, for instance) and environment (court surface).

Equipment

Your tennis equipment includes your racket, strings, balls, clothing, and accessories. You can adjust your equipment in a variety of ways to reduce tennis sportforces. In tennis, more than in any other sport, playing with the proper equipment is the key to eliminating sportaches. Literally thousands of players are incapacitated every year by elbow pain that stems from the fact that they are stringing their tennis rackets too tightly. And that's just the tip of the iceberg of equipment-related tennis aches. Don't hesitate to experiment. Ask plenty of questions. You could save yourself lots of unnecessary pain, frustration, and expense.

RACKET

Your choice of a tennis racket is your most important decision as a tennis player. Tennis rackets, like players, differ in a variety of ways. No one racket is perfect for everyone. Consider all of the following points:

Grip Size. Grip size is more important than most players realize. During the past ten years the trend has been to smaller and smaller grips. Many men now use four-and-a-half-inch grips, while women often choose rackets with four-and-three-eighths-inch handles and four-and-a-quarter-inch handles. However, if your grip is too small for your hand, your racket is more likely to twist when you hit a shot even slightly off center. To resist torque, you'll have to squeeze harder, with a greater impact force load then being transmitted to your arm. A racket with the proper grip size can therefore help you reduce stress.

How can you determine what size handle you need on your tennis racket? For maximum control and minimum torque, most experts favor a grip that's slightly too large over one that is too small. A relatively large grip also makes it less likely that you'll be hitting with excessive wrist motion.

Caution: A grip that is excessively large can impinge on the bone in the bottom of your hand, causing wrist pain. So make certain your grip is large enough to minimize torque, but not so large that it will cause other problems.

Chances are that your present grip is too small. That doesn't mean you have to buy a new racket. Your current grip can be removed and a layer or two of tape wrapped around your handle to build up your grip size. Then the leather grip can be re-wrapped.

Grip Condition. Grip condition is another simple equipment consideration that can prove surprisingly important. Early pros, like Don Budge, had no fancy leather grips on their wooden racket handles. Leather is a definite improvement in terms of comfort. But when it gets wet or worn, leather can become slippery, and that's dangerous.

If your grip tends to slip, your forearm muscles will have to work that much harder to keep control of your racket at impact. The more work you ask of your forearm muscles, the more you increase effective impact forces.

Old leather grips are especially slippery. You should invest in a new grip from time to time. A raised grip — one with ridges — may be easier for you to hold on to than a smooth grip. If your racket still twists and slips, do what the pros do. Keep a little rosin or sawdust in your pocket and apply it frequently to your grip — between games or even between points. On Har-

Tru or clay courts, try pressing your wet hand onto the court, then rubbing the granules that stick to your palm onto your handle. Gauze grip tape, available at most pro shops and equipment stores, is helpful, as is a towel. You may also want to try a tennis glove. As a last resort, at least dry your hand frequently on your shorts, shirt, or skirt.

Racket Composition. The composition of your racket will determine whether it's stiff or flexible. With dozens of rackets to choose from, made of various materials with confusing trade names, your best source of information about the relative flexibility of your racket is likely to be your local pro or racket salesperson. Some manufacturers are beginning to indicate on a racket whether it's stiff or flexible, but the disclosure process is slow. Still, rackets are constantly tested, and information on their degree of flexibility is increasingly available.

There's a common misconception that all wood rackets are stiff and that all metal, composite, and Fiberglas rackets are flexible. This is *not* true. There are, for example, some relatively flexible wood rackets as well as some extremely stiff metal ones.

Remember that what's best for you depends on your playing style and conditioning. Experts agree, however, that most players should avoid both very stiff and very flexible rackets. It's true that a flexible racket will absorb some impact forces that would otherwise reach your arm, thereby reducing effective ball impact force. But you may have to work harder to generate power on your shots. A moderately flexible racket is the most sensible answer for most players.

Experiment with various possibilities before buying a racket. Most pro shops nowadays have "demos" that you can borrow. Play a set with a friend's racket before you go out and buy one just like it. Remember, what works for someone else may wreak havoc with both your game and your health. Find the racket that's right *for you*.

Racket Design. In addition to flexibility, racket design can be an important consideration if you are concerned about tennis sportaches. A racket with an open throat, for example, can seem easier to swing and therefore easier on your arm than a comparably weighted racket with the traditional single shaft design.

The big debate about racket design began a few years ago with the development of the first "oversized" racket. Some experts swear that switching to a large-headed racket is the best possible decision most recreational players can make if they are concerned about tennis-related aches. The larger racket face, they reason, provides a bigger area where balls can be hit with minimum resulting torque. But other experts insist that an oversized racket alone makes no significant difference. The debate continues. However, it now seems plain that although the "sweet spot" is no bigger in an oversized racket, the comfortable hitting area may be.

Meanwhile, more and more recreational players are switching to oversized rackets. Since no one has yet argued that they actually exacerbate elbow or wrist problems, it seems reasonable to advise anyone concerned with tennis aches at least to try playing with a larger racket.

Racket Weight. The question of racket weight is relatively straightforward. As baseball players and golfers know, the heavier your bat or club, the harder and farther you can hit, at least if you tighten your grip as you swing and if you meet the ball solidly.

Weight increases momentum. Momentum increases force at impact. However, the heavier the object you are swinging, regardless of your sport, the stronger your arm must be, and the more strain each swing places on your wrist, elbow, and shoulder.

In tennis it's quite possible to develop a sportache in your arm simply because your racket is too heavy. You should experiment with different rackets — on the court, not in the pro shop. An overly light racket creates its own problems, as any adult knows who has tried to hit with a junior racket. But if you're worried about your arm, be certain your racket is not too heavy.

Racket Balance. The balance of your racket is even more important than its weight. A head-light racket is harder on your arm than one that weighs the same but is more evenly balanced.

Some manufacturers are now marking their frames according to balance. But if your favorite racket doesn't come with information about balance, be certain to test it with your pro or salesperson. If you swing half a dozen different frames, all of which are supposedly the same grip size and weight, you'll be able to feel differences in balance that measurement will confirm. You may also feel differences in grip size and weight, despite identical markings. This is worth remembering. Not all four-and-a-half-inch light frames are alike, for example, even ones that are meant to be identical.

Experts talk about the "center of gravity" and the "center of percussion." And they point out that the proper balance for you depends on where you place your hand on the grip. However, one thing is clear. Most players should avoid head-light rackets. In fact, to counter the forces of a mis-hit, you're better off with a racket that is slightly head-heavy. At least be certain your racket is evenly balanced and not head-light.

Age and Condition of Racket. The age and condition of your racket represent one final important consideration, especially if you play with wood. Wood rackets can warp, and a warped racket will be hard on your arm because of the additional torque created every time you hit the ball. Even if your racket isn't actually warped, it can lose its feel after a few months or years of play. Characteristics of flexibility can also change with age, both in wood and metal frames.

The solution is simple. Treat yourself to a new racket from time to time. It's a lot less expensive and less painful than tennis elbow.

STRINGS

The stringing in your tennis racket is crucial. What kind of strings you buy and how tightly you have your racket strung can make a big difference in the sportforces generated each time your racket collides with a tennis ball.

Gut or Nylon. Your first basic stringing decision is the choice between gut and nylon strings. There are many different types of synthetic strings available, but most experts agree that gut is still worth the extra expense, particularly if you are anxious to minimize arm strain.

Although it's never been proven, many top players swear that gut strings generate more power with less effort than nylon strings. They feel they don't have to work as hard to hit their shots at the same pace with gut. Whether or not gut is actually more resilient than nylon, it very definitely does seem to reduce the work you have to do to hit a tennis ball. In the process, the stress your body must be able to withstand is also reduced.

If you opt for nylon strings because gut is simply too expensive or because it breaks too often — perhaps you hit with a lot of spin or it's damp where you play — get the best quality nylon available. Price is generally the most reliable index of good string quality.

String Tension. String tension may be the most important variable in your racket. It's generally agreed that overly tight strings can have a disastrous effect on your arm.

Björn Borg's rackets are strung with gut at an incredible seventy to eighty pounds of tension. Even on TV you can hear the difference between the ping of Borg's shots and the duller thud the ball makes when it hits his opponent's racket. Anyone watching Borg — certainly the outstanding player of his generation and arguably one of the greats of all time — might be

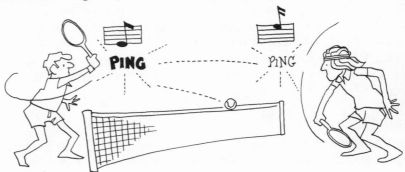

tempted to put tighter strings in his or her own racket. However, what works for Borg hasn't generally worked for his fellow pros and it's even less likely to work for you. Borg is exceptionally strong and well conditioned. Also, his extreme topspin shots allow him to use tighter strings with minimal resulting stress. For the average player, tight strings create excessively high ball impact force loads. Also, if you're really considering imitating Borg, you should know that he routinely breaks five to ten sets of racket strings per week of competitive play. At $30 per racket for gut strings, that comes to more than $5,000 per year for strings alone. Still interested?

What degree of string tension should you use? It depends on both the type of string you choose and the design of your racket, as well as your level of ability and style of play.

Most stringing is done nowadays on stringing machines. It takes no great skill to operate a stringing machine. Consequently, lots of unskilled people are stringing rackets. Mistakes are unfortunately common. Also, the accuracy of some stringing machines is questionable. Stringing a racket at fifty-eight pounds on one machine doesn't guarantee that the result will be identical to a string job supposedly done at the same tension on another machine — especially if two different stringers are involved. Don't be afraid to ask questions if you think you're not getting the string tension you asked for. It's your elbow that is going to start throbbing if the strings in your racket end up at sixty-four pounds instead of fifty-eight pounds.

Here are a few general guidelines about stringing that every player should follow:

1. For an average player using a normal-sized racket with gut strings, fifty-two to fifty-eight pounds of string tension should be sufficient.

2. Only experienced players who are relatively well conditioned and who hit a higher percentage of their shots in the center of the racket should use as much as fifty-eight to sixty-two pounds of tension.

3. If you switch to an oversized racket, the stringing machine setting should be set several pounds higher to achieve comparable tension. In other words, if you've been playing with a normal-sized racket strung at fifty-six pounds and you decide to try a Prince, ask for sixty-two to sixty-six pounds of string tension.

4. Nylon string tension should be about two pounds lower than gut — if you're used to gut strung at fifty-eight pounds and you switch to nylon, ask for fifty-five to fifty-six pounds of tension.

5. The flexibility of your frame is key. With a relatively flexible racket, your stringing should be somewhat tight. If you have a stiff frame, your strings should be relatively loose.

Age of Strings. The age of your racket strings is another important consideration in the management of your tennis sportaches. Time and use result in a loss of tension and resiliency, whether you play with gut or nylon. Overly loose strings are no better for your arm than overly tight strings. If your strings are loose, you'll have to swing harder (faster) than usual to hit with your normal pace. That will result in higher impact force loads as well as greater swing forces. Have your racket restrung regularly, whether or not your strings actually break. It may seem wasteful, but this simple precaution can save you months of needless pain and frustration.

TENNIS BALLS

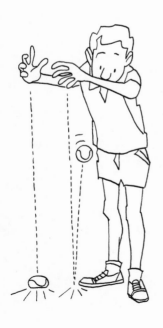

Too many players — even relatively experienced ones — don't pay enough attention to the balls they use. A surprising number of people try to squeeze weeks of play out of each can. Also, players commonly use the wrong balls for their playing surface.

Every tennis player knows that pressurized balls lose their pressure — ''go dead'' — in a remarkably short time. A dead ball has only a percentage of its original resiliency. Prove it to yourself. Drop a new ball and a used ball from the same height. Which bounces higher? If the balls you play with aren't as resilient as they could be, you're going to have to work harder — swing faster — to generate the power and depth you are used to getting on your shots. Therefore, new balls can help you minimize swing forces, as well as reducing ball impact forces.

The pros change balls every nine games. You don't need to buy new balls quite that often, but if you have a sportache, you should certainly consider getting a new can at least every few sets.

What about pressureless balls — ones that come in a box instead of a can? By definition, a pressureless ball can't lose pressure so pressureless balls don't go dead, at least not in the

traditional sense. However, pressureless balls do play differ-
ently as they age and lose their nap. Moreover, pressureless
balls simply aren't as resilient to begin with as their pressurized
look-alikes. Stay away from pressureless balls if you have a sore
arm — or if you're afraid of developing one. The extra effort it
takes to hit a pressureless ball may be all it takes to give you a
sportache.

High-altitude balls are just about mandatory over 1,500 to
2,000 feet above sea level. You won't be able to keep normal
balls in the court at that altitude. But high-altitude balls should
never be used at sea level. They require too much work to hit.
Likewise, grass court and hard court balls should be used exclusively on grass courts and hard courts.

The color of the tennis balls you use isn't only a matter of
aesthetics. If you can see "optic yellow" better than traditional
white, you're probably going to hit your shots more consistently
near the center of your racket. There's no doubt that mis-hits
are an important cause of tennis elbow and other tennis-related
aches. So buy balls you can see. You'll reduce effective impact
force loads and, while you're at it, you'll improve your game.

CLOTHING AND ACCESSORIES

Having the proper clothing and accessories can make more of a
difference to you as a tennis player with a sportache than you
might imagine. A number of things you wear on the court can
play a significant role in reducing tennis sportforces and helping
you eliminate sportaches.

Footwear. Your tennis shoes must give you both proper support
and good footing. If your feet and ankles are not properly protected, foot impact force loads will be higher as you move
around the court. As a result, you'll be more vulnerable to foot,
ankle, and knee sportaches. In addition, if you have trouble with
your footing, you'll have trouble hitting your shots in the center
of your racket. Improper footwear can thus lead not only to
foot, ankle, and knee sportaches but also to tennis elbow and
other upper-extremity sportaches.

You want to make certain your tennis shoes are appropriate
for the surface on which you play. Hard courts require more
protection for your ankles and feet than softer surfaces such as

If you have trouble with your footing, you'll have trouble hitting your shots in the center of your racket.

Har-Tru, clay, or grass. High-friction surfaces (hard courts) also require a certain kind of sole for proper footing. Your tennis pro or equipment salesperson should be able to help you choose the ideal type of shoe for your favorite courts. However, you need to be more knowledgeable about footwear than most people if you want to be certain you're getting good advice — and proper shoes.

It may sound too simple, but improper shoe fit is the single most common cause of foot problems for tennis players. Perhaps you've suffered from the much fabled tennis toe — a sudden, constant, unremitting pressure on one of your toes. Tennis toe can result from a shoe that's too narrow, too tight, too short, or too long. You've probably got tennis toe if you notice a blood blister under a toenail after you play. Other problems can also arise from shoes that don't fit properly in the heel or arch. If you're wearing the wrong size shoe, the built-in stability and protection of your shoe won't be effective. You'll develop an ache, as your feet must repeatedly absorb and transmit ground reactive forces without proper protection.

If your feet hurt on the tennis court, by all means consider new shoes. Make sure you buy the right size as well as checking to see that the brand you choose fits your foot properly. In addition to size, there are a few other important criteria you need to be aware of when you're trying on tennis shoes.

Do you want leather, canvas, nylon, or a combination for the upper? Which works best? The jury is still out. Each material has its strengths and weaknesses. You want a shoe with an upper that holds your foot in its most stable position. If your shoe stretches or gives too much, your feet can be subjected to abnormal stresses. Tennis shoes have traditionally come with canvas uppers, but there are some obvious advantages to leather, at least from the standpoint of support.

The wall around the base of your shoe tends to stabilize your foot. So does the heel counter — the stiff area at the back of the heel. The counter keeps your heel from rolling in or out and upsetting the stable position of your foot. That reduces the possibility of ankle instability and foot fatigue.

Since your feet are constantly twisted and pounded in tennis, often on hard surfaces in hot or warm surroundings, it's wise to have an upper made of material that "breathes." In this regard, canvas or nylon mesh uppers are a plus.

The insole is a two-part package. First, there's the material on which your foot rests. It helps prevent blisters, as well as cushioning your foot and helping your lower extremities to accept the twisting and shearing action of running on a tennis court. Second, there's the unit that cups, cushions, and supports your heel and arch. This part of your insole can either be a single completely formed unit or a combination of components.

The midsole fills the space between the insole and outsole. In most tennis shoes the midsole is either attached to the bottom of the insole and fits into a special cupped area of the tread member, or it's a separate material that fits into that groove. As a rule it is light.

The outsole of your shoe (what you probably think of as the "sole") must provide your foot with traction while at the same time being both light and durable. Since those properties can be mutually exclusive, the outsole has a difficult job. If your foot slips too much or too often, it may be impossible for you to maintain a stable body position at peak force. You may also find yourself mis-hitting more often since you'll find it harder to be consistently at the correct distance from the ball. A too-heavy shoe can cause fatigue. And a worn-out shoe can cause excessive twisting.

Tennis shoe outsoles are part of the bottom covering of what is called a "tread member." The tread member of your tennis shoes is shaped and preformed and includes the wall around the edge so that the upper fits on and into it.

Orthotics (arch supports) can be used in any sport. They're

designed to hold your feet in their most stable position, particularly when they're subjected to peak force loads. Orthotics come
in various shapes and are made of various materials. They can
be purchased over the counter or custom-made by a laboratory
or a doctor.

By holding your feet in their stable position, orthotics prevent
them from rolling in too much. If your feet roll in when they hit
the ground, they cannot properly absorb and transmit sportforces. The result is stress — not only to your feet but to your
entire lower extremity.

Orthotics are like eyeglasses: they don't correct your feet any
more than glasses correct your eyes. Glasses correct your vision. Likewise, orthotics correct your gait, and by holding your
feet in their stable position, they do help. If you need them you
should wear them. (For more about orthotics, see the next chapter.)

Hats. If you're playing outside on a sunny day, wear a hat or
visor. It will not only protect you against sunstroke and other
similar problems, but it will also enable you to see the ball better. You'll hit more balls near the center of your racket and
reduce effective ball impact sportforces.

Sweatbands and Headbands. Wristlets can mean the difference
between a slippery and a dry grip. A slippery grip makes it
harder for you to control your racket. Remember, muscle use
translates into stress. Also, if you can't control your racket, you
may mis-hit your shots.

Headbands serve a dual purpose. They can prevent a drop of
sweat from temporarily blinding you or clouding your vision,
resulting in a painful mis-hit. They also help to keep your hair
out of your eyes.

Gloves. A glove may be the only way to keep your grip from
slipping. If that's the case, it's worth a try. A glove may also
prevent you from loosening your grip if you're suffering from
blisters or a sore hand.

Glasses. If you need corrective lenses to see, it only makes sense
to wear them on the court. How can you hit the ball consistently

in the center of the racket if you can't see it? On sunny days dark glasses are also a good idea.

Warm-ups and Sweaters. Wearing a warm-up jacket or sweater makes sense on all but the hottest days, at least until you've been playing for a few minutes. Warmth promotes circulation which, in turn, enhances your body's ability to absorb forces and withstand stress.

If you have arm trouble, consider wearing a light jacket, long-sleeved shirt, or turtleneck sweater throughout your match or practice session. You need to keep your arm warm. Jimmy Connors has a specially designed neoprene arm-warmer, which he sometimes wears on his left arm throughout his matches despite the fact that he has never had any serious arm or elbow problems.

Warm-up pants or sweat pants make good sense. Some players also wear high socks. If you keep your shins and calves warm, you reduce your vulnerability to lower-leg sportaches.

Arm Braces. Anyone worried about tennis elbow should consider wearing an elbow brace during play. There are several types of braces currently available. The most effective compress your forearm muscle mass gently and keep you from using excess wrist motion during your strokes. Two adjustable bands are joined by a splint running down the inside of your forearm.

Environment

Your environment as a tennis player includes where you play, when you play, and against whom you play. These considerations are surprisingly important in determining the amount of force you have to contend with on a tennis court. Your environment can make the difference between an enjoyable game and a painful experience.

WHERE YOU PLAY
Court Surface. Let's start with the court surface. It can affect your feet, your ankles, your knees, even your arm. Certain sur-

faces generate both higher foot impact force loads and larger ball impact forces.

Hard courts, for example, are notoriously tough on your legs. Clay, Har-Tru, and grass surfaces provide more cushion for your feet and generate smaller ground reactive sportforces.

Friction makes a difference, too. On high-friction (hard) surfaces like asphalt, concrete, wood, and carpet, you have to lift your feet to cover even the shortest distance. Of course, every time you pick up a foot, you also have to put it down. That increases the risk of ankle problems while simultaneously jarring your lower leg. On low-friction (soft) surfaces, you can slide — a big advantage, as any experienced clay court player will tell you.

Hard courts also play faster than most other surfaces. With less time to prepare your shots, you're more likely to mis-hit the ball or hit late. And, since your opponent's ball comes off the court with greater speed, absolute ball impact forces are greater.

Hard courts do have some advantages. For one thing, you usually get a better, more consistent bounce, even if the ball does come off the ground faster than on soft courts. Unless a clay or composition court is in perfect condition, bad bounces can be frequent. Bad bounces result in numerous off-center hits and last-second stroke compromises, increasing your vulnerability to elbow and wrist problems. Grass courts provide a lot of cushion for your feet. However, if you let the ball bounce on grass, it skids and hops unpredictably. Even the best players in the world frequently mis-hit their ground strokes on grass.

In addition, hard courts also encourage you to swing early at your ground strokes, attacking rather than waiting for the ball to drop. It's difficult to play defensively on a hard court. Points tend to be shorter, which reduces the cumulative stress on your body. And because you have less time to prepare, you'll probably shorten your backswing, thereby minimizing wear and tear on your forearm by reducing internal sportforces.

Finally, the fact that hard courts have painted lines can also be to your advantage. It's something you can appreciate only if you've played regularly on dirt or clay courts with plastic or linen lines. When the lines are painted onto the court, balls can't bounce erratically off the lines and you can't slip or trip on the tape.

All things considered, however, most experts agree that the recent dramatic increase in the number of hard courts all over the world has been a major factor in the development of an epidemic of tennis sportaches. If you have a choice, especially if your legs or arm(s) are bothering you, minimize your play on hard courts. Certainly try to avoid hard courts that are in poor condition, as they are in too many parks and playgrounds.

Indoors or Outdoors? Should you play indoors or outdoors? Your local climate often makes that decision for you. But you should know about the benefits and risks of each environment.

Indoors there's no sun to blind you, no wind to bother you, no extreme heat or cold. Good backdrops usually enhance visibility. The major disadvantage is the artificial lighting, which frequently isn't as good as natural light. Some recreational players who rarely mis-hit outdoors have trouble hitting solidly inside. When you do move indoors, wear your corrective lenses and watch the ball carefully. Also, don't let the strange acoustics indoors cause you to hit too hard.

WHEN YOU PLAY

The most important considerations here are wind, sunlight, and precipitation — all factors only if you play outdoors.

Wind. Playing in the wind can prove difficult. At least avoid playing against the wind if you have arm problems. Every player knows how tiring it can be to hit into a strong wind. You have to

generate much greater swing forces just to get the ball over the net. The extra effort and strain may be all it takes to cause your elbow, wrist, or shoulder problems to flare up.

Sunlight. Tennis courts should be built facing north and south. That helps to minimize the problem of direct sun except at mid-day. Many courts, however, aren't constructed at an ideal angle. Even if they are, morning and evening sunlight can still make it difficult to see at certain times of the year. Avoid playing early or late in the day if the court is laid out so that you'll be blinded by the sun on one side. If you don't have a choice, and especially if you have an arm problem and are therefore wary of mis-hits, try to play on the shady side.

Precipitation. Should you play in the rain? It's not as silly a question as it might seem. With court time at a premium, a few raindrops, even a light drizzle, usually won't stop a match, but be careful. Tennis balls pick up moisture — and water weight — quickly. Wet, heavy balls don't do your strings or your arm any good.

In addition, court surfaces, hard and soft, become slippery when wet. If you're lucky enough to avoid a twisted ankle or a strained knee, you still may lose your balance enough to mis-hit.

PICKING YOUR OPPONENT

To protect your weak elbow or wrist, you may simply have to decline to play against hard hitters. Except when you are serving, you have to contend with the force of your opponent's shot. Every player has played against someone who clobbers the ball. Returning hard shots creates exceptional stress in your forearm. If you don't have to do it, you probably shouldn't. After all, you're not Björn Borg, faced with the choice of playing Roscoe Tanner under lights or defaulting the U.S. Open.

You should also avoid opponents who hit with lots of spin. Chances are you won't be able to hit your shots consistently in the center of your racket. If there's any shot more difficult and painful for someone with a sore arm to return than a cannonball serve, it's a heavy twist serve.

Hitting against a backboard can be very good practice. It can also be very hard on your arm. If you're successful, the ball keeps coming back. That means your rallies against the wall are much longer and more tiring than most of your rallies when you play. The ball also comes back quicker and harder than it does in a match. Remember, both the wall and the surface beneath your feet are almost always made of concrete, cement, or asphalt. Also, you're much closer to your "opponent" than you would be on a court.

For practice, a ball machine is a much better substitute opponent, at least if you program it to deliver only a moderately hard ball, and at reasonable intervals. However, you should be sure that the machine isn't filled with dead or pressureless balls. Otherwise you'll have to swing much too hard just to get your shots over the net.

Finally, for the preservation and protection of your arms and legs, you should probably play more doubles than singles. In doubles you hit fewer balls, serve half as often, and have only half the court space to cover. But you must be especially alert when you're at the net. Keep your racket up in front of you. The sudden need to lunge at a ball or to jerk your racket up to protect your face or body can create stresses unique to doubles. Most singles players don't spend that much time at the net. And when they get there, they're naturally more alert because they know they don't have a partner covering for them.

Velocity

There's nothing complicated about the concept of velocity in tennis. The faster you swing, the greater the forces you generate in key joints of your upper extremity as you prepare for and recover from your shots. Also, the faster your motion, the greater the ball impact force if you hit off center. Think of the collision between your racket and a tennis ball as if it were an auto crash. If you know you're headed for a collision, would you prefer to be driving ten miles per hour or fifty-five miles per hour? By slowing down, you reduce impact forces. Can you now understand why you also want to avoid playing against hard hitters, at least if you have a sore arm?

A fast swing generates greater internal and external sport-forces. If you have a sportache, you need to reduce forces. You must, therefore, reduce velocity.

Tennis pros always tell their students, "Swing slowly!" It's much easier to control your shots with a slow, deliberate swing. By reducing velocity you not only reduce forces and minimize aches, you also improve your performance.

Obviously, if you swing too slowly, you'll never get your shots over the net. But you'll be surprised to discover how little effort it takes to hit an adequate tennis shot. The following two guidelines may help:

1. *Prepare your racket as early as possible.* Particularly on ground strokes, try to get your own racket back and ready as soon as the ball leaves your opponent's racket. Most recreational players don't even start their backswing until the ball bounces on their own side of the court.

Watch your friends play. When do they begin their backswings? Do you think you get your racket back faster? Late preparation often results in a hurried, fast swing. That places much more stress on your arm and makes it more difficult for you to control your shots. Your racket should be back and ready at the latest by the time your opponent's shot crosses the net.

Jimmy Connors and Chris Evert Lloyd are prime examples of the advantages of early racket preparation. Both players hit the ball with plenty of pace, but their swings are rarely hurried and are fairly slow. Neither has ever suffered major arm problems.

2. *Try for control, not speed.* Want a sure way to hurt your arm? Just clobber the ball early in the season or before you're thoroughly warmed up. That should do it.

Especially during your warm-up, try pushing your ground strokes instead of slapping or hitting them. Tighten your grip, concentrate, and press into the ball with your legs. Accelerate your racket gradually and guide the ball over the net.

Similarly, when you're at the net, punch the ball instead of swinging at it. At least for the first few games, press your serve into the opposite court instead of trying to clobber it.

Perhaps you're not interested in hitting the ball hard anyway. It's spin you want. There's a common misconception nowadays that all good players utilize lots of topspin. Attempts to imitate the exaggerated topspin ground strokes of superstars like Björn Borg and Guillermo Vilas have caused considerable frustration and pain for many recreational players. Both Borg and Vilas are strong and flexible, especially in their upper bodies. Vilas, for example, can play and practice as much as six to eight hours a day, seven days a week. Does that sound like your training schedule?

Hitting with heavy topspin requires just as much effort (and creates just as much stress) as clobbering a tennis ball. To reduce both swing forces and ball impact forces, don't try to imitate Borg or Vilas. Swing slowly. Be satisfied with the natural topspin you'll get by starting your racket below the level of the ball and swinging up, keeping your racket face perpendicular to the ground.

It makes sense to spend your energy and strength on a tennis court wisely. If you have arm problems, for example, try hitting most of your first serves at half pace. You'll get more of them in and thus you won't have to serve twice on virtually every point. Nothing is more tiring and counterproductive than blasting first serves that rarely go in.

If you insist on smashing your first serves, you're doing yourself a double disservice. First, you're creating greater force loads than necessary by hitting hard. Second, you're increasing the cumulative force loads you must absorb by hitting unnecessary shots.

After you've done everything you can to ease the stress on your body by reducing sportforces, only three choices remain if you are a tennis player with a sportache. You can (1) increase your body's ability to withstand stress, (2) play in pain, or (3) quit.

If adjusting your equipment, environment, and velocity doesn't eliminate your sportache, then try increasing your tolerance for sportforces. Sportaches occur when the connective tissue that holds your joints together is subjected to more stress than it can tolerate. Your joints can withstand considerable stress if they are stable. As a tennis player, you need to ensure that an aching joint is as stable as possible when it must absorb and transmit sportforces. As in other sports, the key to joint stability in tennis is technique and conditioning.

Increasing Your Tolerance for Stress

Technique

An incredible amount of material — books, articles, films, and more — has been generated on tennis technique. Thousands of tennis teachers earn millions of dollars every year teaching people how to play. Nevertheless, no two teachers will tell you exactly the same thing. If you're anxious to perfect your game and you read various books and articles as well as take lessons from different pros, you may end up very confused. However, when it comes to eliminating sportaches, only two matters of tennis technique are really important:

First, you need to reduce forces by cutting down your velocity. You must swing slowly. Second, you must learn how to

keep key joints in your arms and legs as stable as possible as you move around the tennis court and hit your shots. That's where the technique phase of the McGregor Solution comes in.

Most important, of course, is the position of your wrist, elbow, and shoulder at the moment of peak ball impact force — the moment when your racket collides with the ball. As it happens, what most teaching pros and instruction books tell you about tennis technique to help you improve your game also helps you increase your ability to withstand stress. Classic tennis technique usually places the key joints of your hitting arm in their most stable position. The proper way to hit a ball is also the least stressful.

Performance and health on a tennis court are both enhanced by the same good habits. So if trying to change your strokes seems difficult (or even hopeless) as a solution to the problem of an aching arm, don't be too quick to look for other answers. If you can learn to hit your shots correctly, you may not only eliminate your ache, you may also start to play better tennis.

This book isn't designed to teach you tennis. But if you're experiencing pain when you play, it's a safe bet that you could use some instruction. Basic adjustments in your technique could save you considerable frustration. Probably your pro won't talk about the stable position of your wrist, elbow, or shoulder. However, while teaching you how to hit with more control, he or she will also be helping you increase your body's ability to withstand the stresses of your game.

The following general observations about tennis technique should help you minimize your exposure to tennis elbow, as well as eliminate wrist problems and shoulder pain. Healthy technique is a straightforward proposition. You can play without pain if the joints of your hitting arm are as stable as possible at all times. The position of your elbow and wrist at the moment of ball impact is especially important. Also key is the amount of wrist motion and shoulder rotation you use in your strokes.

ELBOW

If your elbow is excessively bent when your racket collides with a tennis ball, you'll feel the stress of ball impact primarily in or around that joint.

Prove it to yourself. Hold your racket in front of you as if you were going to hit a backhand, with your elbow bent at a 90°

angle. Now have a friend push gently on the center of your strings, simulating ball impact. Try to push back toward the net. Where do you feel the strain?

Next, keeping your arm bent in exactly the same way, have your friend push again, this time off center, while you continue to push back toward the net. Try to keep the racket from twisting. You should feel stress on the outside of your elbow. And you should feel significantly more strain when your friend pushes off center, thereby creating torque. In effect, you have experienced the feeling of the classic "poke" backhand, which has contributed to hundreds of thousands of cases of tennis elbow. Your elbow should never be bent at anything like 90° when you hit any of your tennis shots.

When you hit your backhand, you do need to bend your elbow slightly. In fact, you never want to lock your elbow completely when you hit a tennis ball. To avoid fully extending your arm and locking your elbow, you must move to the ball instead of lunging or reaching with your racket to hit your shots. However, you don't want to get so close to the ball on your backhand that you have to poke at it. Likewise, on your serve, your ball toss shouldn't force you to reach way up or hyperextend your arm. Locking your elbow on your serve can be a prime cause of shoulder problems and elbow strain.

WRIST

Both your wrist and elbow are vulnerable to aches if you use excessive wrist motion on your shots. One of the most common mistakes made by players on all levels is to hit a variety of shots with too much wrist. Wristy strokes not only fatigue and stress the muscles that move and stabilize the joint, they also increase the likelihood that your wrist will be out of its stable position at impact.

You do *not* want to roll your forearm to achieve top spin on your forehand or backhand, despite the apparently wristy ground strokes hit by some of today's superstars. Spin is vital for control in tennis, but neither spin nor speed should be generated with an excessive wrist snap or roll. To achieve topspin on your ground strokes, learn to hit from low to high with your wrist firm. Likewise, to hit a twist serve, try rotating your shoulders instead of snapping at the ball with your wrist.

You can easily prove to yourself how dangerous it is to meet the sportforces of ball impact with your wrist unstable. Prepare to hit your forehand — but pretend you're going to hit the ball late. If you're a right-hander, a late forehand is hit off your right pocket instead of at a point even with your left foot. To get your racket face at a proper angle to send such a forehand over the net you'll have to bend your wrist at impact. In that position have a friend press your racket back, first pressing in the center of your strings and then simulating torque. Where do you feel the stress? Both your wrist and the inside of your elbow should feel the strain.

Every tennis player must understand the relationship between wrist motion and elbow strain. In brief, the forearm muscles you use to extend and flex your wrist, as well as to roll your forearm in either direction, are attached by tendons to your elbow joint — either on the outside (for extension and supination) or on the inside (for flexion and pronation).

Hold your hitting arm out in front of you with your wrist in its stable position. Now put the fingers of your other hand on the outside of your elbow joint. Bend (extend) your wrist — as if you were slapping someone with the back of your hand. What do you feel under the fingers that are resting on your elbow? If you like, try the same test with your fingers on the inside of your elbow and your wrist bending the other way (flexed).

Wrist motion is just as likely to result in tennis elbow as it is to give you a sore wrist. When your forearm muscles tire, the stress ends up in your elbow. To avoid tennis elbow you must not only keep your elbow in as stable a position as possible, you must also minimize the amount of wrist motion in your strokes.

STROKE PARTICULARS

Grip. How do you hold your racket? Your grip can make a tremendous difference in both your performance and your health. The continental grip, which requires you to twist your wrist at least slightly on most forehands and backhands, is more likely to result in wrist and elbow problems than a proper eastern forehand and a proper eastern backhand grip. If you use a continental grip, your wrist is unlikely to be completely stable when you hit your ground strokes. You'll also have to use your forearm muscles to twist your racket face enough to get your shots to go in, risking stress to your elbow. Of course, there are some advantages to a single-grip system, especially on slower surfaces where the ball stays low. But the potential for grip-related aches far outweighs any real advantages.

Similarly, if you've had any elbow trouble or if your forearm isn't highly conditioned, try to avoid all extreme grips. A western forehand grip may work for Björn Borg, but it could prove painful and disappointing for you. The same goes for an extreme backhand grip on your serve. Sure, you'll get lots of overspin. But you'll twist and snap your wrist much more than you should. A moderate continental grip would be a better choice for your serve. And if you're bothered with chronic arm problems, you might even be better off with a forehand grip for serving.

Many teaching pros advocate a one-grip system for net play. "There isn't enough time to change grips," they say, "and you don't need a grip change anyway." It's true that your reaction time is relatively short at the net. But if you don't change grips, you'll have to twist your wrist to volley anywhere but cross-court. That means your wrist won't be in its stable position at impact, and your forearm will have to absorb considerable stress. Solution: Try to keep your racket up in front of you at the net. Maintain a loose grip with your racket hand and cradle your racket at the throat with your other hand. Use the hand on the throat of your racket to twist your racket and thereby effect a slight grip change just before you punch your volley. There's really more time for reaction at the net than you think. Especially on your backhand volley, a proper grip will mean less strain for your wrist and elbow.

A western forehand grip may work for Björn Borg . . .

Preparation, Before You Hit. You should prepare early for both your ground strokes and your volleys. With early preparation, you should be able to reduce both impact and swing force loads, as you'll automatically slow down your swing.

How you prepare is also crucial. What kind of backswing you take may affect how stable your joints are at peak force. Books, articles, and teaching pros offer a wide range of advice about how to get your racket back. Many of today's players utilize relatively elaborate backswings, which you may feel you should imitate. Don't. These pros are all superb athletes, blessed with remarkable timing and coordination. The flourishes of a Borg require the talents and strength of a Borg. The more flourishes you make with your racket, the less likely it is that your wrist will be in its stable position at the moment of peak force.

The key to healthy preparation in tennis is simplicity. To get your racket ready, you want to use your body, not just your arm. On your forehand, for example, try drawing your racket back by turning your shoulders. Don't rely on an isolated arm movement that takes your shoulder out of its stable position. Take your racket straight back, without excessively opening up or laying back your wrist. Likewise, on your backhand, turn your shoulders to prepare your racket. Your backswing should be straight back, slightly below the level of the ball. For your volleys, a half turn of your shoulders is all that's required. In contrast, your serve and overhead should begin with a full shoulder rotation (shoulders at five o'clock instead of toward the net) — that's the only way you'll be able to achieve power without putting too much stress on your arm.

Impact, As You Hit. You must remember to watch the ball, of course. But that's only part of what has to be happening at the moment you hit your shots. To reduce your chances of developing a sportache, you must also minimize wrist snap or roll, avoid reaching or lunging for a ball so that your elbow locks, and remember to try for control instead of speed.

The experts talk about transferring your weight when you hit a tennis ball. This may not be as easy as it sounds. But if you're concerned about your elbow or wrist, weight transfer is an important part of good tennis technique. If you don't lean forward as you swing, your arm muscles will have to work harder than they may be able to without strain. It isn't always possible or even desirable to take the traditional step forward just before you swing your racket. But at least you want to be leaning forward at impact. If you're consistently off balance as you hit, you're practically certain to develop arm problems.

To "lean in" as you hit a ground stroke or volley, you must swing before the ball gets to you. On your service, you must toss the ball slightly ahead of you. If your toss is straight up over your head or behind you, you'll have to rely exclusively on your wrist to generate both control and power. And that's not good for your health or your performance.

Follow-Through, After You Hit. Many wrist and elbow problems result from excessive twisting (pronation or supination) of your forearm during follow-through. Your forearm pronates when you roll your wrist over to hit a topspin forehand or a heavy twist serve. It supinates when you try to hit a topspin backhand by flipping your wrist over the ball.

Your follow-through offers perfect evidence of what your forearm and wrist were doing as you hit any particular shot. To minimize your chances of developing a sportache, particularly on the inside of your elbow, you want to finish your forehand ground strokes without pronating your forearm or rolling your wrist. Keep your racket face perpendicular to the ground. Likewise, a good backhand follow-through will find your racket pointing on edge across the net, not flipped over or pointing behind you.

You should complete your service motion with your racket across your opposite side, not with a snap down on the same side as your racket arm.

Finally, on both your forehand and backhand volleys, keep your wrist firm. Your follow-through should be minimal, both for good performance and for good health.

A Special Note on Two-Handed Strokes. A number of authorities claim that a two-handed backhand is a virtual guarantee against tennis-related elbow problems. Your second arm, they reason, will effectively share the force load of each stroke, thereby protecting the elbow in your hitting arm. If you have persistent lateral elbow pain, or if you're afraid of developing classic tennis elbow, you may want to consider a two-handed backhand. In fact, a few great players have even hit two-handed forehands as well as two-handed backhands.

However, before you rush out for a series of two-handed stroking lessons, be aware of four points. First, lateral elbow pain is not the only tennis-related sportache. Even if a two-handed backhand can minimize your chances of developing lateral epicondylitis, it won't necessarily prevent your developing medial elbow problems, as well as wrist or shoulder pain.

Second, a two-handed backhand is difficult to learn. If you are young and talented, and if you move very well, you may not find it too hard. But most recreational players are unable to switch from a one-handed to a two-handed stroke without considerable effort and frequent mis-hits. Two-handed strokes require better than normal footwork since with your second hand on the racket, you significantly reduce your reach. For most people, uncertain footwork leads to an increased number of off-center hits. Having your second hand on the racket isn't very productive if as a result you double effective sportforces.

Third, two-handed strokes tend to be hit with excessive wrist. Watch Borg hit his backhand. His racket flips over the ball and ends up pointing behind him, off his right shoulder. Borg hasn't reported any wrist or elbow problems thus far, although he has begun to complain periodically of shoulder pain. But you may not be as fortunate. Even if you don't develop an elbow problem, your attempts to hit a two-handed backhand may result in a wrist sportache.

Finally, golfers, who frequently complain of tennis elbow in their leading arm, offer clear evidence that two-handed swings can result in elbow problems.

Not many recreational tennis players hit two-handed backhands. Therefore, it seems arguable that the authorities who talk so enthusiastically about two-handed strokes as a means of avoiding tennis elbow are forgetting that the two-handed strokes they have studied for the most part belong to exceptional players with superior coordination, footwork, and conditioning. Though there's little doubt that a two-handed backhand will, in part, reduce the peak impact force that must be absorbed in your hitting arm, it may not completely protect you from elbow problems.

TENNIS TECHNIQUE IN GENERAL

What determines your body's ability to withstand the stresses of tennis? It can't be repeated too often. The key is the position of the joints in your arms at the moment they're required to absorb and transmit sportforces. And how can you utilize sound tennis technique to help eliminate or prevent sportaches? Here are some general suggestions:

1. *Watch the Ball.* Some pros will tell you to watch the ball hit your strings. But if you've ever tried to follow that advice, you know it's virtually impossible. Don't worry about it. Just try to relax and concentrate on each ball as it approaches your

racket. Remember, by hitting more of your shots closer to the center of your racket, you automatically reduce effective ball impact force loads.

2. *Keep Your Feet Moving.* Stay on your toes. Maintain your balance. That's the essence of good footwork in tennis. The key is to take small steps and to keep your feet moving. Think of how a boxer dances, darts, and shifts body weight. Watch how a football linebacker shuffles his feet constantly as he gets ready to protect against a pass. That's the secret of staying on balance. As a tennis player, you need to take several small steps even to cover a short distance. With small steps you should be positioned well enough when you arrive so that you can make smooth contact, thereby reducing effective ball impact force loads. Moreover, if you avoid giant steps, jumps, and lunges, you'll improve your chance of avoiding common ankle and knee sportaches. Lower-extremity problems are often caused by sudden spurts of effort that result in intolerably high foot impact force loads, as well as by footwork that leaves you leaning one way while your feet are pointing another way.

3. *Loosen Your Grip between Shots.* The best players grip their tennis rackets tightly only during the brief instant of impact. Learning to cradle your racket with your ''other'' hand between shots should help you relax, thereby avoiding continual muscular tension and stress in your forearm. But you *must* have a firm grip when you actually make contact.

4. *Don't Hit Unnecessary Shots.* If your opponent's serve is out, don't clobber it back. It's impolite. More important, it places unnecessary strain on your arm. Likewise, don't swing at shots your opponent hits over the base line. Avoiding unnecessary shots is the easiest way to reduce cumulative force loads in tennis. By the same token, you shouldn't run for balls you can't get!

Tennis Conditioning

The remaining way to gain the margin you need to withstand the stresses of tennis is through conditioning. It's a resource every bit as important as adjusting your equipment, environment, and velocity, as well as doing whatever you can to improve your technique. You may not think of it as fun, but conditioning doesn't have to be as onerous or time consuming as you may

think. Also, it works. In fact, without a minimum of conditioning, nothing else you do can really guarantee your protection from tennis sportaches.

The first question for you as a tennis player is whether your muscles are strong and flexible enough to permit you to achieve and hold a stable position in the joints of your hitting arm and legs during peak force. Regardless of your technique, you cannot withstand the stresses of tennis safely unless your general conditioning is good.

The second question is whether you will make it a habit to limber up before you play, to warm up slowly once you're on the court, and to warm down for a few minutes after you finish. No general conditioning program can guarantee that you'll be able to avoid or manage tennis aches if you insist on starting cold, hitting your first few balls as hard as you can, or sitting around in damp clothing after playing.

In fact, the cornerstone of a successful tennis conditioning program is healthy playing habits. The only way you can expect your body to withstand the stresses of the game — to absorb forces without developing aches — is if you can train yourself to use common sense before, during, and after you play.

General Conditioning

The general level of conditioning of tennis players is relatively poor. It hasn't really improved much since the first English players interrupted teatime to "knock a few balls." As a result, tennis sportforces can be especially destructive. In fact, the only saving grace for the average player is the recovery periods built into every match or practice session. During changeovers, as well as between shots, points, and games, your body has regular opportunities to recover. Such recovery periods are not available to athletes in repetitive action sports like running. Take advantage of them. Pause whenever you can on the tennis court. Even a few moments of rest may make a real difference.

A general tennis conditioning program should include both strengthening and stretching exercises for the muscles you use most in tennis. Tennis is a total body sport, involving both your lower and upper extremities. Although most tennis aches, especially tennis elbow, can be managed, if not avoided, by keeping your forearm in good shape, strengthening and stretching your shoulder and leg muscles is also important. Your pro should be able to advise you about specific tennis conditioning exercises, or you can take your pick among the many books and articles that have appeared recently on the subject.

Most recreational players, even superior athletes, don't have particularly strong forearm muscles. Many players are especially weak in the muscles used to hit backhands. After all, muscle strength is a function of use. What other sports or activities require you to make a backhand motion? Aside from the racket sports, there's Frisbee. And that's about it. A variety of hitting and throwing sports as well as numerous other activities call on the muscles you use to make your forehand and serving motions. However, chances are that certain muscles needed for tennis are nevertheless relatively weak. As Stan Smith put it in a recent interview with my co-author, Steve Devereux:

> To me, no matter how strong you are — guys who are ex-football players, weightlifters, and so on — everyone can get elbow problems. It seems crazy in a way, but your technique in hitting a tennis ball may be wrong, and no matter how strong you are elsewhere in your body, your forearm muscles may not be that strong or well developed relative to the demands you are putting on them.

The best way to develop the kind of forearm muscle strength you need for tennis is to hit a lot of tennis balls. Of course, you must be careful to increase the demands you place on your body very slowly. Early in the season, or if you are a beginner, you should only gradually increase the amount of tennis you play. It's much better to play three or four times a week for thirty minutes than to play two hours once a week. Build slowly toward regular practices and matches of an hour or more. Infrequent two-hour sessions won't promote muscle development and may even result in the sudden appearance of a sportache such as tennis elbow.

There are a variety of forearm strengthening exercises you can do at home, at the office, on a plane, in a car, even on the tennis court between points or games. If you are planning to make tennis your "lifetime" sport, you should start now to achieve and maintain forearm muscle strength.

The flip side of strength is flexibility. If you're not careful, the stronger you get, the less flexible you become. Dr. James D. Priest and two of his associates at the Stanford University School of Medicine proved it. Their study, published in the *Journal of Sports Medicine* (May/June 1974) and entitled "Elbow Injuries in Highly Skilled Tennis Players," surprised the sportsmedicine community. Dr. Priest's team studied eighty-four world-class players, almost half of whom revealed that they had experienced significant elbow pain during their careers. This shocked various experts who'd always theorized that faulty technique and inadequate muscle strength were responsible for tennis elbow. How could the pros, strong players with generally flawless strokes, have elbow problems in such astonishing numbers? A subsequent study of world-class players provided the answer. Although the pros generally have forearms that are significantly stronger than the forearm of the average recreational player, their hitting arms are also much less flexible.

You can easily test your own forearm flexibility. Hold your arm straight out in front of you with your fingers together. Now bend your wrist up and down. If you are properly flexible, you should be able to point your fingers almost 90° in either direction. However, most world-class players cannot bend their wrists beyond 60°.

You can promote forearm flexibility with several stretching exercises that are easy to do. Many can be done while you're also doing something else, like reading, watching TV, driving, or talking on the phone. You can do them at home, in the office, even on the tennis court between points.

Try to make periodic forearm stretching part of your daily routine, especially if you are playing a lot of tennis or if you already have relatively strong forearm muscles from another sport or activity. Unless you have been working at flexibility, a strong muscle is likely to be a tight muscle. And tight muscles make it difficult, if not impossible, for key joints to achieve their stable position. That increases your vulnerability to sportaches.

Your forearm may be your primary concern, but you must also strengthen and stretch other muscles to be generally in shape for tennis. Your serve and overhead clearly stress your shoulder. Therefore, you should try strengthening and stretching exercises for your shoulder muscles, too. Don't forget to exercise both shoulders, to keep your body in balance.

If exercises just don't fit into your daily routine, remember that there is no better training for the muscles you need for performing a certain activity than the activity itself. Instead of rallying all the time or playing doubles, where you serve only fifteen or twenty times per set, take a basket or bucket of balls at least once a week and practice your serve. Start each session slowly and build up gradually, until you're able to hit fifty to one hundred serves during each twenty or thirty minutes of practice. In addition, practice your overhead from time to time, against a ball machine or with an opponent who lobs well. Both your serve and overhead will become more effective and your shoulder will become stronger and less vulnerable to tennis sportaches.

As for your legs, tennis requires both agility and endurance. Agility and endurance require both flexibility and strength. If you jog several times a week, you'll build strength in your legs. But you'll tend to become inflexible unless you also swim, do calisthenics, or stretch.

Nevertheless leg strength is important. In particular, the large static forces generated as you crouch in your ready position demand strong quadriceps and calf muscles. To promote lower-body strength, try walking instead of riding in a car or bus. Or climb the stairs instead of taking the elevator. You'll be surprised how much better you'll feel late in the third set with a little more strength and endurance in your legs. And since your mind won't be on your legs, you'll play better too.

Remember, a fatigued muscle exposes the connective tissue of your joints to undue stress. If your legs tire quickly when you play tennis, the likelihood that you'll develop ankle and knee sportaches increases. Tired legs can also lead to arm problems. Rather than moving close enough to the ball to absorb impact forces in your body instead of your forearm, you'll start reaching and mis-hitting when your feet just won't carry you that extra step.

There are dozens of different lower-body strengthening and stretching exercises. Tennis players should be especially interested in general conditioning for the muscles of the lower leg, as well as the muscles that extend and flex the knee joint.

Limbering Up

Imagine that you arrive for your regular tennis game fifteen minutes before your scheduled court time. Or you get to the court at the appointed hour and find that your opponent isn't there. He or she arrives ten or fifteen minutes late. How would you use the fifteen minutes before you can start playing? If you are like most recreational players, you might sit by the side of the court waiting or stroll around watching other people play. Be honest. Would you spend the fifteen minutes limbering up?

Bill Norris, the most successful and respected trainer in men's pro tennis today, was recently asked for a single reason why recreational players suffer so much from tennis elbow and other tennis sportaches. Without hesitation he replied:

Why not limber up?

> Ninety-nine percent of the tennis players in the United States and around the world never even think about limbering up or warming up before they play. Visit any club or playground where there are courts. You won't see anyone limbering up. People just step out onto the court and start banging away.

The way you should limber up before tennis depends on your general level of conditioning as well as the amount of time and energy you have before a match or practice. Remember, the strengthening and stretching exercises you do as part of your general conditioning program do not take the place of a regular limbering-up routine. You *must* limber up before you play — *every time*.

Where should you start? At the very least, do a few calisthenics and some easy stretching at courtside. Even if it's only for five minutes, you'll be much better off than if you start cold.

An ideal way to limber up your forearm and shoulder is simply to swing your racket. You may want to keep the cover on to provide a little extra wind resistance on each swing. Take fifteen or twenty swings per minute, starting slowly. In about three minutes your arm will be warm and ready to go.

Skipping rope is an excellent prematch warm-up for both your legs and arms. Keep a jump rope in your racket cover or in your bag. You'll make effective use of it — and you'll probably enjoy yourself too. Running in place is another fine limbering-up exercise for your legs as well as for your circulatory system.

You should be able to devise your own limbering-up routine. But if you'd prefer to save your imagination for those crucial moments on the court, the following ten-minute program is just about ideal.

1. Calisthenics: jumping jacks, windmills, and so on. Two minutes.
2. Skipping rope or running in place. Two minutes.
3. Easy practice swings with a covered racket. Three minutes.
4. Gentle stretching, especially for the hamstrings, calf muscles, Achilles' tendon, and forearm muscles. Two to three minutes.

If you have twenty or thirty minutes available before you play, by all means increase the time you allot to each of the above exercises. If you're at a club with locker room facilities, you may also want to take a three-minute hot shower before exercising, especially during the winter when your muscles are likely to be extra cold. If time and weather permit, why not bicycle or run to the courts? You'll arrive far more limber than if you take your car.

When it comes to limbering and warming up, television has misled a lot of recreational players. Perhaps you've watched your favorite pro walk onto the court, drop an armful of rackets at courtside, stride to the base line, hit for four or five minutes, and then start playing all out. You figure that if the pros do it, so can you. Wrong. As is frequently the case, TV has not shown you what goes on behind the scenes.

Every tennis pro warms up on a practice court for thirty minutes to an hour before a match. Most pros nowadays also do a variety of other limbering-up exercises. Before your favorite star appears on television, hits for five minutes, and then plays a grueling three- or five-set match, he or she has probably completed a lengthy limbering- and warming-up routine. Fifteen to thirty minutes of stretching and calisthenics are followed by thirty to sixty minutes of on-court practice, including a number of serves. The most disciplined players then put in another ten to fifteen minutes of stretching and warming down before taking a warm shower, changing into dry clothes, resting for a bit, and then doing another few minutes of stretching and limbering up just before match time. Do you still think ten or fifteen minutes of limbering up is more than you can manage before you play?

Warming Up

If you've upgraded your general level of conditioning and spent at least a few minutes limbering up before you take to the court, you're on the road to healthy tennis. But you're not there yet, not if you fail to take the single most important step in the prevention and management of tennis sportaches. *Start slowly!* You *must* warm up!

You limber up *before* you step onto the court; you warm up *on* the court. Your first few minutes of play are crucial in all sports, and tennis is no exception. You must start gradually. Your first ten or fifteen minutes of hitting constitutes your warm-up period.

You should usually start with ground strokes, at least if you're concerned about your arm. Why ground strokes? Because when the ball bounces, the force of your opponent's shot is significantly reduced. The only time ground strokes may be harder on your arm than volleys is on a surface where you get consistent bad bounces. If you play on grass, for instance, you might want to warm up at the net before retreating to the base line.

A good warm-up drill — at least for players with sufficient ball control — is to rally from service line to service line. Try to keep the ball going gently back and forth, letting it bounce before you hit it and aiming no deeper than the middle of the opposite service box. The force of ball impact is minimal in this drill, and because you don't need much backswing, internal forces are also reduced. However, you will have to move your feet, follow through carefully, and watch the ball — just as you'll need to do when you eventually move back to the base line.

Regardless of whether you start at the base line, the service line, or the net, during your warm-up you should never lunge or jump for shots. Keep your feet moving, but resist the urge to race after an errant ball. Don't be overly concerned with your accuracy; just try to meet each ball in the center of your racket and push it up over the net toward your opponent. Never try to clobber the ball during your warm-up.

When they both were regulars on the pro tour, Arthur Ashe and Bob Lutz offered a sharp contrast in tennis styles, both in their play and their warm-up. Ashe, lean and sinewy, was a master of control. Even during the heat of a match, he would frequently dink his passing shots, slice his first serve, and chip his returns, rather than trying to blast balls past his opponent. Lutz, built like a football fullback, always enjoyed crunching the ball, just as he did fifteen years ago as a top junior player growing up on the hard courts of California.

Steve Devereux was watching Ashe and Lutz warming up together before Ashe was to play singles for the United States in the Aetna World Cup in 1979. They had been hitting base line to base line for only a couple of minutes when Lutz moved to the net and signaled for Ashe to hit him some lobs.

Arthur lofted his next backhand high over the net. Bob retreated under the ball, cocked his racket behind his head, and held his left hand out in front of him to sight the ball as it drifted down from the rafters. With perfect timing, Lutz grunted and hit an overhead — his first of the day — as hard as he could.

The ball came right back at Ashe, standing just inside the base line. With lightning reflexes — and a minimal backswing — Arthur turned his shoulders for a forehand, caught Lutz's smash on the rise, and delicately placed it back at Lutz's feet. Lutz half-volleyed it into the net.

Smiling, Ashe called out, "Bob, you shouldn't hit the ball that hard." Good advice.

The two hit for a few more minutes. Then Lutz decided he'd had enough. He waved to Dick Stockton to take his place. Half an hour later, American coach Dennis Ralston rushed up to team trainer Bill Norris while he and Steve were chatting off-court. "Will you come and check Lutz's back?" he asked. Shortly, it was announced over the loudspeaker that Stockton would replace Lutz on the American doubles team that afternoon. Ashe went on to win his singles match against John Alexander easily. Lutz spent the rest of the day on the massage table and in the whirlpool.

Whether you are a top pro or a weekend player, you should usually hit five or ten minutes of easy ground strokes before you go to the net to warm up your volleys and overheads. Even then, go for placement, not power. Not until you're just about ready to play should you warm up your serve. Then hit at least ten or fifteen easy serves. Don't try to kill the ball. In fact, you may want to serve at half-pace for the first few games.

If you've had lateral elbow problems, hit forehands and forehand volleys for a few minutes before you try any backhands. If you've had medial tennis elbow, backhands will probably be less of a strain than forehands and serves.

Listen to your body on limbering up and warming up. Slender, loose-jointed types may take less time and tire more quickly than solid, tightly knit players.

Warming Down

This sounds easier than it is. Ideally, after you've warmed up and played for forty-five minutes of your hour, you should finish up with a few easy warm-down drills. What makes it difficult to do this is the competitive nature of tennis. You may find it impossible to convince your opponent to stop playing before the end of that valuable hour just so that you can warm down sensibly while you're both still on the court. You may not want to slow down yourself. For whatever reason, if you end up playing all out right up until you are kicked off your court, at least put on a sweater or jacket and do a few simple stretching exercises before you shower and change.

Another good alternative — if you have the court time and the energy — is to play singles first, and then warm down with an easy set or two of doubles.

Stretching exercises are most effective only when your muscles and joints are warm and supple. That's why it's important to find a way to do a few minutes of stretching after you play. It's especially vital if you play regularly. You might try stretching as you get out of your playing clothes and into your street clothes. Or you might try it in the shower. Ideally, it will become a habitual part of your warm-down routine.

7
Running

ONLY TIME WILL TELL whether the millions of people who took up jogging and running during the 1970s will eventually turn to other fads. My personal conviction is that many of them will continue to run, at least occasionally. However, one thing is certain. If you are one of the many people worldwide who now run, sooner or later you're going to be coping with some problem in your knee, ankle, or foot. Running may or may not continue to be remarkably popular, but it will always be incredibly stressful because people enjoy reaching their limits — and then pushing those limits.

The explosion of interest in recreational running during the 1970s was simply phenomenal. By some estimates there were more than twenty times as many runners in the United States in 1979 as there were in 1970. In many ways running was the perfect activity for the "me decade" — rigorous, simple, and personal.

Running also contributed more than any other recreational activity to the emergence during the 1970s of the sportsmedicine doctor as a legitimate force in the medical community. Runners everywhere had begun to pour into doctors' offices by the end of the past decade, and the members of the medical community who were specializing in athletes' problems were suddenly in tremendous demand.

If you're a runner with an ache, you should find a solution that will work for you in this chapter. EEVeTeC works for runners, as it does for tennis players and other athletes. You won't necessarily need a doctor or a trainer, but you probably will want to consult a knowledgeable shoe fitter, in addition to reading a few books or articles about proper running technique.

The first step toward managing running sportaches is to understand and appreciate running sportforces. Next you'll want to identify your potential aches. Once you have a clearer understanding of sportforces and sportaches, you should find it easy to implement the McGregor Solution. In fact, when you begin to use EEVeTeC as a runner, you'll probably be surprised to discover how much you can do to reduce running sportforces. You may also be astonished to learn how easy it can be to increase your body's ability to withstand the inevitable stresses you must be able to tolerate when you run.

Running Sportforces

The goal of a runner is to move over the ground. Regardless of whether you are setting out to jog a slow mile or struggling to finish a marathon, every movement you make with your arms and legs when you run is designed to help you propel yourself over the terrain under your feet.

The moment when your full weight comes over your foot is the focus of your performance as a runner. It's also the moment when the sportforces of running are at their peak.

Running is an impact sport. When you run, each foot hits the ground approximately 800 times per mile, with an impact force that can amount to as much as three times body weight. Think of that for a moment. If you weigh 150 pounds, each leg is exposed to as much as 360,000 pounds of stress every time you run a mile — approximately 180 tons!

The impact force generated when you run is called *ground reactive force*. Of all sportforces, the ground reactive force to which runners routinely expose themselves is potentially the most destructive. This is for two reasons, in addition to the sheer enormity of the force itself.

First, when you run, only one of your feet is on the ground at any given moment. That's the definition of running. Anything else — two feet on the ground at the same time — is defined as walking. When you run each foot or leg therefore has to be able to withstand peak forces by itself.

Second, running is a cyclical activity with tremendous cumulative stress. You do the same thing over and over when you run, without any recovery period during which your muscles can rest. Scientists who study running talk about the running gait cycle: First one foot is on the ground; then you are airborne; then the other foot is on the ground; then you are once again airborne; and so forth. During the running gait cycle, your knees, ankles, feet, and hips are exposed to rapidly repeating stress.

Running sportforces primarily affect your lower extremities. When you run your lower extremities must be able to withstand the ground reactive force generated as each of your feet hits the ground, in addition to being able to tolerate the internal forces (swing forces) generated within your joints as you make the various movements required to complete your gait cycle. Efficient running requires your body to translate or resolve a variety of forces — the forces of rotation (side to side), rolling in and out, and up and down — into forward motion.

The gait cycle through which each of your legs passes repeatedly as you run can be divided into three phases: preparation, moment of peak force, and recovery. Your body must be able to tolerate certain unique forces during each stage.

Preparation

Each of your lower extremities is in the preparation phase of its gait cycle from the time your foot is farthest back until the moment that it contacts the ground. The forces generated as you complete the preparation phase of your gait cycle are internal (swing) forces. They flow outward — from your hip through your knee, and then through your ankle and foot.

What must happen as you prepare for peak force as a runner is a rather precise combination of rotation and hinge motions. If these motions are not precisely executed, at foot strike (peak force) key joints in your lower extremities are likely to be dangerously unstable.

The size of the internal forces you generate as you prepare for foot strike is a function of several variables, including how fast you are trying to run, whether or not you are running up or down a hill, your running surface, and so on. In other words, the amount of preparatory force the joints of your lower extremities must be able to transmit is a function of the amount of work your muscles have to do to take you as fast and as far as you want to go. Moreover, if you are generating greater internal forces than your body can tolerate, you may be creating a dual problem, since ground reactive forces will often be correspondingly greater as well.

Moment of Peak Force

In tennis the moment when your racket hits the ball is your moment of truth. If you make contact in the "sweet spot" (not necessarily the exact center of your strings), peak force is minimal. Your equipment, racket and strings, will absorb the ball impact sportforces of a perfect hit. However, as your contact point moves away from the center of percussion, effective force loads increase.

There is a similar potential for minimal stress in running. If you wear proper running shoes and land on a flat, cushioned surface with all of your lower-extremity body segments in their stable position, you can reduce peak running sportforces. Conversely, the farther you land from your stable position, the more you increase running sportforces — as well as your potential for sportaches. Unfortunately, not very many runners land consistently in a way that helps to reduce the stress of running.

The principal concern of the runner at peak force is with the foot. Your feet must be able to (1) absorb the impact of your body at foot strike, (2) support and stabilize your body's weight, and then (3) transmit explosive kinetic force to the ground to propel your body forward.

Despite the fact that a runner's feet must be able to absorb and transmit considerable force loads, the stress of running often does not result in an ache — at least not an ache in your feet. The foot is generally able to do everything we ask of it. At one instant, your foot is a shock-absorbing mobile adapter, accepting impact. In the next instant, it's a support mechanism, supporting your body at peak force, on whatever surface at whatever angle. Last, it becomes a rigid propulsive lever, thrusting and lifting you off the ground. At the moment of peak force, an external force flows into your body (ground reactive force) at the same time as internal forces generated during your preparation for foot strike pass through the joints of your lower extremity on their way into the ground. If your feet weren't wonderfully versatile, your lower extremities would ache after only a few minutes of running.

Although peak force can be reduced, there is always a significant potential for stress to your lower extremities when you run. A number of our suggestions are designed to help you ensure that your feet do a proper job of transmitting sportforces. Ensuring that your feet don't fail you at the moment of peak force is an important way to avoid running sportaches.

Recovery

During the recovery phase of the running gait cycle, significant internal forces are once again generated. The muscles in your lower extremities are called upon to return each of your feet in turn with precision and speed to its most rearward position, so that the cycle of preparation, peak force, and recovery can begin again. If key joints are away from their stable position at the beginning of the recovery phase of your running cycle, your muscles and joints must be able to tolerate increased stress.

The farther any key joint is from its stable position at peak force, the greater the sportforces during recovery. If your right knee doesn't extend or straighten enough at foot strike — whether because of tight muscles, poor running technique, hilly terrain, or whatever — the connective tissue within your knee not only must be able to transmit exceptionally high ground reactive forces, but also must be able to withstand the stress of increased recovery forces.

•

The sportforces of running are not confined to your lower extremities. Despite the fact that runners virtually never develop running-related aches in their upper extremities, your arms do play a very definite role when you run. In fact, your arms serve two functions. They balance and stabilize your body, and they

help supply you with power. In the process, your upper extremities go through their own cycle of sportforces.

When you run each of your legs works synchronously with the opposite arm. As your left leg moves forward, so does your right arm. As your left leg moves back, so does your right arm. Your right leg and left arm work similarly. When your knees pass each other, so do your elbows. This alternating back-and-forth motion of arms and legs provides you with balance and stability. The straighter your body, the less the arm swing when you run. Note that when you need power, as in sprinting or running up a hill, you tend to lean forward and swing or drive your arms back and forth.

Running requires precise, predictable patterns. This is true for your upper extremities as well as your lower extremities. Whereas the moment of peak force in your legs occurs at foot strike, your elbows are opposite one another at the moment of peak force in your arms. In addition, there is a preparation phase that involves getting your arms ready for peak force, as well as a recovery phase after peak force.

The sportforces to which your upper extremities are exposed when you run are internal forces; they are generally not significant enough to cause aches. If you hold your arms too high when you run, you may end up with a pain in your neck, but your arms themselves won't hurt. In fact, stress is actually least in your arms at the moment when your elbows are in line with one another (peak force).

Nevertheless, despite the fact that your upper extremities are not themselves in danger of hurting as the result of a run, what you do with your arms as a runner can very definitely increase your vulnerability to lower-extremity pain. If it turns out, for example, that at peak force your elbows are not even with one another at your sides when they should be, the extra effort you'll have to make to bring your arms to their stable position can cause your body to get out of "sync," increasing your potential for knee, ankle, foot, or hip pain.

Obviously, it is desirable to run with "correct" style. Nevertheless, some runners have individual idiosyncrasies or abnormalities that make it difficult or impossible for them to run with arms and legs in perfect harmony. In the end, every runner has to settle for a subjective position of maximum stability.

When it comes to running sportaches, thirty seems to be an important dividing line. If you run more than thirty miles a week, your potential for running sportaches increases dramatically — especially if you are over thirty years of age. Conversely, many runners who are younger than thirty years old and who run less than thirty miles per week are relatively ache-free.

Running sportaches can occur in virtually any joint in your lower extremities. Knee pain is by far the most common complaint among runners, but ankle and foot sportaches also occur, and hip problems are relatively common.

Many runners eventually develop lower-back pain or some other ache in the many-jointed complex known as the back. However, your back can also be the site of a variety of other potentially serious problems. You can easily develop a bona fide sportache in your back as a runner. EEVeTeC may supply the solution to your backache. Many a runner has eliminated persistent backaches by obtaining proper running shoes, using orthotics, and strengthening or stretching key muscles, particularly in the legs and abdominal area. However, we have chosen not to discuss the back in this book for two simple reasons.

Running Sportaches

First, your back is a very complicated part of your body. Its many problems defy generalization. Second, no one should treat backaches on their own without first consulting a doctor — there are simply too many serious complications that can ensue if you underestimate or misdiagnose your problem. By all means use EEVeTeC, but only after your doctor assures you that you do not have a medical problem requiring medical treatment.

When you run each of your legs is alternately lengthened and shortened. With a stop-action camera, you'd see that as your body thrusts forward at toe-off, the leg that is being lifted off the ground is moving away from the center of gravity of your body — extending to its full length. Similarly, at foot descent, just before heel strike, you bend in foot, ankle, knee, and hip effectively to shorten your leg. This shortening continues through midstance or peak force. Obviously, it is important that the hinge joints of your lower extremities be in good working order.

Some joints hinge only — knee and ankle. Other joints hinge and rotate — hip and foot. There is minimal rotation around your knee, but it's still a functional hinge. When a joint acts as a hinge, one muscle stretches while the other contracts. The vast majority of running-related aches occur because the motion of a hinge joint has been hampered — either because of faulty design, muscle imbalance, or a sportforce that has subjected the joint to more rotation than it can tolerate.

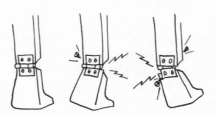

Your problem may also be a "short" limb. Or is it a long limb? Either way, if one of your lower extremities is longer than the other, you may develop aches because of asymmetrical limb length, a not uncommon situation. For most people such a difference (usually a matter of several tenths of an inch) isn't a problem. But with increased force loads and the increased stress of running, even slight asymmetry can create any of a number of running sportaches. Precise measurement of your limbs is difficult and the cause of your aches may not be immediately identifiable. However, no runner should discount the very real possibility that running-related aches are a function of a manageable limb length discrepancy.

Your feet are remarkably good at absorbing and transmitting sportforces. Your knees, being less versatile, are much more vulnerable to ground reactive forces. Also, of course, your knee is the first joint after your hip to be subjected to the internal forces generated within your body as you prepare for peak force (foot strike) and recover from it.

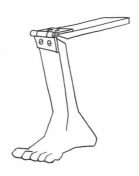

It should come as no surprise that knee problems head the list of runners' aches. Like your elbows, your knees are primarily hinges. They cannot be twisted very far without pain. To use the same image we employed in explaining tennis elbow, if you are having difficulty envisioning what happens to your knee when you run, think about twisting a towel at both ends. That's right. It knots up in the middle. Your knee is in the middle of that kinetic chain called your lower extremity. Like the middle of a towel being twisted at both ends, your knee is stressed by dual forces when you jog or run — both external and internal forces tend to twist your leg before, during, and after peak force.

If running doesn't make your knees ache, the sportforces of running may find a weak link in one of your ankles or feet. That makes sense because ground reactive forces — by far the most important forces your lower extremities must be able to withstand at the moment of peak force — have to pass through your feet and ankles before they can reach your knees.

Finally, there is hip pain. If you develop an aching hip as a runner, chances are that the internal or swing forces you're generating as you prepare for and recover from peak force are at fault. Swing forces travel from the core of your body through your lower extremities. The first joints through which they must pass, of course, are your hips. Also, some hip pains can be caused by impact.

Knee Sportaches

Your least versatile joints generally have the most difficult time with sportforces, which explains why the functional hinge joint in your knee is likely to be the first victim of the stresses to which you expose yourself as a runner. The inherent stability of that hinge lies in the combination of shapes of the bones that make up your knee joint, the placement of the ligaments that bind the bones together, and the capsule that is the final protective sleeve around the joint. In fact, your knees are not very stable.

The hinge action of your knee is made possible by the muscles and tendons that span the joint. The precise location of each of these structures highlights its role as either a mover or a stabilizer, at least so long as your knee functions as it was meant to. When your knee doesn't function like a hinge, it is stressed by twisting at your hip or your foot. Your feet, in particular, may twist for a variety of reasons when you run, including either too much or too little motion in your ankles.

One other aspect of knee joint function is vital in identifying and understanding knee sportaches. It's the bending, flexing, and extending that take place principally through the action of the muscles in the front and back of your thigh. Chief among those muscles are the quadriceps, four muscles bound together and ending in a common tendon that crosses the front of your knee and anchors in the top and front of the major bone in your lower leg.

The patella (kneecap) is a movable bone within the quadriceps tendon. It acts as a fulcrum, making extension of your knee less stressful. It is also designed to slide in a specifically contoured groove in the upper leg bone, the femur. Though not a joint in the strictest sense, this junction of patella and femur is classified as a joint. Many sportaches are the result of faulty design or function of the patello-femoral joint.

FRONT-OF-THE-KNEE SPORTACHES

Although there are a few notable exceptions, as a general rule all front-of-the-knee sportaches, in either the patella, its tendon, or the muscles that act on the patella, are caused by either faulty design or muscle imbalance.

If the patella and the groove in which it slides aren't in harmony, grating and irritation often result under the exceptional stress of running. Point this out to a patient like the forty-five-year-old male executive I saw recently and you always hear, "How come it's taken all these years to hurt?" I usually answer, "The stress of running was the straw that broke the camel's back." After a lifetime of cumulative stress, some knees are just waiting for that one final moment of stress before they break down. Of course, the same rule applies to all joints.

Normally, the strength ratio between the quadriceps muscles in the front of your thigh and the hamstring muscles in the back of your thigh is six to four. When that ratio is out of phase and the muscles in the front or back of your thigh aren't strong enough, your patello-femoral mechanism is weakened and your patella tends to drift. The result is often a front-of-the-knee sportache.

Imbalance can also be the result of inflexibility. The most common problem among runners is overly tight hamstrings. Since we tend to spend a significant part of our lives sitting, with our leg muscles neither challenged nor stretched, inflexibility is a widespread problem in the modern world. If you haven't been making a conscious effort to stay flexible, either your hamstrings or your quadriceps are probably too tight, creating an imbalance that can result in knee pain when you take up jogging, change your running routine, or suddenly increase your weekly mileage.

SIDE-OF-THE-KNEE SPORTACHES

Pain on either side of the knee joint is usually the result of a pinching or twisting of the hinge. Faulty design or malfunction may be the cause.

Knock knee or rotating knee, sometimes called knee wink, is a function of faulty design. Do you have knee wink? To find out stand with your feet parallel. If your kneecaps tend to "wink" (slightly face) at each other, you've got knee wink. Your knees will not withstand running sportforces well.

With faulty function, your knees either cannot or do not get into the proper hinge relationship. For instance, when you walk or run, do your toes and kneecaps naturally point outward? In other words, are you what we call the "ten minutes to two" walker? If your feet form the hands of a clock at ten minutes before two, the slue-foot position, they will roll in excessively. Your knee will tend to cave in, "pinching" either the inner or outer side of the knee. Sportaches around your kneecap can also be caused by this excessive rotation or pinching.

•

Knee sportaches carry fancy labels like runner's knee, jumper's knee, chondromalacia, and patellar tendinitis. Sometimes even I use such labels. My favorite is patellar stress syndrome. However, I'm never happy about using medical terminology, at least not when a patient is complaining of pain during or after a run that can't be reproduced during an examination. Knee pain is knee pain — at least until you develop acute or chronic inflammation or suffer a direct injury.

You have a knee sportache from the moment you begin to notice recurring knee pain during or after a run. You can wait, as many runners do, to see if your pain will become incapacitating. Chances are that it will. Then you'll have to stop running and spend time and money treating your inflammation before eventually using EEVeTeC to avoid a relapse. Your alternative, of course, is to use the McGregor Solution right away — at the first sign of a knee sportache — and save yourself lots of pain, frustration, and money. It's your choice.

Ankle Sportaches

Running can be described as the repetitive lengthening and shortening of a limb. Your knees and ankles — both hinge joints — are key in this extension and contraction, with your hips also playing a role. It must be a complete action. If not — if one of your limbs doesn't get long enough or short enough — sportaches can result.

Incomplete range of motion, which spells trouble for your knees, can be disastrous in your ankles as well. If one of your feet can't extend down far enough or up far enough to achieve the important lengthening/shortening relationship required when you run, ankle sportaches can occur.

What causes incomplete range of motion in the ankle? As with the knee, muscle imbalance may be the problem. However, a restricted range of motion in one of your ankles may also be the result of a block or impingement of the bones in either the front or the back of the joint.

In the back of the ankle, your problem is usually a superfluous or extralarge bone, most often an inherited defect. In the front of the ankle, pain commonly results from a proliferation of bony prominences, often a consequence of long-forgotten blows or stresses you may have experienced during other sports like football, basketball, soccer, rugby, or baseball — a condition that can be confirmed only by X-ray.

No matter what your problem, if your ankle cannot do what it has to do when you run, the muscles and tendons that move and stabilize the joint will begin to hurt. Eventually, you may develop a serious ankle sportache.

Ankle aches usually occur in the back of your ankle somewhere from the attachment of the Achilles' tendon in the heel bone to a point four or five inches up the tendon itself. Alternatively, you may develop an ache in one of the several tendons that pass in front of your ankle.

Foot Sportaches

Next to the knee, the foot is the most common site of runner's sportaches, again as the result of either faulty design or faulty function.

Faulty foot design can cause either not enough motion or too much motion. A foot with insufficient motion, either a rigid, high-arched foot or a rigid, "flat" foot, may be effective as a propulsive lever, but inadequate as an absorber and adapter. In contrast, a foot with too much motion will absorb shock and adapt like clay, but it will fail as a support mechanism and propulsive lever. Which foot is yours? Look at the print you leave when your foot is wet. If you can't see much tread, you have a rigid, high-arched foot. If you see excessive tread, you have a rigid, flat foot. Otherwise, your foot is mobile.

It is often argued that there is a "biomechanical" or natural selectivity to some activities. For instance, when you ski, your hips accomplish the necessary rotation while your knees and ankles absorb shock. Since your feet are fixed to your boots (and hence to your skis), you don't want or need much foot motion. As a result, the high-impact, rigid foot is well suited to skiing. As a matter of fact, the same foot is perfectly adequate for cycling, swimming, and even tennis. However, it is not suited to long-distance running. If you have high-impact, rigid feet as a runner, ground reactive forces tend to cause heel sportaches. Also, because it is not a particularly good shock absorber, a rigid foot causes sportaches in all the joints above it, from the ankle to the knee and even through the spine. High-arched, rigid feet tend to roll to the outside, putting stress on the outside structures of the ankle and knee. Low-arched, rigid feet tend to roll to the inside, putting stress on the inside structures of the ankle and knee. A rigid foot also flexes less at the ankle.

If you have feet that are hypermobile (too much motion), you're likely to develop foot aches as a result of too much movement in the joints of your feet. In addition, heel pain can arise at the points where the tendons or other supporting structures attach. Your foot collapses with each step, resulting in a constant pull on your heel bone. At its worst, such irritation can stimulate excessive bone growth, resulting in the much-fabled heel spur.

Even if you don't have a problem with faulty design, faulty foot mechanics or faulty function can still result in foot sportaches. An otherwise healthy or well-designed foot is subjected to abnormal sportforce loads if it is placed on the ground improperly. An example is the slue-foot position, where your feet form the hands of a clock at ten minutes to two.

The area of the ball of your foot, where your toes join the rest of your foot, can also have problems. High-arched, rigid feet often have cocked up toes and downward depressed bones on the ball of the foot.

Lower-Leg Sportaches

Several sportaches can arise in your lower leg. Many of them parade under the nondescript and imprecise term *shin splints*. Most lower-leg sportaches are a function of the fact that either your foot is not doing the right thing at the right time or it is doing the wrong thing at the wrong time. Remember that all the muscles that originate in your lower leg end up in your foot. If your feet fail you — for example, if one, or both, rolls in too much — the result is often a lower-leg sportache.

The other major reason for lower-leg sportaches is either the weakness or inflexibility of key muscles. When the muscles in the front of your lower leg contract concentrically, they bring your toes closer to your leg. When they contract eccentrically, your toes move away from your leg. Running requires a precise series of shortening and lengthening motions. If the muscles in your lower leg that enable you to raise and lower your toes are not strong enough, they can be easily overstressed. Likewise, if the muscles in the back of your lower leg — your calf muscles — are too weak, or if either set of lower-leg muscles is too tight, the result can be an ache.

Hip Sportaches

Hip sportaches generally occur because a muscle or tendon is being pulled excessively over the bony prominences of your hip. This potential problem often first becomes evident when you try to increase your stride length.

If the muscles that stabilize your hip are too weak to do their job, you may also develop hip sportaches. Remember that running requires total support on a single limb. The muscles in each of your lower extremities must be able to support three times your body weight 800 times per mile. You can strengthen weak stabilizing muscles by running. It's your best conditioning tool. Sometimes, however, conditioning may not be enough. It's not uncommon to find that runners with hip pain have a bony limitation of motion in their hip that makes proper rotation of their thigh impossible.

Toe Pain

Ask any runner who is at all familiar with the host of material written about foot problems, "What's Morton's toe?" and you'll get one of two answers: (1) short first toe (this answer is partially correct), or (2) cramping and pins-and-needles sensation of the fourth toe (this answer is also partially correct).

Why are there two different answers? Well, you've probably guessed it already. There were two different Mortons.

In 1909 Thomas G. Morton, a Philadelphia surgeon, was the first to describe a painful, cramping, burning, pins-and-needles sensation, usually of the fourth toe, sometimes the third, and rarely the second. Further investigation brought out the fact that this condition was usually caused by a thickening or enlargement of a nerve in the foot. Morton called this a neuroma — the suffix -oma means swelling of the neur, nerve. To allay any misgivings that the -oma was caused by invasive cells, often found in cancers, Morton's toe was called a traumatic intermetatarsal or interdigital neuroma. That is, it was caused by irritation at the nerve that ran between the metatarsals or toes, a neat, precise description of what was in fact going on.

Then, in 1939, Dudley Morton, a New York orthopedist, described a rather precise series of circumstances that he believed were present in 25 percent of the human population. They were: (1) short first metatarsal, (2) long second metatarsal, (3) excessive motion between the bones at the base of the metatarsal, (4) rearward displacement of the sesamoid bones under the first metatarsal, (5) possible skin callus under the second metatarsal head. He called this Morton's syndrome, a collection of findings, and hypothesized that it represented a throwback to our quadripedal heritage. Morton's syndrome has also been described as the "aristocratic foot." Dr. Morton believed that the condition he named after himself was the cause of a large number of foot problems.

In the recent flurry of medical writing about running, Dr. George Sheehan, among others, has lionized Morton's toe or Morton's syndrome. It has reached the point where patients flood doctors' offices with self-diagnoses of Morton's toe and demands for instant action. I'm ready for them. Whenever someone tells me, "I have Morton's toe," I respond, "I wonder if he's missed it yet."

Bone Pain

Always be suspicious of pain in a bone anywhere in your lower extremities. Until a doctor tells you otherwise, consider such pain to be a stress fracture. Anyone practicing sportsmedicine who claims never to have missed diagnosing a stress fracture is either a liar or in the first weeks of practice. Why? Because stress fractures are quite common among athletes, in addition to being very difficult to diagnose, at least in their early stages.

A stress fracture is a slight crack of the cortex or outer shell

of a bone. It usually occurs when a bone undergoes extreme stress, most often rotational stress, which it isn't strong enough to resist. The alarming thing about stress fractures is that you may have the classic symptoms of a stress fracture some time before anything will show up on an X-ray. The use of radioactive scanning or some other sophisticated diagnostic technique may be required before a doctor can see your fracture and confirm the diagnosis. It is even possible that no scientific wizardry will ever confirm your problem. Despite the fact that your symptoms seem unmistakably those of a stress fracture, neither you nor your doctor will be completely certain how to treat your problem.

What can you do? I don't believe in heroics. I've seen and heard of too many relatively "simple" stress fractures that have turned into disabling, completely displaced fractures. Therefore, I never allow any patient who might have a stress fracture to undertake an inappropriate activity or resume a sport too early.

I know it's no fun having to wait on the sidelines, especially if it means sitting out all or part of a season. But your ache is your own responsibility. Are you willing to gamble while you try to work your way through your pain? If you're a runner with bone pain and you insist on trying to "run through your pain" because your X-rays don't reveal a fracture, you may end up on the sidelines for a lot longer than it takes a minor stress fracture to heal.

Stress fractures can take anywhere from six weeks to four months to heal completely. Also, treatments can vary. I've found that it's usually wise to restrict motion and/or weight bearing until pain goes away. This can be done with crutches in the case of hip and thigh fractures; plaster immobilization in extreme cases of thigh, leg, or foot fractures; and removable casts, splints, or wooden sandals in the case of leg or foot fractures.

Once a patient can ambulate without pain, unaided by artificial devices, I recommend a gradual return to increased non-weight-bearing activity — swimming, bike riding, even running in water above knee level. When all diagnostic signs are negative — negative bone scan, healed cortex as viewed by X-ray — then running, tennis, and most other sports can be resumed. I understand how many recreational runners feel they must "use it or lose it." However, in the case of bone pain, I'd add that it's crucial not to "abuse it."

Accidents and Injuries

Runners are no less prone than other athletes to a variety of common and not-so-common accidents and injuries. In the same sense that running-related sportaches can usually be prevented or managed with EEVeTeC, the accidents and injuries that can befall you as a runner are often more avoidable than many runners might admit, at least if they run in a normal running environment where there are automobiles, animals, trees, curbs, rocks, and other people.

Probably the most serious running injuries involve automobiles. As more and more runners take to city streets and country roads, a growing number of people will inevitably be hit by cars. Sometimes it seems that drivers purposely come as close as possible to passing runners. I've never heard of a situation where the automobile loses in a showdown between runner and driver. So be careful.

I advise running against the traffic, even if that is contrary to local ordinances and laws. At least you'll have a few seconds' warning if a car is bearing down on you. Obviously, it also helps

to wear light-colored clothing or a reflector if you run at dusk or in the dark. Finally, you should stick to the sidewalk as much as possible, at least if traffic is heavy where you run.

If you do run on the sidewalk, of course, watch out for bicyclists and pedestrians. Tangling with a ten-speed or a baby carriage may not leave you in quite as bad shape as the thousands of runners each year who are hit by trucks or cars, but you still may be very sorry you weren't more careful.

Avoiding a collision is not your only challenge if you run anywhere near traffic. You'll also want to avoid near misses. At least once a month, some runner comes into my office with a muscle pull in the back of the lower leg or thigh. The story is always the same: A car jumped or ran a traffic light or the runner misjudged the speed of a vehicle and suddenly had to sprint. I always point out to such a runner that he or she is lucky to have sustained only a pulled muscle.

Runners need to be alert at all times to their surroundings. Running with your dog, for example, can be delightful for both you and your pet. But it can be dangerous. Our dog, Taffy, always seemed to be a natural running companion. She never needed any instruction, was just far enough in front of me or behind me, never in the way. That is until one day during September 1978 when I was passing in front of the local armory in the last half mile of a sixteen-mile training run. At that point I confess I was thinking more about a cold beer than Taffy. Sud-

denly, she was met by four dogs who streaked across a nearby lawn to say hello. The next thing I knew I was on the ground, having tripped over Taffy and two of her newfound friends. When I eventually picked myself up, I started a slow trot, only to discover that with every step there was a pain in my right rib cage. Subsequently, I learned that I had cracked a rib when I fell. That was the end of my plan to run the 1978 New York Marathon. In fact, I didn't feel really well for months.

By far the most common running accidents and injuries result from running on uneven surfaces or in conditions where you can't see rocks, roots, or holes in the ground. Unfortunately, such conditions are quite common. As a result, very few runners can hope to avoid the occasional ankle or knee injury that results from tripping or falling during a run. In fact, if you just sprain or twist your ankle from time to time, you're lucky. Thousands of runners actually break an ankle, foot, or leg every year. Nevertheless, if you're alert when you run, you should be able to minimize such accidents. Also, as John Robinson, former world orienteering champion, once explained to me, a determined cross-country runner can train to avoid pitfalls.

Running in the woods or along a tree-lined river bank can be very pleasant. Watch out for low-hanging branches and twigs, however, as there are regular reports of runners being badly scratched or injured when someone ahead is careless or when the light is poor.

And then there are the bizarre running accidents and injuries — the ones you hear about but can't quite believe. Jon Lindholm, an old running friend from Boston, recently told me about

an incident he witnessed while jogging on vacation in northern Florida. Jon was running on the edge of the seventeenth fairway of the golf course at the resort where he was staying. The ocean was across the road to his right. On the other side of the fairway to his left was a lagoon. As he was gazing across the fairway, Jon saw a golfer tee up and hit across the lagoon toward the nearby sixteenth green. As Jon watched in dismay, the golf ball curved and hit an older woman who was jogging across a footbridge normally reserved for golf carts and golfers. The woman was stunned. She staggered and fell over the guardrail into the water. Jon sprinted to her rescue, but before he and the golfers could fish her out of the lagoon, the unfortunate runner had almost drowned.

Running Solutions

Running sportaches can be eliminated; EEVeTeC works well for runners. The easiest way to manage the pains of fitness as a runner is to reduce forces. This may be as simple as making a basic adjustment in your running equipment, changing your running environment, or adjusting your running velocity. If reduction of running sportforces isn't enough to eliminate your running sportache, you'll want to consider increasing your body's ability to withstand running-related stress. Increasing your tolerance requires an adjustment in either your running technique or your conditioning.

Remember, sportaches are often the result of overuse — doing "too much, too often, too soon." To decide where to start in your effort to employ the McGregor Soluton, you need to begin with a personal sports history.

If you're now suffering from a running-related ache, you need to determine whether you've done anything lately that might account for your problem. Have you bought a new pair of running shoes? Did you just have your old shoes resoled? Have you recently switched from running on a cinder track to running roads? Have you started running at a different time of the day? Are you running more often now than in the past? Have you been trying to go faster than before? Have you changed your running technique? If it's winter and the days are shorter, are you not taking as much time as you know you should to warm up because you don't want to "waste" precious daylight after work? Think carefully. Any of these seemingly minor changes, and others like them, can be at the root of your problem.

If you can pinpoint the origin of your present running sportache, you may also have found its solution. If thinking about your recent running history reminds you that you bought a new pair of running shoes just before your current knee pain really started to bother you, what you ought to try first in your application of the McGregor Solution is clear. However, even after you experiment with other running shoes or decide just to get your old pair resoled, you may still have to make additional adjustments in your running EEVeTeC. At least for awhile you may have to run less often; slow your training pace; avoid hills and uneven running surfaces; and limber up, warm up, and warm down thoroughly before, during, and after every run.

Even once you figure out how to begin using EEVeTeC in your effort to eliminate your running-related ache, you may nevertheless have to make a variety of additional adjustments to rid yourself entirely of your pain. Let's begin at the beginning — with the reduction of running sportforces.

Reducing Forces

Ground reactive sportforces are your primary concern as a runner. Therefore, reduction of running sportforces is largely a matter of reducing the impact force generated each time your feet hit the ground.

First, there's *absolute impact force*. Running on concrete exposes you to a greater force than running on hard sand or on a cinder track. Likewise, if you run downhill, you'll encounter greater absolute impact forces than on level terrain, and so on.

Absolute impact force is the amount of force generated when your foot collides with the ground — regardless of how much of that force is actually transmitted into your lower extremity. Obviously, the greater the absolute force, the greater the potential stress to your feet, ankles, knees, and hips. There are a variety of adjustments you can make in your running equipment, environment, and velocity to reduce absolute impact forces. At the same time, you'll probably succeed in reducing stress.

Second, there's *effective impact force* — the amount of absolute impact force that actually travels through your running shoe and up into the various joints of your lower extremity. Among the variables you can adjust to reduce effective impact forces, the most important is, of course, your running shoe. In addition, since effective forces increase if your joints are unstable, you'll be exposed to smaller effective forces on a flat, even surface where your footing is relatively sure. Likewise, effective impact forces can be reduced if you don't run in the rain or on slippery surfaces, and if you don't run at night or when you can't see the ground under your feet.

A number of the tips that follow are designed to help you reduce effective impact forces. The key is to adjust your equipment and your environment to maximize the cushion between your feet and the ground and to minimize bad footing. If you do everything you can to ensure that effective forces are at a minimum, you should have relatively few aches even if absolute ground reactive forces are considerable — as they will be, for example, if you train or race on roads or hills.

Of course, ground reactive forces are not the only sportforces you must contend with as a runner. Reduction of running sportforces also means you have to minimize the internal forces generated during the preparation and recovery phases of your running gait cycle. These internal forces are basically a function of velocity. As a rule, the faster you run, the greater the sportforces generated within the joints of your lower extremities. Also, if you lengthen your stride (even if you don't also increase your speed), you increase the amount of work that key muscles

within your joints must do to prepare for and recover from peak force — thereby increasing the internal forces you generate when you run. Finally, if you run on a surface or with equipment that requires you to work relatively hard — as you'll have to if you run in soft sand, for example, or in an overly cushioned shoe — greater internal forces are generated with each step you take.

Equipment

Tennis players, golfers, and skiers have a variety of adjustments they can make in their equipment to avoid and manage sport-aches. Runners, in comparison, have substantially fewer choices. If you run, the only equipment adjustments you can make in your effort to manage a bothersome ache involve your running shoes, orthotics, socks, and clothing. But these are so important, they may suffice.

Don't hesitate to experiment with your running equipment. You may save yourself lots of unnecessary pain, frustration, and expense.

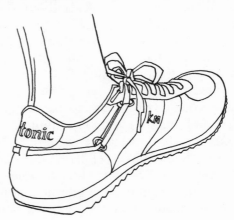

RUNNING SHOE

The running shoe is to running what the racket is to tennis, and the club to golf. Your shoe is at the crucial interface during peak force — when your foot meets the ground. No single equipment decision made by any recreational athlete is more important than the choice of a running shoe by a runner. The incredible evolution of the running shoe during the past decade offers proof positive that everyone — designer, manufacturer, and wearer

— now considers the running shoe as equipment. No longer is your shoe merely an extension of your running wardrobe.

Only a few years ago there was no real distinction between training shoes (which now compose 90 percent of the market) and racing shoes. In fact, distance running, at least as we know it today, didn't exist. Distance runners were either on high school or college teams or were part of a small group of "fanatics" who ran the Boston Marathon. Most training was done in shoes like racing shoes, which typically didn't have much of a heel raise and provided only minimal protection throughout the whole bottom part of the shoe. If you developed an ache as a result of the fact that your running shoes didn't offer adequate cushion or protection for your feet, you simply had to quit running.

Like many runners, I started running in tennis sneakers. I didn't wear my first training shoe — a New Balance Trackster I — until the early 1970s, at which point I'd been running a mile or two every once in a while for several years! I remember that one of the New Balance innovations was a slight wedge along the underside of the shoe, designed to provide both support and stability. The shoe was light and flexible but provided minimal protection. Its ripple sole was better than nothing, but like many other runners, I soon discovered that it wore out quickly on the outside and had to be replaced.

Nevertheless, the introduction of the Trackster I marked the dawning of an incredible era in the running shoe industry. Sales, which amounted to just a few million dollars in 1970, have increased astronomically. The several manufacturers that existed ten years ago have proliferated, with literally hundreds of available shoe models replacing the original few.

Today's running shoes are not only more numerous and diverse than those of ten years ago, they are much better. Manufacturers have made amazing advances in both the design and production of running shoes. As the designer of a popular shoe, I'm delighted that this progress hasn't occurred in the relative vacuum of the research and development labs of the major shoemakers. It has come in public, right out in front of the consumers, the runners themselves.

Runner's World, the magazine, has paralleled and, in some ways, led the running boom. It has grown from a mimeographed newsletter, cranked out by a high school student named Bob Anderson at his home in Kansas, to a multimillion-dollar publishing enterprise now based in Mountain View, California.

Since *Runner's World* first started evaluating running shoes in 1972, its annual survey has become the bible for runners who are serious about their feet. The *Runner's World* panel, as well as the shoe experts who write for other running publications — notably *Running Times* — use increasingly sophisticated electronic and mechanical equipment to quantify certain predetermined qualities in running shoes. Still, there's an inherent weakness in the process of ranking shoes. As accurate and reproducible as the data is, what does it all mean to the average consumer-runner? Since no two runners are the same — we all vary in foot size and construction, body weight, and running style — the value of standardized shoe data is really questionable.

The running shoe that is good for someone else — or that is rated number one by *Runner's World* — isn't necessarily the best shoe for your foot and your running routine. Choosing a shoe can become both confusing and frustrating. However, there is help, someone you can turn to for advice. Be sure to consult your local equipment technician — the man or woman who sells running shoes in the local sporting goods shop or running shoe store.

More and more, shoe fitters are functioning like the old neighborhood pharmacist. Remember when you used to ask the person behind the counter at the drugstore for medical advice? "Say, what do you have for a sore throat?" Or, "You got anything for an earache?" Invariably, the druggist would have a solution. Well, the next time you're in a store that sells running shoes, close your eyes and listen to a typical conversation. You'll hear consumers asking for help — and getting it. "My heel hurts. What kind of shoe do you recommend?" Or, "I'm getting a knee pain. Do you think my shoes are the problem?" If you didn't know better, you might think you were in a doctor's office.

As a doctor, I'm very grateful to the shoe fitters in my area for helping hundreds of runners use EEVeTeC to eliminate their own aches — so they don't have to waste time and money in my office. I call these shoe fitters first-point practitioners in my sportsmedicine community.

As a matter of fact, I've given clinics all over the United States, Japan, and Europe for shoe fitters. I know that doctors in general and podiatrists in particular have provided voluminous instructional material for shoe fitters since the running boom began during the 1970s. Therefore, during my office "call-in" hours, I often tell runners to check with their shoe fitter before setting up an appointment with me. If a given problem appears unrelated to equipment, then I see the patient, of course. But first I like to rule out the shoe, and I trust the people who fit running shoes to help me do so.

•

What should you look for in a running shoe if you're anxious to avoid running sportaches? To be effective, a running shoe must fulfill three important requirements:

1. It should fit.
2. It should protect.
3. It should support your foot in its most stable position. Your leg should be at a right angle to your foot, and your foot evenly balanced on the ground.

Remember, the real test of your running shoe comes at the moment of peak force, when your foot must be able to absorb and transmit a ground reactive force equal to three times your body weight for as many as 800 steps per mile!

Fit. No researcher, no magazine, no survey can determine which running shoe will fit you best. You are the only judge. During twenty-nine years of active general podiatric practice, I've seen thousands of problems caused by what I call shoe-foot incompatibility. That is, the shoe and foot don't get along. And the foot usually loses.

Notwithstanding, during the last eight years as an active sportsmedicine practitioner, I've seen only a few examples of shoe-foot incompatibility among runners. That means two things. First, running shoes generally fit and function well. Second, running shoe buyers generally make intelligent choices. The one common exception to this last rule of thumb is the runner who intentionally buys shoes that are too short or too tight, on the theory that they will provide ''a better feel of the road.'' To that runner I say, ''It's your problem.''

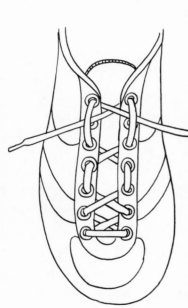

I believe that one reason today's running shoes work so well for most runners is that they don't generally get in the way of your feet. Running shoes actually complement and aid your feet in their job, which is running. In contrast, high heels, for example, make walking (much less dancing or running) a precarious activity indeed.

The fit of your running shoes can sometimes be enhanced through changes in the lacing system. The example shown in the accompanying illustration is a variation of a lacing system that has gained national popularity. I've found it particularly useful because it grips your shoe to your foot and improves heel fit, especially for those runners with narrow heels.

A colleague first showed me this special lacing system the day before the 1978 Boston Marathon. I used it in the race — and I've used it every day since. It doesn't work as well if your running shoe has a six-eyelet stay, and it's practically useless with four-eyelet shoes. However, if it will work in your shoes, it can be effective in many sports besides running — sports like soccer, where you want your shoe to function as part of your foot.

Protection. Sometimes I think that ''protection'' is really more of a concept than a measurable quality in running shoes. Shoemakers emphasize this "important feature." But I'm not always sure they have a clear idea of what they mean.

For one thing, although you definitely want your running shoe to reduce the shock generated when your foot hits the ground, you don't necessarily want that shock completely absorbed. Does that sound strange? It shouldn't. It's important to you as a runner to have some of the energy you generate at foot strike returned to you. That's the secret of energy-efficient running. Therefore, if what shoe manufacturers mean by "protection" is shock absorption, it's not necessarily true that the more protection a shoe offers, the better it will be for your feet and lower extremities.

Running in shoes that absorb all the shock of foot strike is like hitting tennis balls that come at you with no pace. You have to do more work, even though impact forces are less. Eventually, work can generate its own problems and aches. Remember that no muscle or group of muscles actually propels your body forward when you run. Momentum is what keeps you going. But your muscles have to work to keep your body in a position where momentum can be effective.

If you want an illustration of the importance of running in a shoe that returns some of the energy generated at foot strike, try running in shoes that feature high shock absorbability and low energy return. After a while you should notice exceptional fatigue in the leg muscles you need to help propel your body. That's because you're forcing your muscles to work too hard. It's like running on sand, where the surface beneath your feet is returning very little energy. Running on a beach, you may not develop aches as the result of impact forces. However, you're very likely to hurt after a while. Eventually, tired muscles will begin to expose your connective tissue to more stress than it can tolerate.

Recent innovations in shoe design include prefilled air pillows. These are available on a limited number of shoes. Most manufacturers whose shoes have air pillows are using laminates of various light, energy-absorptive and -dispersive plastic materials to protect your feet. For some runners the prefilled air pillows and other similar cushions are a blessing. If you are a runner with a minimal or diminishing fat pad under the heels or balls of your feet, you need all the protection your running shoe can offer. Otherwise just be careful you don't buy so much protection in your shoe that you don't have enough energy to run in it.

Support. The third requirement of a good running shoe is that it hold your foot in its stable position. Recent biomechanical research by Penn State's Dr. Peter Cavanaugh indicates that the proper vertical relationship of your leg to your foot can be enhanced by the counter in your shoe. Cavanaugh's findings have been confirmed by Dr. Barry Bates, a biomechanist at the University of Oregon. Running shoes with a proper shoe counter can thus help prevent sportaches. The counter supports the rear part of your foot in its stable position, thereby helping to avoid excessive rolling in, or rolling out, of your foot.

The material used in constructing the sole of your running shoe can also play an important role in determining whether you can avoid running sportaches. Materials used in running shoe soles range from those that wear like iron, and are about as comfortable, to those that are as soft as butter and last about as long. Each one has its advantages and disadvantages. You want a sole on your running shoe that is firm enough for your use but not so firm that you feel as if you're running in horseshoes. If the sole of your running shoe is too inflexible, you increase the work you have to do with the muscles in your legs.

You should check regularly to see whether you need to repair or replace your running shoes. Ill-worn or outworn shoes can cause all sorts of sportaches. In fact, there is probably no other more important single cause of running problems related to equipment than outworn shoes. If, for example, the outside of your sole is worn thin at the heel, the sole or heel of your shoe automatically forms a wedge. That's a problem. A good rule is to keep the soles on your running shoes as even as possible, using glue, plastics, or little add-on clips. If the sole on your shoe is worn out but your upper is not distorted, worn over, or worn out, then resole the shoe. If the upper is distorted, replace the shoe. If you try to run in a resoled shoe with a distorted upper, your foot will be twisted on the new flat sole, increasing the likelihood that you'll develop a sportache.

ORTHOTICS

Orthotics are custom-made arch supports. They work like eyeglasses. Glasses don't usually correct your eyes; they correct your vision. Similarly, orthotics don't correct foot problems; they correct gait stresses by helping to hold your feet in their most stable position. Orthotics make your feet function better. In the same sense that glasses can't make you read faster, orthotics can't make you run faster. But they can help you run without unnecessary pain.

Orthotics are custom-made arch supports.

Do you need orthotics? People ask me that question all the time. Again, it's like eyeglasses. You don't know until you try. Deciding whether you need glasses is relatively simple for the eye doctor. He or she can examine your visual acuity through the use of a series of lenses. Unfortunately, there's no similarly simple exam for your feet. Also, even if an examination establishes that you may need orthotics, they are not actually called for until you develop an ache or some other symptom.

We can establish certain findings, such as the relationship of the angles and segments of your foot and leg, in an examination. But whether we should do anything about these findings isn't always obvious. Frankly, it's hard for me to take mere findings too seriously. There are too many people passing me in races without orthotics and with feet far "worse" than mine. Still, if there are symptoms — sportaches — then orthotics should be considered.

You don't necessarily need expensive, custom-made orthotics to support your feet and prevent running aches and pains. Many foot, leg, and knee sportaches can be eliminated with homemade arch supports. They're your feet and it's your ache. Don't be afraid to experiment. You may need something to keep your foot in its most stable position. If so, tissue paper may do the trick, and if it doesn't, you may end up relying on anything from prefabricated "arches" built into your shoes to prefabricated "over-the-counter arches."

If you finally decide to go to a doctor to get custom-made orthotics, you should know that there are a variety of kinds. Orthotics can be made of anything from light, self-forming foam to unyielding steel, nylon, or Plexiglas.

How long should you wear your orthotics? When can you stop wearing them? I tell my patients nowadays that if they want to find out whether they still need their orthotics, all they have to do is try running without them. If they get their old aches back, obviously the orthotics are still needed. If they can run without pain, the orthotics may no longer be necessary.

When I started practicing sportsmedicine, I didn't realize that a runner might simply outgrow the need for orthotics. However, I learned that lesson relatively early in my career. I was standing at the starting line, ready for a race, chatting with several other racers. Suddenly, a patient spotted me and rushed over, gushing: "Dr. McGregor, if it weren't for you, I wouldn't be here. Gosh, isn't it great to see you. You must meet my wife." As he led me into the crowd, I remembered that this particular patient — whom I hadn't seen for more than a year — had come to me originally with a routine problem, one easily solved with orthotics.

"Cathy," the man said, "here is the guy who saved my running and our marriage. This is Dr. McGregor."

I blushed. Next thing you know, I thought, he'll have me demonstrating running on water. I wanted to change the subject.

"Tell me, Tom," I said brightly. "How are the old orthotics working?"

"Orthotics?" he responded. "I don't need them anymore."

I was dumfounded. Here was this guy raving about my saving his running career and his marriage, and he wasn't even using the orthotics I had prescribed for him.

During the ensuing race, I thought a lot about Tom. Did he really need his orthotics in the first place? Or were they just a means to an end and not the end in themselves? When should doctors intervene? Would his problem have been solved without intervention? I resolved never again to assume that a runner needs orthotics unless his or her feet and legs are actually hurting. Moreover, I realized that a runner obviously could need orthotics one year and not the next.

As a sportsmedicine practitioner, one of the toughest lessons I've had to learn involves when to do nothing. A teacher I remember vividly, Dr. Paul Norton, used to tell me: "Rob Roy, the easiest thing for a doctor is to do something. You know, operate or prescribe. The hardest thing to make yourself do is to treat a patient with studious neglect."

If you have a running-related ache by all means try an arch support. Consider custom-made orthotics. If your ache goes away, try running without your "crutch." If you get away with it — if you have no pain — perhaps your feet have rebuilt themselves into good working shape. Be glad and stay in shape.

SOCKS

I don't object to runners racing without socks. But training without socks is just asking for trouble.

If you alternate between wearing and not wearing socks when you run, remember that you are constantly changing the way your running shoes fit. Without socks, your shoes are going to be slightly loose, and are not, therefore, going to do nearly as good a job of supporting and protecting your feet. Moreover, if your shoes are loose, you're likely to develop a blister. There's no quicker way to develop an ache than to change your running technique because of a blister.

If your feet are simply too hot with socks, perhaps you need to look into shoes that "breathe" and socks, even Peds, that wick the perspiration to the outside where it can dry. If wearing socks can prevent blisters and irritation, wear them.

CLOTHING

Clothing plays a simple but important role in the prevention of running sportaches. Your body must be properly protected from sun, heat, and especially cold when you run. How you feel affects how you run. If you're cold when you begin a run, for example, you're very likely to start off at a faster pace than is healthy just to try to warm up. A combination of hat, mask, gloves or mittens, pants, and socks provides the answer.

If you run in the cold, you should experiment with your attire. If you make a mistake, it makes sense to err on the side of excess. It's easy to take off and carry extra garments such as a wind shirt, mock turtleneck, mask, or mittens. And it's better than freezing. Don't forget the wind-chill factor and the direction of the wind. These considerations can be particularly tricky if you run after dark.

The other problem of being too cold, of course, is that your muscles simply don't do as well at protecting your connective tissue until they are warm. In other words, it's difficult to limber up and warm up if you're not dressed properly.

Environment

Your environment as a runner includes where you run, when you run, and with whom you run. These considerations should never be underestimated when you are calculating the amount of stress you undergo as a runner. By carefully choosing and adjusting your running environment, you can significantly reduce sportforces. Environmental considerations are most important at the moment of peak force, although some factors play a role throughout the complete running cycle.

WHERE YOU RUN

Surfaces: Soft versus Hard. According to the law of conservation of energy, if you do your running on overly soft surfaces like sand or wood chips, your body must work harder. Impact forces are reduced, but internal forces are significantly greater. In addition, soft, unstable surfaces also increase the chance that you'll develop an imbalance or suffer an accident.

Hard surfaces, on the other hand, have their own set of disadvantages. Concrete, for example, is very hard. I still remember the grueling 1979 New Orleans Marathon. The first twenty-four miles were run on a straight, flat, concrete causeway over Lake Pontchartrain. As mile bled into mile, the surface seemed to become harder and harder. The impact forces we had to be able to withstand that day were incredible.

One runner summed up the situation perfectly. I was running and chatting with Jim Fixx around the sixteenth mile, when a young man passed us. I heard him take the Lord's name in vain and mutter: "Every time my foot hits this road, my ears ring."

It's ideal to run on a surface that absorbs some of the shock of impact without being so soft that you have to strain to keep going. If you can't find a surface that is hard but resilient, at least try to switch regularly from concrete to asphalt to hard ground to whatever so that you vary the stress to which you subject your body.

Runners nowadays tend to run as much on the dirt next to so-called running or bicycle paths (usually made of asphalt) as they do on the paths themselves. River banks in every major city are dotted with runners, and golf courses, parks, and beaches are being literally overrun. If you stay off roads and sidewalks, you'll probably do your body a favor as well as minimize the chance of being hit by a car or tripped by a pedestrian. However, you need to be certain that the surface you run on is free of surprises — holes, stones, and so on. If you can't see the terrain beneath your feet, you'll tend to steer your foot as it goes to the ground. If you're steering your foot, it's not being held naturally as you prepare for foot strike and is therefore predisposed to injuries. When you steer your foot, it doesn't strike the ground in a relaxed or stable position.

Surfaces: Level versus Bevel. Highly crowned or canted roads can be a problem for you as a runner, especially if you always run on the same side of the road. Patients frequently complain that they've suddenly developed pain on one side of a knee or pain on the opposite sides of both knees. Upon questioning, I often discover that they've recently run a race in which they were obliged to run on one side of a slanted road. Running on a slight slope for several miles is enough to throw anybody off balance.

During the same New Orleans Marathon in which I learned once and for all about running on a hard surface, I learned something about the importance of being able to vary the angle at which your feet hit the ground over long distances. The New Orleans causeway was not only hard, it was also absolutely flat. Partway through the race, I began to notice a nagging pain in my hip. "If only I could find a cant in the road, some kind of slope," I thought. "If I could lift my foot somehow, then maybe this pain would go away." However, New Orleans is run on a causeway without a cant. I had to solve my problem myself. I decided to cup my arch as I ran. That did it. A few miles later, when I went back to my regular posture, my hip pain did not recur.

You should ideally run over ground with regular changes in terrain. Even better, try to run in the middle of a humpback road, where there's a little canting on each side of your body. Both of your feet will tend to land in their most stable position, minimizing effective impact forces.

If you run on a banked track, make certain you change direction every few laps. Otherwise, you are virtually certain to develop an ache.

Surfaces: Flat versus Hills. The muscles in the front of your body are antigravity muscles. They keep your skeleton erect. Downhill running, especially if your skeleton is held too far back at an angle, can cause problems.

If you have to run hills, you can reduce the strain of going downhill by remaining as perpendicular to the surface as possible, or, if this causes unmanageable acceleration, walking downhill.

In running uphill it's best to (1) lean forward, (2) shorten your stride, and (3) supply increased power by pumping your arms.

When you run hills, key joints in your lower extremities are much less likely to be stable at peak force. Your knees in particular become vulnerable. They tend to be bent to an extreme when your feet hit the ground. Also, you subject your knees, feet, ankles, and hips to greater internal sportforces. On the way uphill, you have to work harder to retain your momentum. Work

translates into stress for your connective tissue. As you run downhill, you tend to go faster than normal, as well as to increase your stride length. Internal forces are increased if you do permit yourself to go faster, and ground reactive forces are, of course, also greater. If you strain to brake your speed, your muscles and connective tissue are subjected to considerable stress as a result, even if you do manage to slow down. It only makes sense to avoid hills if you are a runner with a lower-extremity ache.

WHEN YOU RUN

The most important considerations about when you run are wind, temperature, precipitation, and time of day.

Wind. The wind can be an important factor in determining how hard you have to work when you run. Regardless of the temperature, running into a high wind is never easy. Running into the wind can cause you to adjust your running technique. That can increase sportforces *and* sportaches. You'll certainly have to work extra hard, generating greater internal sportforces.

If you must run one part of your course into the wind, run that leg first. Running into the wind first is particularly important in cold weather, when you can develop a chill if you run into the wind on the way home. Anyway, whether you're warm or cold, you'll probably be more tired on the return leg, so it's better to have the wind at your back. Running with the wind means you

won't have to bend into it. However, you'll tend to go faster than normal, possibly even opening up your stride length.

Given a choice, try to run with the wind at your side, and work out on roads with trees. Summer or winter, trees provide protection from the wind.

Temperature. Extreme temperature and humidity should be avoided. Noel Coward wasn't advising runners when he wrote that "mad dogs and Englishmen go out in the midday sun," but he might as well have been.

With the increase in popularity and participation in road racing, race organizers have learned that early starting times are mandatory in hot and humid weather. The Honolulu Marathon starts at 6:30 A.M. on the second Sunday in December, with the runners setting off into the rising sun. Magnificent!

If it's excessively hot or humid when you run, your muscles will warm up quickly. Also, you shouldn't have a tendency to go faster than you normally do, as you may during cold weather. However, you may find that you gradually begin to lose the spring in your step if you run in the heat. Each foot seems to hit the ground harder and harder. As you stagger forward, ground reactive forces may affect your joints more. You'll tend to slump a bit, making it unlikely that key joints will be stable at peak force.

Precipitation. Precipitation can be a factor if you run outside. Runners nowadays think nothing of training and racing in wet weather. Obviously, when you run in the rain, you have to be careful of your footing. When it's slippery, you automatically tense your muscles and steer your foot — making it much more likely that your feet won't be in their relaxed, stable position at foot strike.

The most treacherous weather for running is when the temperature hovers around freezing and it's raining or wet. When the ground is icy, you're really asking for trouble if you run. You'll have to strain all the time to keep your balance and stay on your feet. If you don't actually fall and injure yourself, you're likely to develop an ache.

Running on snow can provide a nice cushion for your feet. However, you won't be able to see rocks or holes in the ground.

Again, if you don't twist an ankle or break a leg, you're likely to develop an ache, since poor traction can result in muscle stress.

Time of Day. What time of day you choose for your regular run can make the difference between pain-free running and a bothersome sportache. If you run first thing in the morning, you may find that you simply can't get limber or warm before your run. Your body will be tight after a night's sleep. Also, early morning is usually the coldest time of the day. Finally, if you're like many of us who run before work, you'll probably find that your limbering-up and warming-up time is sacrificed any time you oversleep or start to fall behind schedule.

Alternatively, if you run late in the day, you're likely to be running at twilight, or even in the dark. Again, the pressures of finishing quickly to get home for dinner or whatever may tempt you to skimp on your limbering-up and warming-up routine. After a hard day's work, you may want to get right out onto the road and work off your frustration — maybe even going faster than you should at the beginning of your run. Finally, if you run late enough in the day so that you can't see properly, your footing may be a problem.

DECIDING WITH WHOM YOU RUN

Nearly all who enter a road race discover that they run faster than they thought they could. The other runners tend to pull you along in a race. You go faster because the people around you are going faster.

This phenomenon is not restricted to racing. You'll also tend to go faster than normal if you train or jog with someone who normally runs faster than you do. Let's say you've developed a comfortable pace and suddenly find yourself straining to keep up with a friend, spouse, or co-worker. You may well develop an ache. The faster you go, the greater the internal sportforces your body must be able to withstand with each step. Likewise, if you suddenly start running with someone who's taller than you are, you may find yourself lengthening your stride to keep up. Finally, be wary of situations in which you are under pressure to go farther than you normally do. That extra mile may be all it takes to cause your body to start to ache.

Changes in how fast you run and how far you go must be

made very gradually. If you suddenly start running with someone who encourages you to step up your pace or lengthen your
distance overnight, you're heading for an ache.

Velocity

Even if you're superbly conditioned and trained, the faster you
go when you run, the greater the internal sportforces you must
be able to withstand. When you run at top speed, you are exposed to minimal sportforces at foot strike, because your contact with the ground is so brief. Nevertheless, the swing forces
you generate during both preparation and recovery can be pun-
ishing. So even if you feel like "flying," it may make sense to
go slow if you have a running-related sportache.

I once watched and "listened to" Bill Rodgers when he set
several American and world records in a one-hour run. That's
right, *I listened*. The race was outside, with the runners doing
lap after lap around the Boston University track. As the leaders
passed me, I'd lay my ear to the ground. Rodgers's steps were
barely audible. In contrast, most of the other runners were
pounding hard as they rounded the banked turns and accelerated
in the straight-aways. Obviously, the impact forces Bill Rodgers
had to withstand that day as he almost literally "flew" around

the track at Boston University were minimal. But the internal forces he was generating must have been awesome.

If you're anxious to reduce forces as a runner, one of your easiest solutions may be to reduce your velocity. Unless you float like Bill Rodgers, cumulative sportforces generally increase as you accelerate.

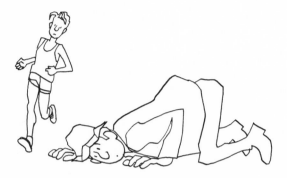

After you've done everything you can to ease the stress on your body by reducing running sportforces, you should turn to technique and conditioning — making adjustments designed to increase your body's ability to withstand stress. As a runner, you need to ensure that an aching joint is as stable as possible when it must absorb and transmit sportforces. As in other sports, the key to joint stability in running is technique and conditioning.

Increasing Your Tolerance for Stress

Technique

Unlike tennis, golf, and skiing, running has not yet spawned an industry of running teachers or teaching pros. Nevertheless, during the past ten years, there have been hundreds of articles and books written about how to run. Most theories about the proper technique of long-distance running are very similar. Remember that what an article, book, or coach will tell you about running technique from the standpoint of improving your performance as a runner also tends to be what you ought to do to minimize running-related stress.

When it comes to eliminating or avoiding running sportaches, two matters of running technique are key. First, you want to find a running pace that generates sportforces you can manage.

There is a saying, often attributed to long-time Oregon coach Bill Bowerman, that almost everyone in the running world has heard or seen. Nevertheless, it bears repetition here, as it is the cornerstone of proper running technique: "Train . . . Don't Strain."

Second, you must learn to keep key joints in your lower extremities as stable as possible as you move over the ground. That's where the technique phase of the McGregor Solution comes in.

Bill Emmerton is a long-distance runner who has become a legend in his own time. By his own count, Bill has now run almost 150,000 miles. Speaking at the American Medical Joggers Association Meeting before the 1978 Boston Marathon, he put the matter of distance-running technique in its proper perspective, saying: "If you land with your lower leg over your foot, your knee over your leg, your hip over your knee, and your shoulder over your hip, you'll be able to run a three-and-a-half-hour marathon." The following day, I made an effort to do as Bill Emmerton had advised and I did in fact cross the finish line in three and a half hours. I also found myself unusually ache-free. What Emmerton had done, of course, was to describe a technique for jogging or running that is both energy efficient and safe.

But running is supposed to be freeform! Perhaps you're now asking if you really have to worry about how to run. The answer to that question is simple. You only have to worry if your technique is contributing to the development of an ache.

Improper technique can produce a variety of running sport-aches. If you overstride, for example, you're reaching too far forward for your *normal* stride sequence. As a result, when each of your limbs finishes its preparation phase and gets to peak force, your foot must be held back longer than usual. The muscles in the front of your leg that have the job of holding back your foot become overworked. The result can be shin splints. Proper technique is no guarantee against shin splints. However, if you develop shin splints despite proper running technique, then you know you don't have any choice except to condition the muscles in the front of your leg to do their job better.

Overstriding is a classic example of bad running technique. It can cause other problems, in addition to shin splints. If you overstride, you can interrupt the otherwise "normal" relationship of key muscles in your hips. As you strain to reach out farther with each step, the muscles on the outside of each of your hips are pulled against the protective bursa at your hip bone. The result can be a hip sportache, possibly bursitis.

For years coaches have advised their distance runners to run on the white line in the center of the road. This advice, like Bill Emmerton's, is loaded with practical considerations. Think about the stable position of your lower extremities. If you run so that each of your feet lands squarely on the center line in the road, you are keeping key joints in your lower extremities as stable as possible.

Foot position is perhaps the most important single aspect of proper running technique. There's no way that the complicated chain of events that takes place when you run can occur safely if your feet are slued out like clock hands at five minutes to one or ten minutes to two. Of course, you can move across the ground with your feet pointed out at an angle. Lots of people do. But you do so at considerable risk. If your feet don't land pointing straight ahead, each foot is required to withstand peak force loads in a position of stress, with various bones and joints far from their stable position. The muscles that are supposed to stabilize the joints in your foot are also subjected to considerable stress. The most likely result is a sportache.

If your running technique doesn't ensure that your feet stay parallel, you have a potential for aches elsewhere in your lower extremities, as well as in your feet themselves. Where are your knees if your feet are pointing out, for example? Not in their stable position. Not only are your knees also pointing out, but when your foot rolls in for toe-off, the inner aspect of your knee tends to roll in with it. Because your knee is not in its stable position either at foot strike or at toe-off, you will tend to develop knee sportaches. Therefore, knee problems can often be eliminated by learning how to run properly — with your feet (and therefore your knees) parallel, rather than turned out.

In his book *The Joy of Running*, Dr. Thaddeus Kostrubala offers this deceptively simple piece of advice about running technique: "Run as if someone were pulling your knees with a string." Even if you are already minimizing knee strain by land-

ing with your feet and knees parallel, this hint can help you eliminate knee aches. If you imagine someone pulling you forward with a string attached to your knees, you should be able to avoid the excessive bobbing motion that is all too common among runners and joggers. Your knees must absorb and transmit sportforces equivalent to three times body weight when you run. Proper running technique is one way of being certain that you don't further complicate matters by bobbing up and down unnecessarily.

Improper positioning of the trunk of your body can also cause sportaches when you run. Leaning forward not only increases the stress to your back, trunk, and arms, it also impairs your running style, causing unwanted knee bending and toeing out, with the potential for subsequent sportaches.

I once had an important revelation about running technique while watching a race from above. I stood on a bridge as hundreds of runners ran toward, under, and away from me. Watching from above, I couldn't help but notice that a number of runners were generating a lot of side-to-side, swivel motion as they ran. Most of those runners were women.

The swivelers are usually found at the back of the pack in a race. This is because they are wasting considerable energy going sideways. As in the case of many women with naturally wider pelvises, that kind of motion is often a function of the runner's skeletal make-up. If that's your case, there may be very little you can do about it, although you should certainly try to streamline the waggle.

An improvement in running technique can make a difference

if the reason you swivel when you run is because you don't know better. At a recent Bonne Bell running camp in Colorado where I was a guest instructor, we found that running with a ski pole in each hand, holding it in the middle with the shaft parallel to the ground, made several women acutely aware of how much arm swing was occurring as they ran. To keep the poles from crisscrossing in front of them, the women had to minimize their natural swivel. It was easy for them to do once they put their minds to it, and they were amazed with the results.

For runners there is no formal instructional system. Nevertheless, the number of opportunities to learn about running technique is growing. Many track and running clubs offer periodic clinics. Instruction is often available from adult education courses, YMCAs, YWCAs, and health clubs. Also, we are now witnessing the emergence of the running camp — not unlike the tennis camp in its design and structure. Finally, you can pick up valuable hints about running technique at many fun runs. And there are the countless books and magazine articles, all aimed at helping you better understand how to run — from the standpoint of both performance *and* health.

If you are concerned about a running-related ache, it just makes sense to see if you can improve your running technique. Follow Bill Emmerton's advice and try to run erect. Avoid overstriding. Check to see if your feet land parallel to one another by seeing if you can run along a straight line. Try running as if someone were pulling you along with a string attached to your knees. Go to a running clinic or check some running books out of your local library and read the sections on technique.

If you want to know how you're doing, ask a friend or coach to watch you run. If you run alone, watch your shadow on the side of the road, or your reflection as you pass store windows. The best thing, of course, is to get someone to take a movie or video tape of you as you run. What you want to see is that key joints in your lower extremities are in their stable position as much as possible when you run — especially at the moment of peak force.

How you run can make a difference in how you feel during and after each run. Unlike tennis or golf technique, running technique is simple and straightforward. It is definitely worth the effort to learn how to run properly, at least if running is your sport and you are doing twenty miles or more per week. You'll be able to run farther and faster. More important, you'll increase your tolerance for running-related stress.

Running Conditioning

The first question for you as a runner is whether your muscles are strong and flexible enough to permit you to achieve and hold a stable position in the joints of your lower extremities at peak force (foot strike). Regardless of your technique, you cannot withstand the stresses of running safely unless your general conditioning is good.

The second question is whether you limber up before you run, warm up slowly once you've actually started, and warm down for a few minutes after you finish. No general conditioning program can guarantee that you'll be able to avoid or manage running aches if you insist on starting cold, taking off as fast as you can, and sitting around in damp clothing after you run.

The cornerstone of a successful conditioning program for a runner is the development of healthy running habits. The forces generated when you run are considerable. The only way you can expect your body to withstand the stresses of running — to absorb forces without developing aches — is to train yourself to use common sense before, during, and after each run.

General Conditioning

Running requires both strength and flexibility in the muscles of your lower extremities. Unlike most other recreational activities, running generates nonstop stress. There is basically no recovery period between moments of peak force. Your general conditioning must be good if you expect to run very long or very far without developing an ache.

A general conditioning program for running must include both strengthening and stretching exercises for the particular muscles you use as a runner. Competition runners find that they can enhance their performance by improving their upper-body strength as well as by conditioning their lower extremities. If you are competing at any level, you might follow their example. As a recreational runner, however, your primary concern should be your legs.

The best way to promote strength in the muscles you use as a runner is to run. Of course, you must be careful when you increase the demand you put on your legs. Don't try to develop strength by suddenly running twice as far as normal or twice as often. Increases in your weekly mileage must be very gradual. One rule of thumb is no more than 15 percent per week.

If you are going to try to develop the strength you need in your legs as a runner while running, don't be afraid to vary your running routine from time to time. Try running backward for a quarter of a mile every day. This will provide a new challenge for your lower-extremity muscles. Skip instead of run for a quarter mile. This will strengthen calf muscles. Run sideways. This will help strengthen hip muscles, which are otherwise rarely exercised. If you have access to a beach, run in soft sand, but wear running shoes, as running barefoot can be particularly stressful to key foot and leg muscles. Better yet, if you really want the ultimate running workout, run a few hundred yards in water up to your midthigh or waist. Remember, to build strength you have to push your muscles to the point of fatigue. However, there's a fine line between a tired muscle and an aching joint. Don't overdo.

As you increase your strength, you must also increase your flexibility. By far the most common problem for runners is rela-

Try running backward.

tive inflexibility. If you feel that you are not as flexible as you should be, you're going to have to stretch regularly for as long as it takes to develop adequate flexibility. Otherwise, you are certain to develop a running sportache.

Stretching is relatively more effective when your muscles are warm. Therefore, the best time to stretch is during or after a run. Stop after you've gone half a mile, stretch key muscles, and then start to run again. You'll promote flexibility much more effectively this way than by trying to stretch first thing in the morning. Alternatively, try to find fifteen minutes for stretching between your run and your shower.

Limbering Up

The word *limber* means to bend, loosen, or flex. Before you run, it's crucial that you limber up. You are trying to bend, loosen, or flex your joints. Your joints don't move independently. They move when the muscles that span and stabilize your bones contract and relax. But the connective tissue of your joints doesn't permit easy, effortless movement until it is lubricated, and it isn't properly lubricated until you are limber.

The goal of any limbering-up routine is to take key muscles, tendons, and connective tissue through a complete range of motion before you actually start to run. As slow, gradual motion takes place, your normal joint lubricating mechanism has a chance to be called into action. Likewise, the various elements that make up your connective tissue are given the chance to stretch and contract. If you limber up key joints gradually before you run, the chance of unnecessary or excessive stretch or contraction during a run is lessened.

One important point bears repetition. The purpose of limbering up is to take each joint through its full range of motion — whatever that range is. If you have a less than complete range of motion in any given joint, limbering doesn't increase that range — it just takes you to it. Regular stretching is the only way you can increase your range of motion. Don't confuse limbering up with general conditioning. If all you do is limber up, you may be nothing more than a limber but nevertheless inflexible runner.

It follows that the later in the day you run the less you will have to limber up. You're naturally stiff in the morning. Nevertheless, no matter what time of day you run, I think it's best to start with what I call the "Hello, Body" maneuver. It lets you say hello to yourself, and in the process find out how limber you are at *that* moment. If you repeat the same test after you limber up, you'll find out how limber you are after limbering up — a good way of deciding whether you're ready to start your run.

How do you say "hello" to your body before a run? Stand with your feet parallel and approximately twelve inches apart. Lean as far back as you can with your arms hanging down and your knees bent. Stand in that position briefly, and then very gradually straighten your upper body, raising your hands directly overhead. Continue your gradual forward bending, bringing your arms to the downward position, fingers extended, knees slightly bent, and hold for a moment. Take notice of the distance your fingertips are from the floor. When you repeat the exercise at the end of the limbering-up session, your fingers should be closer to the floor. In between, what should you do? You can make up your own routine. I'd include rotation, side-to-side and back-and-forth motion of your arms and trunk, simple stretches of the muscles in the front and back of your thighs and legs, bent-knee sit-ups, alternate toe touches, and finally jumping jacks.

What if you're a runner with chronic muscle or tendon contractures or a recent injury? Harry Connover is a good example of a runner with those kinds of special problems. Harry claims that even a chronic condition can be managed if you want to run and are willing to dedicate yourself to doing what you need to do to run without pain. Previous football and ski injuries have left him with: (1) one knee that tends to be "stiff," although X-rays do not reveal any bony-joint changes; and (2) a somewhat tight Achilles' tendon. Since his daily schedule permits only early morning running, when Harry tends to be stiffest, he starts his day with a hot shower. While in the shower, he stretches both knees and ankles. After routine limbering exercises, Harry will pedal his stationary bike for five to ten minutes. If he's not at home, he jumps rope for the same amount of time. Harry's routine not only limbers him up but gets him ready for the warm-up phase of his run.

Warming Up

Warming up before you really start running is crucial. You are preparing your muscles and connecting tissue to help your lower body carry up to three times body weight as many as 800 steps per limb per mile. The fact of the matter is that your body is only fully warm after six to nine minutes of exertion. That's why the first mile of a run can be so disagreeable.

Depending on how I feel as I set out for a run, the first mile is when I sometimes wonder why in Heaven's name I'm engaging in such foolishness. Fortunately, once my body is warm, things always look up and I feel better. Then I know *why* I'm out there. As George Sheehan explains: "The first half-hour of every run is for my body; the second is for my soul."

The first six to nine minutes of every run should definitely be done at slower than your regular pace. If there is any single conditioning mistake runners routinely make, it's the very common mistake of starting too fast.

When it comes to racing, imitate the front runners. By the time the starter's gun goes off, they are already *warmed up*. That's the only reason they can take off at race pace.

For those of you who tend to be flexible and in good shape, I'll offer my own half-mile warm-up:

1. Start with a "Hello, Body" stretch.
2. Run very slowly for 100 yards (three telephone poles, whatever).
3. Stop and do several alternate toe touches.
4. Run slowly another 100 yards.

5. Stop and do several alternate knee presses. Standing on one leg (a warm-up and conditioning exercise in itself), grasp the other knee as close to your chest as possible; hold for an instant. Reverse the procedure with the other knee. After several of these, standing on one foot, grasp the other foot from the back, pull it to your rump, and hold. Reverse the procedure.

6. Run a little faster for 300 yards.

7. Stop. Do a couple of dozen jumping jacks.

8. Run 400 yards, faster still.

9. Stop. Do another "Hello, Body" stretch. Mark your progress.

10. Then take off. By this time you've covered approximately half a mile. Your total warm-up should have taken no more than five or six minutes.

Warming Down

Ideally, every runner should walk the last quarter mile of every run, do some stretching, and then promptly shower and change into dry clothes. However, most of us do not warm down properly after a run.

The physiological concern about suddenly stopping after a run is that your blood tends to pool in your lower extremities. Blood is drawn from your heart and brain. I've seen runners faint after stopping suddenly. Though the fit body can handle such a sudden shift, even if you're in great shape it puts an unnecessary burden on your system to stop running without warming down.

There is another reason for warming down. You need to stretch out those muscles that tend to become contracted in the process of running. My friend, John Cedarholm, adds some features to his warm-down routine that tend to startle the unwary or uninitiated. He will run backward for quite a distance, stretching various lower-extremity muscles. Then he hangs from a tree limb, stretching his whole body. Try it. You too may want to imitate Tarzan at the end of every run.

8
Other Sports

NO FEWER THAN 112 different sports and activities are listed in the *Oxford Companion to World Sports and Games*. We've just discussed two of them, tennis and running, in considerable detail. In addition, you have found references throughout the previous seven chapters to various other sports, including golf, bicycling, skiing, bowling, swimming, baseball, football, and racquetball. However, there's no denying that we've totally ignored many of the other sports listed in the *Oxford Companion*, such as bandy, aquabobbing, korfball, stoolball, and pétanque.

How did we choose tennis and running for such in-depth analysis? First, as we've already explained, I'm an experienced runner as well as the designer of a popular running shoe, while my co-author, Steve Devereux, has been a tennis player and tennis coach for most of his adult life. Naturally, we feel most comfortable talking about the two sports we know so well. Between us, Steve and I have more than thirty years of experience in running and tennis. We've seen all the different sides of the running and tennis worlds. Also, we have each experienced many of the sportaches that plague runners and tennis players. Steve's runner's knee first put him in touch with me. More important, his frustrating experience with tennis elbow made him an enthusiastic believer in EEVeTeC. And, of course, my own running sportaches as well as the complaints of thousands of runner-patients finally prompted me to formulate the McGregor Solution.

Second, although tennis and running are comparable in terms of their immense popularity, they have very different sport-forces, sportaches, and solutions. In fact, about the only thing tennis and running have in common, aside from their immense popularity, is the fact that they are both impact sports. No two other popular sports embody as many different aspects of the McGregor Solution or provide better examples of the versatility of EEVeTeC.

Almost every conceivable way EEVeTeC can help you avoid and manage sportaches is illustrated in either chapter 6 or chapter 7. If you study the tennis and running chapters, you should have little remaining doubt about how EEVeTeC can work for you — even if you've never been near a tennis court or a running track.

The outlines that follow are designed to help you use EEVeTeC if you participate in golf, racquetball, squash, bowling, swimming, or bicycling. We've consulted a number of experts about these sports and compiled a list of tips that should get you started using the McGregor Solution. You'll have to complete the analysis of your own favorite activity yourself, and you may well come up with solutions we haven't even alluded to.

If your favorite sport is not among the activities profiled in the following pages, don't be discouraged. EEVeTeC will still work for you. Take a quick look at the following outlines and then make a similar outline yourself for your own favorite sport.

You know your sport as well as we do — at least if you do anything other than run or play tennis. We know that the McGregor Solution works. We've already shown you how it can save you endless frustration, pain, and expense if you take your recreation on a tennis court or a jogging trail. Now it's your turn. Good luck.

Golf

Sportforces

Golf is an *impact* sport. Peak force occurs each time your club head strikes the ball or the ground behind the ball. Although a golf ball is not moving when you hit it, there is a significant external force generated at impact. The shock of ball impact travels up your club, through your hands and into your body, depending, of course, upon how solidly you hit your shots. In addition, considerable ''swing'' forces are produced within your joints during your backswing, downswing, and follow-through — except, of course, when you're putting.

Golfers don't have to run, jump, and change direction the way recreational athletes do when they play tennis, squash, or racquetball. Nevertheless, golf can stress much of your body, including your lower extremities. The external forces that flow into your body at impact usually come to rest in your wrists or elbows, while the internal forces you generate as you wind up and swing your golf clubs frequently result in stress to your shoulders, your lower back, your lead hip, your lead ankle, your back knee, and your back foot.

Sportaches

''Golfer's *hip*'' is the best known golf-related sportache. One of the first lessons every golfer must learn is to rotate his or her lead hip on the downswing. Unfortunately, the rapid hip rotation required in golf often results in chronic hip pain. Your lead hip also absorbs some of the shock of impact in golf, contributing to the development of hip sportaches.

''Golfer's *elbow*,'' though hardly as widespread as tennis elbow, is nevertheless a serious, painful, and alarmingly common ailment. Among golfers elbow problems seem to crop up just about as often in the lead arm as they do in the back arm. If you play right-handed, for example, your left arm must absorb most of the external force that flows into your body at impact, while your right arm does much of the twisting and straining during your downswing and follow-through. Both of your elbows are susceptible to pain.

Likewise, the fact that you must first cock and then rotate your wrists during a normal drive or iron shot can result in a sportache in either *wrist*. Your wrists are also the first joints that must be able to withstand the ball impact forces that travel up your club and into your body.

Shoulder problems, while not nearly as common as elbow or wrist sportaches, can present a real threat to the unprepared golfer. *Knee* problems are also a possibility, especially in your back leg. Your back knee bears the bulk of the stress you generate as you thrust forward in an effort to get extra power.

Finally, *ankle* and *foot* problems are not unheard of among the golfing population. Even those golfers who avoid the obvious strain of walking eighteen holes and who would never dream of carrying their own golf bags occasionally complain of ankle and foot sportaches. The usual problem area is in your lead leg, which must bear your full body weight as well as absorb considerable torque during your follow-through.

Solutions

EQUIPMENT

Choose your golf clubs carefully. Remember, your clubs must be right *for you*. If you swing extra hard, you may want to consider clubs with relatively stiff shafts. On the other hand, if you feel you need additional power, you should probably choose clubs with flexible shafts. Stiff shafts don't absorb impact forces particularly well, however, while flexible clubs tend to transmit relatively more vibration into your arms and body. A set of clubs with regular shafts may be your best compromise selection.

Regardless of whether they are made of metal or graphite, most golf clubs have standard size grips. Golfers' hands, however, vary dramatically in girth. If your grips are too small for your hands, you'll have to squeeze extra hard to resist torque. Your grip may slip needlessly no matter how hard you squeeze. Have your pro alter your grips. It's easy to do. You may also want to buy a golf glove, which should not only help to prevent painful blisters that can trigger other aches, but may also keep your hands from slipping.

If your hands slip consistently, or if you have to strain to hold onto your clubs, you may eventually develop a wrist or elbow sportache. Therefore, if you play in the rain, a towel becomes your most important piece of equipment. No matter what the weather, try to keep your grips and your glove as dry as possible. Also, replace your grips when they become old and slippery.

Just because one of your burly friends can swing a D10 driver effortlessly doesn't mean that you should try. Obviously, the more your club heads weigh, the farther your shots will carry if you're strong enough to generate sufficient club head speed. However, you're also likely to experience greater forearm stress with each swing. Anyway, a heavy club is no guarantee of a long drive. You'll probably get more consistently long drives with a lighter club that is easier for you to control.

Club length is another important equipment consideration. Longer clubs can reduce the stress of a fully crouched stance. Long clubs may also produce longer shots, at least if you connect solidly. However, a long club increases leverage and therefore amplifies torque if you mis-hit a shot. Moreover, the longer clubs tend to vibrate more at impact. Make certain your clubs are the appropriate length for your height and your game.

Be certain to wear golf shoes on both wet and dry surfaces. You need the support and traction, especially if you want to avoid ankle and knee problems, as well as minimize painful mishits.

Finally, don't wear tight clothing on the golf course. Tight pants, such as blue jeans, are especially inappropriate, as they can effectively block hip rotation, increasing knee, ankle, and foot strain. A tight sweater or jacket can also be a problem, restricting motion in key upper-extremity joints. Dress warmly but in loose clothing. Wear a hat to keep both sun and sweat out of your eyes. And don't forget dark glasses if you need them.

ENVIRONMENT

If you play golf in cold weather, don't expect the ball to fly as far. Be careful not to underclub, making it likely that you'll force your shots. Make an effort to warm up thoroughly, in addition to dressing warmly and wearing gloves on both hands.

In hot weather dress appropriately. Pace yourself. If you allow yourself to become exhausted or dehydrated, you're likely

to become careless and start overswinging. Play efficiently. If it's 90°, for example, don't circle the green ten times to line up a six-inch putt.

Be careful in the wind. Remember not to underclub when you're hitting into the wind. The vast majority of golfers underclub all the time, especially in the wind. When the breeze is in your face, choose a longer club and resist the temptation to swing harder.

If it's wet out, remember that your golf balls won't fly as far. Also, your clubs will feel heavier. Wet grass will offer more resistance, even if it's not actually raining when you play. In addition to using a towel to keep your grips dry, by all means wear a golf glove, make certain your footwear is providing you with maximum support and traction, and keep your glasses dry. You should also be extra careful not to take a soggy divot. Make every effort to strike your shots solidly. And don't underclub.

On a hilly course conserve your energy. Don't try to overhit when your lie is on a hillside — too often you'll take a divot anyway. Likewise, avoid the temptation to blast out of deep rough or a sand trap. You'll be doing your wrists and elbows a real favor to be certain you hit the ball solidly, without trying to move or lift too much grass, dirt, or sand.

Many pros refuse to watch their opponents hit. They fear that what they see may affect their own play. If you're playing

against someone who consistently outdrives you, don't start to overswing in an effort to compete. There's no better way to guarantee an ache than to start forcing your shots. Capitalize on your short game. Play the course, not your opponent.

VELOCITY

The harder you swing a golf club — the more you try to force your shots — the better the chance that you'll hook or slice if you hit the ball at all. If you try to force your shots, you're also more likely to hit fat, sending tremendous shock waves into your body. And even if you hit the ball perfectly when you wind up and try to clobber it, the swing forces you generate with a fast swing are unnecessarily stressful.

Learn to swing as slowly and with as much control as possible. Keep your backswing very deliberate, and try to accelerate smoothly from the top of your backswing down to the ball and through. Both your score and your body will benefit.

TECHNIQUE

Keep your lead arm firm but flexible, both so that you will make a full backswing turn and so that you won't "shock" your elbow if you mis-hit. A radically bent arm is no better than a locked elbow, but you shouldn't be afraid to flex your lead arm a little bit.

Keep your head steady during your swing. Too many golfers allow their heads and bodies to sway during their backswing. If your center of gravity shifts toward your back leg as you wind up, your club head may well come up short, behind the ball. You'll hit fat consistently, and both your score and your body will suffer. To keep your head in its original position, try facing slightly toward your back leg before you start your swing, as Jack Nicklaus does. This trick should help you avoid turning your head during your swing.

For most golfers technique problems begin even before the start of each swing. Experts agree that the vast majority of recreational golfers address their shots improperly. In addressing the ball, try not to stand too close or too far away. Be certain that you're comfortable — neither too upright nor too cramped. If you have any doubts about this important aspect of your technique, ask your pro to check your position as you address the ball. If you address your shots correctly, you'll tend to strike more of your shots in the precise center of the club head, thereby minimizing effective impact forces.

You may also want to have a pro check your grip. If you're like many golfers, you probably grip your clubs too firmly, with your hands turned too far clockwise. As a result, certain muscles in your forearms are obliged to twist and turn unnecessarily during your backswing and downswing to ensure that your club face meets the ball properly. Wrist and elbow problems are often the result.

Natural wrist motion is the key to both performance and health in golf. Don't cock your wrists as soon as you begin to draw back your club. Premature wrist motion only inhibits a good backswing and increases your chances of hitting behind the ball. Instead, let your wrists break gradually until your club head is parallel to the ground at the top of your backswing. Try to delay the uncocking of your wrists as you bring your club through, leading instead with your hips and lower body.

To minimize shoulder strain, try not to overswing at the beginning of your downswing. Golfers who "hit from the top" are likely to spin their shoulders, generating extra stress — as well as a nasty slice. Instead, lead your downswing from the hips. Then, once your swing is well under way, drop your arms into a proper hitting position and accelerate through the ball. Another possibility, of course, is to flatten your swing, emphasizing hip rotation instead of coiling your body and stressing your shoulders.

To minimize hip strain turn your lead foot out slightly in the direction of your swing. Keep the tempo of your swing as consistent as possible. Don't try to clobber the ball. If all else fails, do as Gary Player and other pros occasionally do, and "walk through" your shots. After hitting the ball, just step through naturally with your back foot. This should decrease stress to both your hip and your back, and shouldn't be too detrimental to your score, at least after you practice doing it for a while.

CONDITIONING

Lots of golfers develop sportaches because they mistakenly believe that golf is not particularly stressful. They routinely ignore a few simple conditioning rules that would be second nature if they were playing some other sport. Because there is so much recovery time between shots in golf and most golfers nowadays neither walk the course nor carry their clubs, you don't have to be in great shape to play eighteen holes a couple of times a week. But you do have to follow a few conditioning guidelines if you want to avoid common golfing sportaches.

Never overdo. What do you expect will happen, for instance, if you take the winter off and then try to play seventy-two holes in forty-eight hours during the first decent spring weekend? And how smart is it really to take an early season lesson and then rush over to the driving range and smack 200 balls?

Keep your forearms and back strong and flexible. One conditioning suggestion should be easy to follow: Keep a light weight or barbell by the phone and do regular wrist curls to build up forearm strength. Also, don't forget the importance of building up abdominal strength to protect your back. Fifty sit-ups every night before bed can buy you a lot of insurance for two minutes of effort.

Limber up before you play. Do back rotation and stretching exercises by placing a club behind your back and twisting it around. Take a number of slow practice swings before you actually start hitting your shots. Hit a few practice balls before each round, starting with three-quarter pitching wedges, gradually working your way up through your short and middle irons to your woods, and concluding with several drives.

Warm up slowly, even after you begin your round. Make a special effort to swing slowly and smoothly on all your shots during the first few holes. Continue to take easy practice swings before each shot.

Practice after each round. Rest for a few minutes and then go to work on the weak points of your game. Your muscles and joints will be loose and better able to absorb the punishment. Nevertheless, don't automatically head for the driving range. You may be able to do a lot more for your game by working on chipping and putting, and your body will love you for it.

Racquetball

Sportforces

Racquetball, like tennis and squash, is an *impact* sport. Each time you swing your racket, your body must be able to tolerate the shock of ball impact, in addition to absorbing considerable internal or "swing" forces. Your lower extremities are also subjected to considerable stress when you play racquetball. Because the game is so fast, with all four walls as well as the ceiling in play, racquetball players typically leap and dart about the court, making leg ailments alarmingly common.

Sportaches

A racquetball racket is lighter than a tennis racket and shorter than either a tennis racket or a squash "bat." However, the ball used in racquetball is relatively heavy — about 1.4 ounces. Also, racquetball players generally have extremely wristy strokes. Since the speed of a normal game results in numerous off-center hits, the majority of racquetball-related sportaches not surprisingly occur in the *elbow* and *wrist* of your playing arm.

Racquetball players seem to complain of medial (inside) elbow pain just as often as lateral (outside) elbow pain. Wrist sportaches, however, are even more common. In addition, unlike squash, racquetball has its own peculiar *shoulder* ailment. The unique ceiling shot used in racquetball often produces a syndrome not unlike "swimmer's shoulder."

Then there are your *knees, ankles,* and *feet*. According to a recent California study, leg ailments outnumber arm problems by about five to one among racquetball players. That statistic no doubt reflects a great number of injuries — ankle sprains, twisted knees, and torn muscles — but lower-extremity sport-aches also occur as the result of racquetball. Your knees are particularly susceptible if your footwork isn't good or if you play against someone who has you twisting and jerking to dig the ball out of a back corner.

Solutions

EQUIPMENT

Make sure you're playing with a racket that is the proper com-position, weight, and grip size. The best way to choose the right racket is to experiment with the various models and sizes avail-able for rental at most clubs. Only by trying a racket on the court — instead of in a shop — can you tell if it's right for you.

Most racquetball players nowadays use either aluminum, Fi-berglas, or graphite rackets. Aluminum and graphite models generally offer more power, while Fiberglas seems to provide more control. A number of tournament players prefer Fiberglas, but aluminum or graphite should be easier on your arm and less prone to breakage.

Rackets vary in weight from 245 to 280 grams. Women gen-erally choose rackets that weigh around 265 grams and men generally settle between 275 and 280 grams. A heavier racket may provide you with power, but it may also create extra strain in your shoulder and arm. Some pros even switch to a lighter racket in the middle of a tournament to minimize tightness in the back of the shoulder. Make certain your racket isn't too heavy for you.

The grip on your racket may be anywhere from three and seven-eighths to four and a half inches around. An overly small grip may cause your racket to slip and twist in your hand, thus placing undue stress on your arm. An overly large grip, in com-parison, can cause your wrist and hand to hurt. Make sure your grip is the right size for you. Also, try a terry cloth grip or a raised grip if your palm tends to become slippery.

Don't forget that string tension can also make a difference, both in your game and in your health. The vast majority of racquetball players have nylon in their rackets, often at more than thirty pounds of tension. If you develop wrist or elbow problems, however, you may want to experiment with looser strings.

When the ball you've been playing with starts to go dead, spend the money for a new live ball right away. A dead ball will oblige you to swing harder on your shots, thereby generating greater sportforces, as well as creating unnecessary stress to your hitting arm.

Make certain your footwear provides you with maximum support, both for your feet and ankles. You'll also need plenty of traction. Lightweight tennis shoes may be inadequate for racquetball; many recreational players nowadays opt instead for high-top basketball shoes. Running shoes, which are not designed to support your feet during quick changes of direction and side-to-side movement, should never be worn for racquetball.

Dress warmly in the racquetball court, but wear loose-fitting clothing. By all means wear an eyeguard. Too many players have suffered unnecessary eye injuries as the result of racquetball, with occasional reports still of accidents resulting in blindness. Also, be certain that you, and your opponent, use the wrist thong on your racket. If you need glasses to see the ball, wear them, although shatterproof lenses are a must. Try a wristband or a glove as well as a headband if you sweat a lot. Get an elbow splint or brace if you are concerned about elbow problems.

ENVIRONMENT

Make certain it's not too cold in the court where you play. There's a direct relation between the temperature where you play and how hard you'll find yourself swinging at your shots. Of course, a warm court can create its own problems. A hot ball really travels and may prove impossible to hit with any degree of control.

Also, make certain you don't play in a racquetball court with "dead" walls. As a rule, wood walls are best, as wood is more resilient than most other surfaces. If the walls where you play are resilient, you won't have to swing as hard to hit your shots with your normal pace.

As in both squash and indoor tennis, court lighting in racquetball is crucial. If you can't see the ball perfectly, you will undoubtedly hit off-center more than is healthy.

Finally, choose your racquetball opponents carefully, at least if you are worried about a sportache. A hard hitter like Marty Hogan may do things to the ball that will leave your arm and body far from stable as you attempt your returns. Likewise, if your opponent is a retriever who regularly forces you to play extra-long points, your arm and body are bound to suffer, as cumulative stress will mount, and fatigue may cause you to become careless.

VELOCITY

Try to learn how to hit at least some of your racquetball shots with finesse rather than pace. The fact that all four walls and the ceiling are in bounds in racquetball means that recreational players routinely rely on power rather than control. However, hitting the ball as hard as you can every time you swing your racket is bound to lead eventually to sportaches. Don't do it. Learn to mix in drop shots, spins, and lobs. Both your health and your game will improve.

TECHNIQUE

Racquetball is a wristy game, but that does not mean you should rely exclusively on your wrist when you're hitting your shots. Get your racket back early on both sides, and work at shifting your weight forward as you hit. Ideally, your racket should end up parallel with your shoulders, and your weight should end up on your front foot.

Keep your feet moving all the time, taking lots of little steps as you move around the racquetball court. Watch the ball. On ceiling shots try to keep your arm directly over your shoulder and contact the ball in front of you. Grip your racket firmly as you hit each shot, but try to relax your grip between moments of impact.

CONDITIONING

You've got to be in top shape to play racquetball. It's a good conditioning exercise in and of itself, of course, but racquetball can be very stressful. If you're not careful, while you train your heart and lungs in the racquetball court, you'll also be developing wrist, elbow, or knee problems.

You may want to do some long-distance running between racquetball games to develop lower-extremity endurance. If you have problems running, ride a bike — either stationary or free-wheeling. You may even want to try some wind sprints to promote quick acceleration in the court. By all means do some rope skipping for agility and endurance. Make stretching part of your regular general conditioning routine, at least if you are at all tight in key leg muscles or in your forearm or shoulder. Strengthening and stretching forearm muscles would also be wise.

Finally, every racquetball player should develop a limbering-up, warming-up, and warming-down routine. Make certain you're limber before you step onto the court. Then warm up gradually before starting to hit hard or play, and warm down after you finish.

Squash

Sportforces

Squash is an impact sport. Peak force, therefore, includes the external force generated as the ball hits your racket as well as the considerable internal or "swing" forces you produce as you wind up for each of your shots and follow through after impact. In addition, your feet, ankles, and knees are subjected to significant sportforces in the squash court as you scramble, lunge, and jump for most of your shots.

Sportaches

By far the most common sportaches occur in the *elbow* and *wrist* of your playing arm. Squash is a very fast game, with frequent mis-hits and "whiffs." Although both a squash ball and a squash racket are relatively light, your squash racket is almost as long as a tennis racket. There is, therefore, considerable torque every time you hit off-center or strike the wall instead of the ball. In addition, squash players have notoriously wristy strokes and often try to hit the ball as hard as they can. Elbow and wrist problems are virtually inevitable.

Shoulder sportaches are not as common in squash as they are in tennis and racquetball. Squash players rarely use the overhead motion of the tennis serve and smash, and there's no shot in squash comparable to the ceiling shot in racquetball.

Knee, ankle, and *foot* problems are frequent, primarily as a result of the sudden stops and starts required as you dart around the squash court, combined with the fact that the floors of most squash courts are quite hard.

Solutions

EQUIPMENT

Make certain your squash racket or "bat" is neither too heavy nor too light. If you're playing with the new, lighter seventy-plus ball, you may want to get a slightly lighter racket as well. However, if you're still using the old, heavier American ball, don't use too light a racket.

Make sure your grip is the right size for you and won't slip. Try a raised grip or a terry cloth grip if your racket tends to slip. Use an oval rather than a rectangular grip if you have a relatively small hand. Check the balance of your racket. Even if it doesn't weigh too much, it may be head-heavy. Try a more flexible racket if you've been using a stiff frame and have developed an ache. Or try a stiffer racket if you've been using a flexible one.

Don't have your racket strung too tightly. Beginners and intermediates should ask for a string tension around thirty pounds. More experienced players may prefer to play with a racket strung from thirty-five to forty pounds. Try gut if you've been using nylon. Gut is more resilient and therefore allows you to ease up on your swing.

Use the new, lighter seventy-plus ball instead of the traditional, heavier American ball. Note that the type of ball you should use depends on court temperature — the warmer the court, the softer the ball.

Make certain your footwear provides you with maximum support and traction. Try two pairs of socks if you blister easily. Dress warmly, at least as you begin a match or practice session. If you need corrective lenses to see the ball, wear them, although you should definitely make sure your glasses are shatterproof. Try a wristband if you sweat a lot. Get an elbow splint or brace if you have elbow problems.

ENVIRONMENT

The colder it is in the squash court, the harder you'll have to swing to hit your shots with your normal pace. The harder you swing, the greater the stress to your hitting arm. However, if a squash court is too warm, points can be endless, subjecting your body to increased cumulative stress. Try to play in a court that is cool but not cold.

Likewise, wood courts are more resilient than composition courts, which, in turn, are more resilient than concrete. The more resilient the court, the less effort you have to make as a player to generate pace. Court lighting is crucial. If you can't see the ball perfectly, you won't hit it solidly.

Your opponent can make a real difference in how you feel, as well as how you play. Avoid players who hit extra hard. Also, since long points result in greater cumulative stress, don't play with an opponent who is a notorious retriever, at least if you're trying to minimize arm strain.

VELOCITY

Don't swing any harder than you have to. Try to develop touch shots instead of slugging the ball all the time. Perfect your lob serve rather than trying to serve so hard that your opponent has to duck and play the return off the back wall.

TECHNIQUE

Don't just plant your feet on the ''T'' and reach for the ball. Keep your feet moving. Take lots of small, quick steps, playing in a crouch as much as possible. Try to hit most of your shots in front of you, avoiding, if possible, the need to flick shots from behind you or the temptation to blast the ball into the back wall to save a point.

Don't try to hit the ball hard all the time. Use your opponent's pace. Learn to use drop shots and corner shots rather than relying exclusively on power drives.

CONDITIONING

Your general conditioning is key in squash. Recovery time between shots and points is very brief. Moreover, with the new seventy-plus ball and racket, points now routinely last twenty to thirty seconds or longer.

Do some long-distance running for endurance. You may also want to jump rope and do wind sprints to develop agility and speed. You'll probably need to stretch regularly to make certain that key leg muscles aren't too tight. You should also do exercises to strengthen your wrist and forearm muscles.

Every squash player should develop a limbering-up, warming-up, and warming-down routine. Under no circumstances should you go onto a cold squash court without being thoroughly limber. Nor should you start playing without a good ten or fifteen minutes of gradual warm-up, or the results can be disastrous.

Bowling

Sportforces

Bowling is a *release* sport. As every bowler knows, there is a moment of crunching impact when a bowling ball hits the pins. Nevertheless, peak sportforces occur at the moment the ball leaves your hand. There are minimal external forces in bowling, but considerable internal forces do build up within your shoulder and throwing arm as you draw your bowling ball back, swing it forward to the point of release, and then follow through after release. In addition, your lower extremities are exposed to considerable stress during your approach and sudden stop at the foul line, as well as by the twisting motion you probably employ during your wind-up and follow-through.

Sportaches

If you can avoid dropping a bowling ball on your foot, bowling can be one of the safest recreational activities. Nevertheless, bowlers frequently encounter a number of common problems.

Despite the fact that a sixteen-pound bowling ball weighs the same as the shot that Olympians and track stars train for months to heave during brief shot-put events, recreational bowlers think nothing of rolling their bowling balls fifty or sixty times per hour, with little or no concern for their bodies. The result is frequently an ache.

The majority of bowling sportaches occur in your lower extremities. Your *knees* in particular are vulnerable to the sportforces generated during your wind-up, delivery, and follow-through. *Ankle* and *foot* problems are also common among bowlers, as are backaches.

The weight of the ball, your sudden stop at the foul line, and the frequent twisting of your body before, during, and after release, can also subject your throwing arm to considerable stress when you bowl. If you try to twist your *wrist* and forearm to impart spin as you release your bowling ball, you may well develop a wrist ache or a painful case of "bowler's *elbow*." And even if you keep your wrist stable, your *shoulder* and elbow can be exposed to considerable stress. Finally, of course, your *hand* is vulnerable to a variety of problems, including the infamous "bowler's thumb" — usually because of an improperly drilled grip.

Solutions

EQUIPMENT

Just because many of the pros use a sixteen-pound ball doesn't mean that you should automatically do the same. As a matter of fact, most recreational bowlers routinely choose balls that are too heavy. Make certain your bowling ball is the correct weight *for you*.

The balance of your ball is also important. An improperly balanced bowling ball is apt to cause you to perform all sorts of gyrations to prevent it from veering off course. If you feel as though you have to fight to keep your ball from hooking or drifting, switch balls. An improperly balanced bowling ball can easily lead to unnecessary aches.

Grip size is another important factor in choosing a bowling ball. There are several varieties of grips available, with different configurations relating to finger spread and the angle of your grip. Get help from a pro in selecting the proper bowling ball for your bowling style (high backswing, quick downswing, and so on) as well as the size and flexibility of your fingers and your overall conditioning and bowling habits. Make certain that the ball you choose is properly drilled *for you*. A poorly drilled grip can be hazardous to your health. If the holes in your ball are too big for your fingers, you'll really have to squeeze to keep your ball from slipping, thereby stressing muscles in your forearm and making wrist or elbow problems much more likely.

There are two basic varieties of bowling balls: rubber and plastic. Each is an improvement over the original wooden balls used by early bowlers. Rubber and plastic balls both have certain advantages, depending on lane conditions. Choose carefully, after experimenting with the free "loan" balls available at your bowling center.

Your bowling ball is by far your most important piece of equipment as a bowler. However, your shoes are also an important consideration if you are seeking to avoid aches. Even if your local center permits it, you should never bowl in sneakers, running shoes, or street shoes. Improper bowling footwear can cause you to slip, slide, or even stumble — none of which will be good for your game or your health.

Choose your bowling shoes carefully. Make sure they fit correctly and are strong enough to support your feet and ankles fully. If you're right-handed, make certain you buy right-handed bowling shoes. Your left bowling shoe should have leather or some composition material that will permit your left foot to slide during your final approach, while the rubber sole on your right shoe should help you to brake with your right foot. Finally, make certain that your bowling shoes offer the right amount of friction for the lanes where you bowl. Too much friction, generated by either lane or shoe, can be just as dangerous as too little.

Use common sense in selecting your other bowling equipment. Wear loose-fitting trousers or a skirt when you bowl. Tight jeans will restrict your movement and thereby increase lower-extremity stress. If you decide to try a wristband, make certain your wrist is not completely locked. Finally, you'll want to keep your hand dry to prevent your grip from slipping, but you don't want to have your fingers dry slick. Chances are that using the blower, which is part of every ball return machine, will be just as effective as either rosin or a towel.

ENVIRONMENT

Conditions can vary dramatically from one bowling center to another. You should be aware of how certain environmental considerations may affect your body. How slick are the lanes where you bowl? If your approach area is either too slick or too dry, you may develop unnecessary aches. What is the condition of the pins where you bowl? You may find yourself overthrowing if the pins have lost their resiliency. How good is the lighting? If you bowl in one of the many relatively dark bowling centers around the United States, you'll have difficulty establishing your spots on the alley. You may overthrow in an effort to compensate. At the very least, you'll get fewer strikes than normal, increasing cumulative stress to your body as you consistently leave pins standing.

What time does your league bowl? If you are regularly obliged to compete when you're tired, you may unconsciously begin throwing too hard or shortening your approach. What is the level of competition in your league? If you're on a highly competitive team or if you bowl regularly with better bowlers, you may begin to press on each frame, thereby increasing stress to your body.

VELOCITY

Don't hurry your approach. Concentrate on accuracy and forget about trying to deliver a cannonball. Keep the pace of your wind-up, delivery, and follow-through slow and deliberate. There's no opponent pitching or hitting the ball at you as there is in baseball or tennis, but if you're not careful, you'll become your own worst enemy when you bowl. Finally, if you bowl too many games a day, or too many days per week, at too fast a pace — you're heading for trouble.

TECHNIQUE

Your approach is key, both to your bowling performance and to your health. Most pros advocate a four-step approach. Nevertheless, if you watch bowling on TV, you may notice that the top scorers take anywhere from three to six steps. You may want to experiment to determine what works best for you. Your goal, of course, is to develop an approach that leaves you on balance during both your delivery and your follow-through.

Make certain you're not swinging the ball up too high during your backswing. Otherwise, your upper arm and shoulder will be unnecessarily stressed.

Resist the temptation to throw the ball as hard as you can. Trying to explode the pins will place undue stress on your arm and forward knee at the moment of peak force. Also, a cannonball may move through the pins so fast that they'll fail to carry other pins as they fall.

Make certain your arm continues through its full range of motion after you release your bowling ball. Your follow-through should at least bring your arm up to waist level. Try to finish on balance, holding your follow-through the way the pros do after release.

CONDITIONING

Bowling is like any other sport. No bowler should begin without at least a brief limbering-up and warm-up period. Nevertheless, bowlers are generally very unappreciative of the need for any sort of conditioning. Therefore, there are many more bowling sportaches than there ought to be.

Find a way to limber up your throwing arm and shoulder, as well as your legs, before you start bowling. A few light calisthenics and several minutes of stretching should be sufficient. When you're finally ready to throw your first practice ball, do it gently. You shouldn't bowl your first few frames all-out any more than a baseball pitcher would throw warm-up pitches at one hundred miles per hour.

You don't have to do extensive general conditioning to have a healthy career as a bowler, but you should be aware of the need to strengthen your abdominal muscles and stretch your hamstrings to avoid unnecessary back pain.

Finally, don't forget to warm down properly after you bowl. Sitting around in a damp blouse or shirt is a sure-fire way to develop problems.

Bicycling

Sportforces

Bicycling is a *resistance* sport. Peak force occurs each time you thrust against the pedals of your bike. When you thrust out and down on your pedals, your bicycle crank rotates, moving your bicycle chain, rotating your wheels, and eventually moving you over the ground. Meanwhile, your pedals resist any effort to move your bicycle forward. As you thrust against that resistance, considerable stress can be generated in your lower extremities. The internal sportforces you generate when you ride your bicycle flow out through your hips, knees, ankles, and feet, passing into the ground beneath you by way of your bicycle wheels.

Although cycling is essentially a resistance sport, there can be impact forces as well, with which you must be prepared to contend when you ride. You may well develop a sore posterior or aching arms as a cyclist, for example, usually as the result of the continual bumping of your bicycle as it moves over the uneven terrain beneath your wheels.

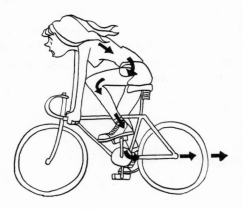

Sportaches

Your legs do virtually all the work when you ride your bicycle. Therefore, it should come as no surprise that your *knees* — which are obliged to flex and extend over and over against considerable resistance — seem to be particularly susceptible to cycling sportaches. Depending on your equipment and technique, you may also develop sore *feet* or *ankles,* but your knees are by far the most vulnerable joints in your lower extremities.

Impact stress, which is usually a problem only if you bicycle over uneven or bumpy terrain, is most likely to result in temporary numbness and tingling in your *wrists* or *hands.* Nevertheless, you may also develop *elbow* problems, especially if you ride with your arms rigid and your elbows locked. Finally, especially if your handlebars are turned down, you may experience stress in your lower *back, neck,* or *shoulders,* with neck problems especially common.

Solutions

EQUIPMENT

Make certain your bicycle frame is the proper size *for you.* You should be able to straddle your frame in your stocking feet. An overly large frame will cause you to rock in the saddle when you ride, increasing lower-extremity stress. Alternatively, if your frame is too small, you'll have to cramp your body on your bike. Riding in a cramped position can be very stressful, especially to your knees.

Once you've selected the proper size bicycle frame, you should consider four additional adjustments. Your *saddle height* is more important than you may realize. According to a recent MIT study, the distance from the top of your saddle to each bicycle pedal at its lowest point should be 109 percent of your inseam. Only if your saddle is at the proper height will you be able to ride comfortably, with your ankles slightly extended at the bottom of each rotation of your pedals and neither leg too cramped at the top.

The *distance between your saddle and your handlebars* can be equally important. If you overextend your arms, you'll have reduced control over your bike. At the same time, you may find yourself more susceptible to elbow pain. On the other hand, if your handlebars are too close to your seat, you'll have to ride with your arms forced into your body, again decreasing control, and this time increasing your vulnerability to wrist sportaches.

The proper distance between your saddle and your handlebars is something only you can determine. However, most experts advocate riding with your elbows slightly bent and your back at a 45° angle to the ground. To adjust the distance between your bicycle seat and your handlebars, you can either move your seat on its post or replace the stem holding your handlebars.

The question of *handlebar height* is relatively straightforward. Comfort and control are usually synonymous. Generally, the top of your handlebar stem should be at the same height as the top of your saddle. If you want to reduce the stress on key joints in your arms, of course, you can shift stress to your posterior by either raising your handlebars or lowering your seat.

The matter of *handlebar angle* can be confusing. There are a number of different hand positions that should work for every rider. Your goal, of course, is to find a handlebar setting that will minimize stress to your hands and arms. Generally, the top of the curved part of your handlebars should be parallel to the ground, and the end of the bar should be at a 10° to 14° angle to the ground. But by all means experiment.

Make certain you have enough air in your bicycle tires. Otherwise, you'll have to work extra hard to pedal your bike.

Try a new saddle, at least if you've been experiencing posterior pain. If your present saddle seems hard, a padded saddle may make a big difference, or vice versa. A wider saddle will help to spread impact forces but may increase the discomfort of chafing. Women may want to try a saddle especially designed for their bodies.

Never wear restrictive clothing such as tight jeans when you bicycle. Bicycling shorts are functional, if not fashionable. Wool or Lycra shorts allow moisture to evaporate and prevent chafing. Gloves or foam handle grips are inexpensive pieces of equipment that can go a long way toward absorbing road vibration. Also, don't forget sunglasses if you need them. Straining to see not only is dangerous but tends to make you tense.

ENVIRONMENT

Where you ride is nearly as important as what you ride. Since a number of cycling sportaches are a function of road vibration, you should obviously pick as smooth a surface as possible on which to ride. Unpaved roads and uneven sidewalks should be avoided.

Ride when and where the light is good. Bicycling at night is not only dangerous because of the increased risk of being hit by a car or truck, it is also more likely to result in unnecessary and painful encounters with potholes and bumps.

Bad weather can also create problems for cyclists. Fighting to maintain control over your bike on wet or slippery surfaces can increase stress to your back and arms. Likewise, attempting to pedal into the wind may be a lot harder on your legs than you may think.

Riding uphill may be all the extra stress you need to provoke an ache. Avoid hills, especially if your knees hurt. Likewise, riding with someone who insists upon going farther or faster than you are used to biking may be an unnecessarily painful experience. Find your own comfortable routine and stick to it.

VELOCITY

Your body is the engine that drives the machine, your bicycle. If you speed, you're asking for sportaches. At the start of the season or after a long period of inactivity, begin slowly. Don't try to cycle too fast or too far. Likewise, even if you're in shape, don't speed at the beginning of a ride or charge the hills.

TECHNIQUE

Unless you're riding an old bike you found in the garage or barn, your bicycle probably has at least three gears. Learning to use the different gears properly is the most important single adjustment you can make in your bicycling technique. Struggling in too high a gear is the most common mistake made by recreational cyclists, as well as an important cause of bicycling sportaches.

Your legs should revolve at a steady pace when you ride your bike, with a relatively constant amount of effort. The gear you choose, not the speed of your legs, should determine how fast you go. Start in a low gear. As you build speed and overcome inertia, shift to progressively higher gears. Try to maintain a constant resistance. Your legs should make approximately the same number of revolutions per minute regardless of your speed.

Every cyclist has a comfortable cadence. Find yours, and maintain it by learning how to use your bicycle gears. A high cadence in a lower gear range is obviously less stressful than a low cadence in a higher gear.

Learn to keep your weight centered when you ride your bike. Try to minimize sideways motion. You can learn by watching an experienced distance cyclist. The legs revolve at a steady pace and there is little, if any, rocking back and forth. Side-to-side motion causes chafing and saddle soreness. And if you don't keep your weight centered when you ride your bike, you'll also increase the chance of developing a lower-extremity sportache.

Make full use of the range of motion in your ankles. Place the ball of your foot, not the area under your instep, on each pedal. You want to be able to flex your ankles as you thrust down to increase power and reduce knee strain.

Finally, switch hand positions often. There are a number of different ways to grip your handlebars that will give you instant access to your brake levers. By remembering to shift hand positions regularly, you can minimize arm fatigue, reducing the risk that you'll develop elbow or wrist sportaches and hand numbness.

CONDITIONING

Bicycling can be more stressful than many recreational athletes believe. An alarming number of people think they can simply climb onto any available bicycle any time and pedal ten miles. How about you? Have you ever considered riding the several miles to work every day or pedaling your bike to the station? Has it also occurred to you that you may need to get into shape before you start to commute by bike? Having the proper equipment and knowing how to use it will help, but some common sense conditioning will nevertheless be required, at least if you want to avoid common cycling sportaches.

You can't expect to ride a bike for the first time in months or years — especially if you plan to go very far or very fast — without aches. And it isn't just sore muscles that should concern you. A long bike ride on the first day of spring may also trigger a bona fide sportache. As in any other sport or activity, you need to build up slowly. If you're really planning to commute by bike starting in April, you'll need to get in shape by riding a mile or two every other day starting in February.

Regular sit-ups will build abdominal strength and give your back a measure of protection. Also, make certain you are flexible enough in key leg muscles, particularly your hamstrings and calf muscles.

Limber up before you bike, at least if it's early in the season and you plan to go very far or start out very fast. Several minutes of calisthenics and stretching should be all that's required.

Warm up gradually as you begin your ride. One of the biggest risks about starting to commute by bike is that you'll end up skipping any limbering-up or warm-up period in a last-minute rush to catch your train or get to work. Try to leave early enough so you'll be able to take the first mile on your bike very slowly and only gradually pick up the pace.

Finally — and this can again be a problem for bicycle commuters — you need to take the time to warm down for a few minutes after you ride. If you can schedule your rides so that you don't have to park and race immediately to your desk, bus, or train, your body will be grateful. Try to cover the last half mile on your bike slowly, leaving time also for a few stretching exercises and possibly a change of clothes before you settle into your office routine or your train seat.

Swimming

Sportforces

Swimming is a *resistance* sport. Floating in a pool, lake, or ocean can be the ultimate in relaxing, nonstressful activity. However, if you try to move through the water — especially if you try to swim with any speed — you'll find that you tire quite quickly. That's because the water in which you are immersed resists the thrusting efforts of your arms and legs.

There's no impact or pounding when you swim. Swimming can therefore be an ideal non-weight-bearing activity. If done in moderation, swimming is very easy on your joints. However, if you decide to use swimming as a cardiorespiratory conditioning tool (as many injured runners have started to do, for example, in addition to swimmers everywhere who work out regularly to "stay in shape") you'll be generating considerable internal sportforces in a variety of joints with every lap you swim. A swimmer's body routinely performs unusual movements in an unnatural medium, thereby creating the potential for a number of alarmingly common aches.

Sportaches

No matter which stroke you prefer, you'll be generating extraordinary stresses somewhere in your body if you take your exercise in a pool. When you swim your muscles are obliged to work against the resistance of the water around you. Work results in stress.

The most common swimming sportaches affect your *shoulders*. Unless you restrict yourself to the breast stroke, side stroke, or dog paddle, your shoulders must absorb peak forces in relatively unstable positions when you swim. If you do the free-style, backstroke, or butterfly, your arms are consistently over your head as you pull against the water, making shoulder pain virtually inevitable if you try to swim very far or very fast.

"Swimmer's shoulder" usually develops gradually. You'll experience pain or discomfort in one or both shoulders after you work out. Gradually, however, your ache will begin to bother you in the water as well, most noticeably when you lift your arm or arms. Eventually, swimmer's shoulder can become just as much of a full-time ache as tennis elbow or runner's knee.

Knee problems are also common among swimmers, especially those who specialize in the breast stroke. The ''frog'' kick commonly used by breast strokers is very stressful to your knees. You may experience pain in or around one or both knee joints, both during and after a workout.

Ankle and *foot* sportaches are less common among swimmers. Nevertheless, complaints do arise. Both the backstroke and flutter (free-style) kicks can create ankle or foot problems. Since you're obliged to keep your toes extended while you kick, neither your ankles nor your feet are particularly stable during peak force.

Solutions

EQUIPMENT

The trend in swimsuits is toward skimpier, lighter, and tighter models every year. Choose your suit for comfort. If you swim in a suit that is too tight around the legs or shoulders, chafing may cause you to alter your stroke — reducing your discomfort, perhaps, but also increasing your susceptibility to sportaches. Women should also avoid loose suit tops, which slip off your shoulders, affecting your arm pull. You may want to tie a shoelace across the back of your suit to tighten the top. Or try a new Lycra suit with a racing back. It may fit more comfortably than your old nylon model.

If you swim in a pool, goggles can be an important piece of

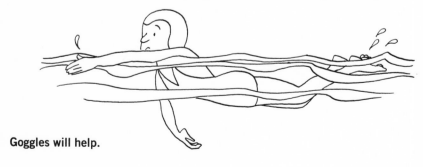

Goggles will help.

equipment to acquire. You'll be able to see the lane markings on the floor of the pool and the walls more easily, eliminating the need to break your rhythm and strain your neck to see where you are. Of course, you'll also keep the chlorine out of your eyes.

A kick board can be useful. A board can enable you to give your shoulders and arms a rest during a workout. Don't press down on the board, however, as that will tend to raise your body too high in the water. You'll do better with a board if you keep your arms relaxed and extended, with your shoulders relatively low in the water.

Obviously, you'll want to avoid working out with a kick board if you have knee, ankle, or foot problems. Likewise, be careful if you decide to try paddles to build up strength in your arms. Working out with paddles can generate increased stress in your shoulders, leading all too often to a bothersome case of swimmer's shoulder.

ENVIRONMENT

Where and when you swim can be more important than you realize. Most municipal and university pools are nowadays quite crowded. In many public pools "circle swimming" has become the rule. A group of swimmers swims up one side of each lane and down the other to minimize traffic hazards and maximize pool utilization. However, swimmers in any given lane are not always equally matched in speed. If you find yourself working out with a group that goes too fast for you, you may inadvertently generate greater sportforces than you can handle, especially while you're warming up. Be careful. Since the fast lanes are usually in the middle of the pool, try starting each workout in one of the slower lanes closer to the wall, joining the "jet set" only when you're thoroughly warm.

If you swim in a private pool without wall markings, you'll find you're constantly breaking your rhythm and lifting your head to see where you are. The result may be an ache. Perhaps you'll need to change pools.

Water temperature is another important factor in the swimmer's environment. Be sure to limber up and warm up thoroughly before diving into relatively cold water for a workout. Otherwise, you'll be tempted to swim all-out as soon as you hit the water — a sure way to overstress your body.

VELOCITY

Whether you swim in a pool or at the beach, the key to healthy swimming is to go slowly — at least until you're thoroughly warmed up. Swim the first several hundred yards of the day at a very leisurely pace. Concentrate on stretching out your body. Vary your stroke from one lap to the next. Even if you're working out in the water, and not merely swimming to relax or cool down on a hot day, you must go slowly as you begin each swim. Speed leads to sportaches, at least if you press too hard too early in a workout. Keep your velocity down if you want to avoid aches.

TECHNIQUE

Proper swimming technique can do a lot to reduce the stress of working out in the water, making you less susceptible to swimming sportaches. Proper technique should also make you a better swimmer. Most swimming technique errors involve your arms. However, there are also important technique considerations in the way you breathe and kick.

Free-style. If you do the crawl (free-style), the path you make with each of your arms as you pull through the water should resemble an inverted question mark. Your elbows should be bent at almost 90° as your hands pass your chin and should remain at least slightly bent as long as each arm is in the water. You want to push as much water as possible back and behind you, not downward. In addition, bending each elbow as your hand pushes through the water should keep you from having to swing your legs to the side as you swim.

Have a friend or coach watch you do the free-style. Make certain you're not like many recreational swimmers, with your arms too low and your elbows locked as you pull yourself through the water. Also, as you breathe you should be lifting your head to the side, not to the front. And when you do the free-style kick, make certain your feet don't come very high out of the water.

Butterfly. Many ingredients of proper free-style technique are also present when you do the butterfly. Again, your arms should be bent as you pull through the water, with your hands tracing the pattern of an hourglass. Don't pull too wide, however, as this will hasten fatigue and increase shoulder stress. When you breathe, raise your head just far enough out of the water so that your mouth is clear — not so far that your chin is in the air. As you return your head to the water, keep it aligned with your body and try to relax your neck muscles. Finally, make certain your powerful butterfly kick comes from your hips, not from your knees.

Backstroke. Too many backstrokers fail to bend their elbows as they pull through the water. As each hand comes past your shoulders, your elbow should be bent at about 90°. Your arm should then gradually straighten out so that as you recover and bring your hand through the air, your arm is straight, but not tense and rigid. Also, if you can learn to roll from side to side as you do the backstroke, you'll find it easier to apply force without overstressing your shoulders and arms.

Breast Stroke. Learning how to kick without straining a knee has always been the biggest challenge for breast strokers. The traditional wedge kick, in which your knees are spread apart and the water is squeezed between your legs, can be more stressful to your knees than the whip kick, during which your knees almost touch your buttocks and water is forced out behind your legs. You may want to learn the whip kick if you enjoy the breast stroke but are concerned about knee pain. Be careful to point your feet at the end of each kick, but don't overdo. If nothing else seems to work, you may also want to try kicking less often per stroke, perhaps using a two-beat crossover instead of a six-beat kick.

CONDITIONING

If you're going to swim to "stay in shape," you should recognize that serious swimming requires a degree of general conditioning, as well as sensible limbering-up, warm-up, and warm-down periods before, during, and after each workout. Don't be misled by the fact that doctors and therapists often prescribe time in the water for the injured, aged, and lame. Someone who rolls from a wheelchair into a pool is obviously not going to work out in the water as vigorously as you are. If you're a serious swimmer, you'd better be serious about getting ready for each workout.

As a recreational swimmer, your most important general conditioning concern should be with flexibility. Make certain to exercise all your major joints through their full range of motion every day. Swimming itself will tend to loosen certain muscles, but you still need to ensure that you are as flexible as possible before you get into the water.

Limber up at pool side before you start to swim. Again, calisthenics and gentle stretching exercises are advisable, at least for a few minutes. A few push-ups and fifty or a hundred sit-ups would also be a good idea before you start to work out.

When you finally get into the water, swim and kick a few laps slowly before you really start to work out. Change strokes often to warm up as thoroughly as possible.

Finally, after you've completed your workout, warm down with a lap or two of slow swimming and then do a few more minutes of stretching at pool side before you head home.

Part IV

WHEN EEVeTeC
ISN'T THE ANSWER

9

Sportache or Medical Problem?

YOU'VE JUST BEGUN your morning run. The temperature is crisp. You feel terrific. Suddenly you notice a twinge in one knee. You slow down, focusing all your attention on the leg that hurts. There it is, a slight pain just as your foot hits the ground. You stop for a minute and curse your bad luck. Then you start to jog again slowly. At first the same pain is still there. Gradually it disappears.

By the end of your run, you've forgotten all about it. But your pain will probably be back. If it's a signal of overuse or misuse, you can expect it to get worse. You have a *sportache*.

•

Your opponent's serve isn't particularly forceful, but her spin is driving you crazy. Your first three returns land in the net. You're feeling frustrated. At 40–love, you figure you have nothing to lose. So you smash your next service return. The ball misses the net and the court, barely catching the top of the fence.

As you change sides, your opponent offers you a couple of practice serves. "No thanks," you say. Without even a practice swing, you wind up for your first serve of the day and hit the ball as hard as you can. An ace! "That'll show her," you mutter.

Later, after you've finally begun to return your opponent's service more consistently, you notice that your forearm aches every time you hit a backhand. With luck, your pain will be gone the next morning. But your elbow problems may be just beginning. You have a *sportache*.

•

Traffic is unusually heavy for a Saturday morning, and you get to the clubhouse just minutes before you are scheduled to tee off. You rush from the locker room to join the other three members of your foursome, waiting at the first tee. Moments later you drive away. Though your first shot lands squarely in a sand trap, you're not upset. You've outdriven everyone else.

As you play out of the bunker, you hit the ball solidly, but you feel a slight twinge in your hip. You've noticed the same pain before. As a matter of fact, it's been bothering you on and off all spring. Your ache is never severe and it always seems to go away. However, chances are, at least if you don't do something about it soon, one of these days your ache is going to get worse. Your hip will hurt all the time. You have a *sportache*.

•

You've heard it before — in the first paragraph of this book — but perhaps you need to hear it again. If you play anything more strenuous than chess, chances are you're going to hurt from time to time. A twinge is just the hint of what can become a serious problem. What makes this a potentially dangerous situation is that the medical profession — to which we are all conditioned to turn whenever we're in pain or discomfort — generally can't do anything to help, at least not until an occasional ache has become unnecessarily acute or chronic.

In its early stages, a sportache only occurs while you are playing your favorite sport. That can present problems if you go to a doctor for treatment.

Let's sit in for a moment on a typical discussion between doctor and patient. The following dialogue takes place thousands of times every day in doctors' offices all over the world. The patient here is a runner complaining of knee pain, but he or she could be any recreational or professional athlete with any kind of sportache.

The doctor begins by taking the patient's history.

DOCTOR: What brings you here?

PATIENT: My knee hurts.

DOCTOR: When?

PATIENT: About the fourth mile.

DOCTOR: Then what happens?

PATIENT: The pain usually lasts until the end of the run. When I stop, it goes away.

DOCTOR: Does this happen every run?

PATIENT: Usually.

Now the scene shifts to the examination room.

DOCTOR: Show me where it hurts.

The patient waves a finger around his kneecap.

DOCTOR: Can you be more specific?

PATIENT: No.

DOCTOR: Why?

PATIENT: Because it doesn't hurt now. I told you it only hurts when I run.

Tension begins to grow.

DOCTOR: Let me see if I can find a painful spot. (He places his index finger on the patient's knee.) Does it hurt here?

PATIENT: No.

DOCTOR: How about here?

PATIENT: Not there.

DOCTOR: And here?

PATIENT: No, not there either.

Sparks are now flying.

DOCTOR: Then where does it hurt?

PATIENT: I told you, when I get to about the fourth mile.

When Steve Devereux and I started to work on this book, we quickly realized that we needed a special word to describe the kinds of problems we are talking about. You won't find the word *sportache* in any medical text. Once we determined that sport-aches are not medical problems, Steve and I decided we had to dispense with the standard medical lexicon.

Our special effort at using nonmedical terminology to separate "medical" from "nonmedical" concerns hasn't made doctors any happier with us. Take my friend Joe, a gifted surgeon. Back in 1978 I tried to explain the basic idea of this book to him. "You're not going to tell a lot of people just enough so that they drive me crazy at my office?" he exclaimed. "Don't you realize how many problems you create when you give a patient a little knowledge?"

I'm sorry Joe feels that way about it. We're not trying to irritate doctors, and we certainly don't want to make the medical community angry with us. Unfortunately, however, Joe's reaction is not uncommon. Doctors have a tendency to see red whenever they think that anyone is urging people to cure their own aches — regardless of the origin of the problems that are causing their pain. For some reason, surgeons in particular seem to resent any suggestion that a doctor sometimes just isn't needed.

I have tremendous respect for doctors like Joe. Surgical intervention is a unique skill. It's hard to imagine the thrill of watching an expert work at the operating table. I know. For many years surgery was a regular part of my practice. Therefore, I also know that surgeons aren't equipped to cope with trivial problems like sportaches. The fact of the matter is that surgeons usually can't help you until you've gotten yourself into unnecessarily deep trouble.

I asked my friend Joe what he'd do for a jogger who came to him complaining of joint pain. "I'd follow my normal procedure," he replied. "After taking a complete history, I'd look for any signs of disease or trauma."

"And what if you couldn't find any?"

"I'd tell him to stop jogging," answered Joe.

"But let's suppose your patient says he doesn't want to stop jogging. Then what?"

"Then I'd tell him that the ache is *his* problem. Come on, Rob, what's the guy doing in my office if he's not going to listen to my advice?"

Of course, I can understand Joe's point of view. He's right. But so is the jogger. The real problem is that Joe, and doctors like him, don't have the solution. And, until now, neither did most athletes.

It isn't surprising that doctors like Joe are incapable of coming up with simple answers to essentially nonmedical problems such as the runner's knee pain, the tennis player's sore elbow, and the golfer's aching hip. EEVeTeC has very little to do with medicine. Nevertheless, doctors around the world are confronted every day with problems that require EEVeTeC. No wonder both doctors and patients everywhere are becoming more and more frustrated.

•

Surgeons tend to look where you point. If you complain of knee pain, they'll look at your knee and only your knee. As a podiatrist, my approach is often quite different. It almost has to be. Podiatrists are different.

Before the fitness revolution, which produced "jogger's heel" among other trendy phenomena, there were no socially acceptable foot diseases. Hiatus hernia, it seemed, made for better cocktail party small talk than common garden-variety bunions.

When I first began to practice podiatry, I was often asked, "How can you look at feet all day?" My standard reply was, "Thank goodness I'm not a proctologist!" So much for those with limited horizons and interests.

For many years, I've given a standard talk, mostly to medical audiences, on the general theme, "What is the role of the podiatrist?" In that speech, I have always tried to make two key points.

First, there are actually a surprisingly large number of people in the medical delivery system who are concerned with the foot. In addition to podiatrists, among others, there are surgeons (general, orthopedic, vascular, plastic, and neurosurgeons), primary care physicians (general practitioners, internists, pediatricians, diabetologists, dermatologists, neurologists, radiologists, osteopaths, and chiropractors), and paramedical clinicians (nurses, physical therapists, athletic trainers, and ski patrollers). Of this great mass, however, only the podiatrist is solely concerned with the foot.

Second, the foot isn't just the "end organ" some people perceive it to be. Your feet, after all, are attached to your body. That's why so many people get so involved with your feet, and that's also why podiatrists are often in a crucial spot. Your feet have a part in almost all sports problems.

Perhaps that's why I approach my athlete patients in a way that used to bother my orthopedic colleagues. Naturally, I begin by checking whatever joint is bothering any patient who comes to me. However, if the joint that's bothering you is apparently normal, I'll probably then check your feet, at least as a possible source of ankle, knee, hip, or back problems.

If you came to my office, I'd want to know everything about your activity, even if it was one about which I was already reasonably knowledgeable. I'd want to know what kind of equipment you use, how conditioned you are, how good your technique is, even where and with whom you play.

When we first put together our group at Sports Medicine Resource, my colleagues frequently expressed doubts about my approach. "Come on, Rob," they'd say, "this guy has a knee problem. Forget his feet and all that other stuff."

I didn't argue. My medical philosophy has always been to do what works best for the patient, even if my approach doesn't exactly agree with that of other practitioners. Every specialty has its place. No doctor has all the answers. I believe that time spent arguing is time wasted.

At Sports Medicine Resource, my point of view eventually began to prevail. To their great credit, my colleagues, despite their long years of training as orthopedic surgeons, eventually began to recognize the difference between sportaches and injuries. Unlike most surgeons, they now routinely ask what they can do for active patients whose aching joints do not require medical treatment or surgery. The answer, of course, is EEVeTeC.

A growing number of doctors have made great strides in separating the pains of fitness from the general mass of athletic and nonathletic injuries. Many practitioners have even begun to treat such problems nonmedically if that's what's called for. For example, Dr. Hank Childs, a friend and colleague, is just one of many primary care doctors in the Boston area who are helping patients improve their quality of life by prescribing running shoes. However, the medical community is still, by and large, unaware of EEVeTeC. And many doctors continue to ignore the difference between sportaches and injuries.

The best way I've found to make it perfectly clear what sportaches are is to say what they are *not*. Whenever you use muscles you haven't used recently, or when you play your sport longer or harder than usual, you can expect to wake up stiff and sore the next morning. But you don't have a sportache. You'll be experiencing normal muscle soreness. Your muscles will hurt. But your pain will pass. In fact, as a result of your exertion, your body will be stronger and healthier. Let me repeat. You do *not* have a sportache.

You also don't have a sportache if you have an ache as the result of a sprained ankle, a twisted knee, a dislocated shoulder or any other joint or limb that has been subjected to sudden trauma. *Trauma* is defined as an injury, wound, or shock. Every sport involves some risk of trauma. But when you sprain, dislocate, bruise, or break something, you do *not* have a sportache, even though you may hurt for a long time thereafter. You have an injury.

•

One of the first things I learned when I began to practice sportsmedicine is that most people don't understand how stressful most sports can be. Many people believe that serious aches and pains are a problem only if you play a contact sport or have the misfortune to suffer an accident during participation in a recreational activity. Everyone knows, for example, that you can drown in rough water or break your neck in a shallow pool. But many people are unaware that recreational swimming also has its share of sportaches. Likewise, people know that cyclists can be hurt by falling off their bikes or being hit by a car. But they don't realize that riding a bicycle can result in the development of knee, wrist, and elbow problems.

Many of us believe that only jocks get hurt. In fact, the opposite is true. Recreational athletes are much more susceptible to certain problems than professional athletes. How is that possible? Think for a moment. Even if you play your sport only occasionally, you are still exposed to basically the same stresses as the full-time athlete. However, you probably lack the pro's superior technique and conditioning.

Every activity has its moments of stress. Everyone who plays any dynamic sport for any length of time will eventually suffer from twinges of joint pain. Whether or not a warning ache becomes a chronic problem is a matter you can control by adjusting the five elements of the McGregor Solution. But be aware that the aches will come. And, if you're relatively underconditioned, your excesses will affect you more than if you were in top shape.

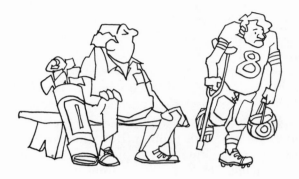

Many of us believe that only jocks get hurt.

Meteorologists love to predict the probability of precipitation on any given day. You can do the same — probably with greater accuracy — when it comes to your relative vulnerability to sportaches. Using the following criteria, you should be able to tell *when* you're likely to develop an ache, if not *where*. Which indexes are most important? The experts aren't sure. But as a doctor and athlete, I feel that at least the following criteria are important.

Age With each passing year, it becomes more and more difficult for you to do the things you've been able to do effortlessly in the past. Carl Yastrzemski knows. The perennial star of my home-town baseball team, the Boston Red Sox, Yastrzemski missed the early days of spring training in 1980. He had pulled a muscle during a preseason weightlifting workout. Carl's problem was his birth certificate. He was forty years old when the 1980 spring training began. He never would have pulled the same muscle fifteen years earlier.

Wouldn't it be wonderful if we could be vaccinated against sportaches as we were, years ago, for smallpox and polio? As youngsters, we seemed naturally immune to joint pain. However, over the years that immunity has gradually disappeared. Unfortunately, there's no acquired immunity, no shot, available to replace it.

Children's bodies are incredibly resilient. Broken bones and bruises are common, of course. But sportaches? They're practically unheard of. Think of the thousands of junior tennis players who hit millions of backhands every year. Have you ever heard of a sixteen-year-old with tennis elbow? There aren't many.

Why does age make us more vulnerable to sportaches? A friend of mine who is a psychiatrist and a former Harvard Medical School professor, as well as a dedicated long-distance runner, once explained it to me in this way: "As you grow older, your connective tissue becomes less forgiving." He's right. In addition, as you grow older, your joints start to hold a grudge. Joint problems increase dramatically for most people after the age of thirty.

After all, what are your joints? A joint is nothing more than a place where your bones are connected by tendons, ligaments, fasciae, and other tissue. Sports require constant joint movement or articulation. So, if you're evaluating your general vulnerability to sportaches, start with your age. If you're in your thirties, for example, you may still feel young. But you can bet that your joints won't be as forgiving as they were a few years ago. If you play your sport with the same intensity and carefree attitude as an eighteen-year-old, you're going to pay the price.

Obesity

Despite the fact that there's no logical reason why being overweight should increase your vulnerability to elbow problems in tennis or golf, a recent study of tennis elbow published in *Physician and Sportsmedicine* revealed that overweight tennis players do suffer a relatively high incidence of elbow pain. In contrast, if you're planning to be a runner or if you're worried about developing lower-extremity sportaches as the result of your participation in any weight-bearing sport, your weight is obviously an important consideration. Excess weight will make you more susceptible to foot, ankle, knee, and hip problems. So, pick your sport and plan your participation accordingly.

Special note to pregnant women: You should be especially aware of the perils of extra weight. Your bodies haven't had a lifetime to adjust to the stresses of obesity. The sudden, dramatic gain in weight you'll experience during pregnancy can cause skeletal imbalance and muscle stress, significantly increasing your susceptibility to joint pain.

Temperament

Your temperament can be a surprisingly good index of your susceptibility to the pains of fitness. If you're aggressive, tense, or hot-headed — we all know the type — you're more likely to develop a serious sportache than someone who's calm, loose, and easygoing. Your vulnerability also escalates if you are obsessive about your sport — as are many of the runners I see as patients.

People who are angry or temperamental or extremely competitive tend to abuse their bodies. Either they can't help themselves or they think that pushing themselves demonstrates a healthy desire to win. But abuse and overuse go hand in hand. Show me someone who uses sports to vent anger, frustration, or aggression, or someone who is obsessive about his or her activity, and I'll show you someone who's susceptible to sportaches.

Existing Aches

Existing aches often lead to other problems.

If you already have an ache that bothers you during or after sports, you're a prime candidate for additional problems. First, your body has already demonstrated vulnerability. Your connective tissue obviously isn't as forgiving as it was when you were younger. Second, as a direct result of your existing ache, you'll probably compensate or alter your technique in some way when you play your favorite sport. An existing sportache tends to disturb your body's delicate balance and can therefore trigger other problems.

A chain reaction of ailments is the rule rather than the exception in sports. Old-time baseball fans point to the case of Dizzy Dean. He suffered a fractured toe when he was hit by a line drive during the 1937 All Star game. Dean tried to come back too soon following his injury. The rest is history. He overcompensated by altering his stride and delivery and wound up doing permanent damage to his arm. It was Dean's arm problem, of course, that ended his pitching career prematurely.

The message is clear. If you try to avoid pain by making changes in the way you play your sport or activity, you will probably create other problems in compensating muscles and joints. Subsequent aches are likely to follow.

Structural Asymmetry

There's one more piece of data you should evaluate in attempting to predict your sportaches. It's structural asymmetry. Your body may not be precisely proportioned. If that's the case, certain joints may never be able to achieve and hold their stable position when you play your favorite sport.

As a podiatrist I know that many of the aches I treat are the direct result of a discrepancy in limb length. Lots of people have a "short leg." The condition may never bother them unless they decide to try running or some other particularly stressful activity. That's when they develop a serious problem, which can be in either the short or long limb.

How can you tell if you have a short limb? It's pretty simple. A man who buys prefinished slacks and finds that the cuffs are uneven should measure to see if he has a short limb. A woman who hems a skirt or dress evenly, yet finds that it's longer on one side than the other may also have a short limb. Or you can simply take a tape measure and check the distance from corresponding points on your waist to corresponding points on each foot.

If you do have a short limb, keep your structural asymmetry in mind if you take up a sport that involves running. A short limb makes lower-extremity sportaches very predictable. An easy solution: Place a lift in the shoe on your short side.

•

After careful consideration of your age, weight, temperament, condition, and body, you should be able to assess your general level of susceptibility to sportaches. It may then be possible for you to adjust your behavior to control or minimize the risk factors listed above. You could lose weight, for example. Similarly, you should be able to watch your temper.

Other factors aren't so controllable. No one has yet found a way to lick the problem of advancing age. Nevertheless, forewarned is forearmed. You can't help but be better off once you become aware of your relative vulnerability to sportaches. Merely realizing your vulnerability can be an important first step toward avoiding and managing certain problems.

In addition to knowing when you are likely to develop an ache, it would obviously be helpful to be able to predict where you're most likely to develop a problem. You could then take every precaution to prevent unnecessary pain.

The last two-fifths of EEVeTeC supply the key to predicting *where* you are most likely to develop a sportache. Technique and conditioning determine your ability to achieve and hold a stable position in a given joint.

If your technique is poor — if it places key joints of your lower and upper extremities in an unstable position when they must absorb and transmit sportforces — you are eventually going to develop a sportache. That's easier to predict than the weather. It doesn't take a great tennis coach to predict that a "poke" backhand or a contorted service motion will invariably lead to elbow or shoulder trouble. Likewise, you don't have to be an Olympic track coach to know that runners who land too heavily on their heels are destined for foot, ankle, or knee problems.

If your arm is usually bent at a 90° angle when you hit a tennis ball, your elbow will eventually start to ache. If your knee is twisted slightly with every step you take when you run, eventually it will begin to hurt. And so forth. The same rules apply to every dynamic sport. Poor technique eventually results in impaired health in whatever joint is farthest from its stable position at peak force.

Good health and good technique are closely related. What a coach will tell you to do in most sports to enhance your performance should also leave key joints of your body as close as possible to their stable position. To the extent that certain sports sometimes require you to function away from your stable position, you've simply got to be in shape.

In the same sense that poor technique can cause joint instability, poor conditioning can also leave key joints unstable and vulnerable. Achieving and holding your stable position requires both strength and flexibility in the muscles that move, stabilize, and protect key joints.

Conditioning may be the key to eliminating your sportaches. What is conditioning? It's *not* just exercises. Your general conditioning is obviously important. You need a certain degree of strength and flexibility to withstand the stresses of your sport. However, our definition of conditioning encompasses three additional steps: limbering up, warming up, and warming down. Regardless of how well conditioned you are for your sport, you must take a common sense approach to getting ready to play, playing, and winding down after play. If you don't, certain sportaches become virtually inevitable.

•

If you do a good job of predicting your sportaches, you should be able to save yourself lots of grief. You'll be able to take corrective steps before you develop an acute or chronic ache. Poor technique, weakness, and inflexibility can all be corrected. If the effort enables you to withstand the forces of your sport in a more stable position, your precautions will have been worth it.

Sportaches, as we've said several times now, are the pains of fitness. Until recently, fitness meant calisthenics, as well as other tests of strength and endurance. "Getting in shape" had all the appeal of a spoonful of cod liver oil. Fitness was something force-fed to you by your physical education teacher or your drill sergeant. It was a real turnoff and distinctly not fun.

Then came the recent fitness revolution. Calisthenics gave way to activities like running, tennis, golf, swimming, and cycling. Memories of the school yard and boot camp disappeared, along with the myth that getting fit was automatically boring and painful. Suddenly fitness became a positive goal, a means of self-expression for millions of people.

I have a standard after-dinner talk, entitled "Fitness Is as Fitness Does." "Fitness," I tell my audiences, "isn't an absolute, defined by the number of chin-ups you can struggle through, the amount of weight you can lift, or your time for the one-hundred-yard dash. Those days are over. Fitness today is simply the pursuit of health, doing something with your body."

There's no one way to achieve fitness. People get fit in a variety of ways — through manual labor, housework, yard work, and so on. Recently, however, many of us have turned to recreational sports as a means of achieving fitness. In contrast to calisthenics or work (whether at the factory, at home, or in the backyard), sports have a special advantage — they're fun. Or at least sports would be fun if it weren't for sportaches.

To eliminate sportaches you must be able to recognize them for what they are. While working on this book, Steve Devereux and I suffered from more than writer's cramp. We also suffered from persistent aches. My problem was a sore right shoulder. Steve was bothered by chronic pain in his right elbow. Both aches evolved from sports. But only one was a sportache. The other was an injury.

My shoulder problem began suddenly on the slopes at Aspen during March 1979. Snow was falling. Visibility was poor. But I had decided to take a final run. It was blissful. I was skiing alone, daydreaming. Suddenly, I caught a tip and went flying. Even while in the air, I sensed I was in real trouble. Therefore,

when I picked myself up and found nothing broken, I was grateful.

I pushed on. By the time I reached the bottom of the mountain, I realized that my luck had been good — but not great. My right shoulder had begun to throb. The pain quickly became acute. I checked in at the local hospital and learned that I'd torn a ligament. My shoulder ached for months. But it wasn't a sportache. It was an *injury*.

Steve's problem was different. A tennis player and coach for more than twenty years, he had been experiencing pain in his right elbow for several seasons. Like most of us, he procrastinated. Steve just never got around to making changes he knew he'd have to make eventually in his game and conditioning.

The result was inevitable. After rushing around New York City one December morning with a heavy suitcase and then playing competitive tennis twice within twenty-four hours, Steve wound up with nonstop pain in his elbow. Rest didn't help. Neither did ice, aspirin, or any of the other standard self-help measures we'll be talking about in the next chapter. Subsequent treatment by three different doctors also failed to produce relief.

Steve's tennis elbow lingered for months and soon triggered other aches. Eventually, after hundreds of anti-inflammatory pills and almost a year of rest, his chronic inflammation disappeared and Steve was able to make appropriate changes in his tennis equipment, technique, and overall conditioning.

Our cases highlight the difference between injuries and sport-aches.

Injuries, like mine, happen instantaneously. One minute you're feeling fine. The next minute you reach for a backhand, turn the corner on your daily run, or fall while you are skiing down a mountain. Suddenly, you're in acute pain. You have a sprained ankle, a twisted knee, a torn muscle, a broken bone, or some other result of trauma. Injuries happen without warning. They always come as a surprise. When you're injured, you shouldn't take unnecessary risks. Seek immediate medical attention.

Sportaches, on the other hand, develop gradually. Your body sends out lots of early warning signals. In the beginning you experience only occasional discomfort. Your pain always seems to go away. When you play your favorite sport, you feel a twinge in a joint or a sharp pain in a muscle. Perhaps the ache is somewhere in your leg as you run. Maybe it's in your elbow, wrist, or shoulder when you hit a tennis ball. Or possibly, it's in your knee as you pedal your bicycle, in your hip as you drive a golf ball, or in your shoulder as you swim.

During the early stages of a sportache, your pain may be transient. If you ignore it, however, sooner or later your ache will become a full-blown, full-time problem, on *and* off the field. In the early stages of a developing sportache, you won't be able to play without pain. But your pain will stop when you finish playing. Eventually, however, your ache may become so acute that it completely grounds you. You may actually find yourself unable to use your affected limb, without pain, even in your daily activities.

To avoid unnecessarily acute sportaches, you have to learn to listen to your body. You must become a connoisseur of pain. While sports participation is never completely pain-free, certain kinds of pain demand special attention.

Every athlete needs to learn to distinguish the laudable or praiseworthy pain of getting into shape and improving performance from the unacceptable pain that is the result of overuse or abuse. On the one hand, you are stiff and sore the next day or simply tired after exertion. On the other hand, you actually experience sharp twinges of pain during exertion.

The trick lies in recognizing sportaches early — so you can prevent them from becoming major problems. After all, would you wait for your rattling car to go dead? For your leaking roof to collapse? For that rip in your suit to become a tear?

So why ignore a sportache? It will usually get worse, eventually becoming acute or chronic. Only there are no warranties, no trade-ins, no replacement parts. Ignore your ache now and you'll pay later.

An injury calls for prompt medical attention. Only a doctor, especially a surgeon, is trained to treat an injury. Sportaches, on the other hand, must be managed by the victims, by the recreational and professional athletes who come down with thousands of new aches every day.

Just as your physical fitness is something only you can control, sportaches are problems you must manage. Essentially, you're on your own. But you're not alone. You can get help from a variety of "expert" sources, including coaches, trainers, and equipment salespeople, as well as other athletes who have been through what you're experiencing.

If your ache has reached the stage where there is inflammation, you may need to see a medical practitioner. A doctor can combat inflammation with a variety of weapons unavailable to the general public. Many of my patients, for instance, are runners whose aches can be alleviated with orthotics (custom arch supports), which I'm trained to prescribe and fit. Often I can also help with a prescription for anti-inflammatory drugs. In a very few instances, I may even use my expertise to prescribe surgery.

However, sportaches generally require therapy — management over a period of time, not one-shot treatment. That, unfortunately, is what frustrates and turns off many doctors. Most medical practitioners cannot provide long-term help, and few have the time or training to administer therapy. Almost any doctor can provide pain relief — treatment for your symptoms. However, it's up to you, the patient, to attack your underlying problem. Otherwise your relief will only be temporary. If you want to continue playing your sport, you will have to use EEVeTeC to eliminate your sportaches.

If your aching joint is normal — if it has never been injured or operated on — you probably should not go to a doctor. What you need is therapy or management, not intervention. EEVeTeC is the answer.

If your joint is abnormal, you are best advised to see your doctor. Despite previous injury or surgery, you may be able to tolerate a surprising amount of stress. However, sportforces may also simply be too much for your already weakened body. Get expert advice before you try to manage your ache yourself.

If your pain has gone beyond the warning stage, your first priority will be to get relief from your pain. Your "ache" has become an "-itis." You now need to learn something about inflammation — the subject of the next chapter. Then you'll have to decide whether you or your doctor will determine the appropriate medical treatment for what has become a bona fide medical problem as the result of your neglect.

You're on your own. But you're not alone.

10
Self-Help
for Inflammation

WHAT HAPPENS when the stress of your activity finally becomes too much for your body? What is going on when your sportache becomes acute or chronic? Simple. You have inflammation.

Suddenly your elbow, wrist, or shoulder hurts all the time. Your knee aches, even when you're sitting at your desk or trying to sleep, and not just when you're running, riding your bicycle, or swimming. Sport pain has spilled over into your everyday life. Some structure in or around a joint has become inflamed. Your body is tired of waiting for you to ease the stress to which you've been subjecting it. Overused (stressed) tissue is demanding your attention.

Twinges of pain are warnings to be careful — to go slow. Occasional pain should flash as a yellow light in your mind. When a particular joint finally becomes inflamed, your body's signals have gone from yellow to red. Inflammation says, "Stop."

Not every sportache involves inflammation. But every ache

can result in inflammation if it is not properly managed from the moment you first notice it. Occasional joint pain doesn't necessarily guarantee that a joint will become inflamed. However, if you fail to heed your body's warning system, inflammation is very likely.

Herb Roth's story is a good example of the inevitability of inflammation. Herb is one of several dozen readers of *Golf Digest* who answered our solicitation for anecdotes when we were researching for this book during the summer of 1979. In Herb's letter he explained that he has been a golfer all his adult life. Recently, he was finally able to retire and move to Florida where he can play golf year round.

Herb had apparently experienced occasional heel pain throughout his golf career. Only after he had retired, however, did his pain finally become a nonstop problem. To quote Herb: "Here I spend a whole lifetime working so that I can eventually play golf as much as I want. Now I have a chance to do it, and what happens? Suddenly I'm laid up.

"I used to finish my game with persistent heel pain. However, by the time I'd go to bed, it would be gone. Then one morning this spring I woke up with my usual pain, and it didn't go away that day. I rested for three straight days and my heel still hurt. Finally, I examined my foot and found that I could also feel some swelling. The bottom of my right heel was hot. I haven't been able to play golf for three months without hobbling."

●

How do you know if you have inflammation? There are four classic symptoms: redness, swelling, heat, and pain. Since inflammation suggests fire, I usually tell my patients that the symptoms of inflammation are the product of their bodies' automatic fire-fighting response. In fact, there is a simple medical explanation for each of the symptoms of inflammation.

Redness occurs because your body automatically increases the blood supply to any area that is diseased or injured. When a sportache is acute or chronic, you have sustained a sort of injury. You've been subjecting your body to stress while playing your favorite game, and key structures supporting a joint have been strained. Your body sends blood to nourish or repair the problem, as it would to combat infection or respond to trauma. It isn't easy to distinguish redness in someone whose skin is black, brown, or red. But it may still be happening.

Swelling takes place because of a chemical chain reaction. Your injury or stress results in damage to body cells, which release chemicals, actually enzymes. These enzymes cause a change in the walls of small blood vessels or capillaries, allowing the escape of fluid into adjoining body space. As time goes on, other chemicals, proteins, clot and wall off the injured area, making the swelling firm.

Heat is the result of increased blood supply. Although heat often accompanies redness, it's possible to experience heat without redness. For instance, your tendons don't have a direct blood supply. Nevertheless, because they are surrounded by a protective tube, the chemical changes described above, which take place as the result of stress or injury, can result in an increased blood supply even in those tissues.

Pain results from increased irritation of nerve endings in the stressed area. It's not completely clear whether this is a result of a chemical reaction or a function of direct pressure of various body tissue upon your nerves.

•

Do all four elements have to be present for you or your doctor to diagnose inflammation? Not really. One element should be considered an isolated finding. However, two or three of the above symptoms make inflammation just about a sure thing.

We had a striking example of this distinction after the 1980

Boston Marathon. As usual after the marathon, our office was flooded with complaining runners. I remember two patients in particular.

Herb Stein explained to me that he had been able to find enough time in his day to conduct a busy law practice in addition to a busy training schedule. He had come into the 1980 marathon looking for his fastest time ever. Herb had qualified well enough so that he started toward the front of the pack.

As he described it, Herb had never quite realized how hard and fast some runners could start until the gun sounded in Hopkinton and the runners broke. He said he felt as if he were in a crowd trying to rush up the subway stairs. Thinking back, he remembered being jostled a good bit. In fact, someone had apparently stepped on the back of his left leg right around the area of the Achilles' tendon. However, in the excitement of the race, Herb quickly forgot about the start, going on to make his personal record.

The next day, when he woke up, Herb felt a kind of stiffness that wasn't unusual for the day after a marathon. He examined his left leg and noticed that there was a welt on the back of his Achilles' tendon. There also appeared to be some swelling. Since he is a serious runner, Herb stopped by to be checked out at our office.

I quickly determined that Herb had no significant pain when I touched his leg or when he moved it. His swelling was minimal, and the redness, I felt, was the result of the blow he finally remembered receiving once I got him to think about the race. Herb was going to be all right without any treatment whatsoever. His lower leg wasn't inflamed.

In contrast, Charlie Johnson came in later that same day with a relatively serious problem. Like many of us, Charlie had not managed to put in all the training miles he wanted before the marathon. His fitness had suffered accordingly. Moreover, during the last five weeks before the race, he had been nursing an occasional pain. Nevertheless, he'd never noticed swelling in his left Achilles' tendon, the site of his pain. His left leg had really bothered him after an eighteen-mile run, but he figured that was only normal. After all, he hadn't run eighteen miles in months.

The 1980 Boston Marathon took place on a warm day. Like many runners, Charlie started off at too fast a pace. With his relative lack of training, Charlie found himself at the bottom of Heartbreak Hill almost ready to quit. However, he had come all the way from Minneapolis to race, and he wasn't going to go home a quitter. He persevered. When we saw him the next day, Charlie had every symptom: swelling, heat, pain, and redness. He limped into my office. My diagnosis? Charlie had an inflamed Achilles' tendon, which required immediate, aggressive anti-inflammatory treatment.

•

The suffix *-itis* means inflammation. If you visit your doctor for help in treating an acute or chronic sportache, he or she may tell you that you have an "-itis." That means you need treatment for inflammation.

How can you control inflammation? Unless your pain and other symptoms are so acute or chronic that you're becoming desperate, you should always consider self-help before turning to a doctor.

We're living in the do-it-yourself age. Most of us can't afford to call a plumber every time the sink leaks. We don't race to a garage every time the family vehicle squeaks or rattles. We can't call a lawyer about every trivial legal problem. And we wouldn't think of hiring an accountant to balance our personal checkbooks. It's simply too expensive not to be basically self-sufficient in the last part of the twentieth century.

Money isn't the only reason we find ourselves on our own with small problems. It's also very difficult nowadays to locate competent people who will provide minor services. Faced with day-to-day problems, most people quickly learn to be self-sufficient.

In no area is informed self-help of more vital importance than in medicine. Medical costs have skyrocketed. Although your insurance may cover a lot of things, it can't cover everything. Also, there's never any guarantee that you'll be able to see "the top man." For that matter, you may not be able to get a quick appointment with any doctor. All of us must therefore learn to cope with minor illnesses, cuts, scrapes, and other ailments.

With sportaches, self-help is essential. Professional medical treatment is not only very expensive and difficult to obtain, in most cases, it's also a waste of time. Even a sports-oriented

physician usually won't be of much help if you have a simple sportache. Doctors are trained to deal with disease and injury. Sportaches are the pains of fitness. When you have a sportache — at least while your ache is only occasional — you aren't sick and you haven't been injured. Therefore, self-help isn't just practical: it's usually your only option.

A sportache that bothers you only while you're playing your favorite sport is *not* a medical problem. Everyone, including doctors, must recognize that the only proper treatment for a simple sportache is self-help. Until inflammation sets in, relief from a sportache can only be obtained through application of EEVeTeC. If you have a sportache, you need to make appropriate adjustments in your equipment, environment, velocity, technique, or conditioning. A doctor usually can't help.

Granted, you may wonder from time to time if you are doing the right thing. In that case, I can only hope you have a doctor you feel comfortable consulting over the phone. Though a "diagnosis," as such, can't be given over the phone, an informed opinion can. If you are so inclined, I would suggest to you, as I do to all of my patients, that you call your doctor and talk about your problem, even if you decide to try self-help first.

Sometimes a doctor can help with occasional aches. I frequently recommend orthotics to my athlete patients. These special shoe inserts often help relieve lower-extremity sportaches. While orthotics don't always have to be designed and fitted by

Chances are, your doctor won't know enough about your sport to help.

an expert, special training in their prescription can make a real difference in whether or not they have the desired effect.

If you're lucky, your doctor may know enough about your favorite sport to make suggestions about equipment, environment, velocity, technique, or conditioning. Chances are, however, that coaches, trainers, and equipment specialists will be more helpful.

•

Unless you think an orthotic or other medically prescribed brace may be the answer in your case, you don't need to see a doctor for your sportaches — at least not unless your symptoms have become acute or chronic. Likewise, even if inflammation has set in, although you'll need treatment for your redness, swelling, heat, and pain, you still don't have to rule out self-help. You have a medical problem (inflammation) that requires medical treatment. However, you may be able to act as your own doctor.

The medical community has many different diagnostic and therapeutic options at its disposal. However, most doctors will attempt to control your inflammation conservatively before deploying any sophisticated weapon. The fact of the matter is that you may be able to do just as well on your own, at least if your inflammation is mild. Therefore, shouldn't you try to obtain relief yourself — before calling the doctor?

Rest, use ice, and take aspirin. If this time-honored treatment works, great. You'll have saved yourself the expense and inconvenience of a medical appointment. On the other hand, if your condition doesn't improve in a week or ten days, then you and your physician will know that your symptoms require more aggressive treatment. Likewise, if your condition worsens despite

your best effort at self-help, you'll be absolutely certain you need a doctor.

Never ignore the symptoms of inflammation. When a sport-ache goes on to bother you all the time, your body is no longer merely warning you to slow down. Nonstop pain is a signal that it's too late to experiment with adjustments in your equipment, environment, velocity, technique, and conditioning. You have a medical problem requiring immediate treatment.

Let's say that your elbow now hurts when you write, shake hands, and shift gears in your car, and not just when you mis-hit your backhand. Or your knee throbs with every step you take as you walk, not just when you run. Or hip pain has you tossing and turning at night and is no longer just a problem when you use your sand wedge. The McGregor Solution could have saved you considerable pain and expense if you had used it when your ache was only occasional. However, it's now too late merely to adjust your EEVeTeC. Still . . . do you really need a doctor? Not necessarily. A variety of self-help procedures are available.

•

If you're going to be your own doctor, you'll have to do some of the same things a doctor would do in the same situation. Compile your own medical history. List any and all previous injuries, surgical procedures, or diseases that might have contributed to the development of your ache. Next, carefully monitor your symptoms. Compare your present discomfort with other occasions when you've experienced significant pain. If your symptoms seem especially acute or your pain seems to be localized in a bone, self-help may be unwise. Likewise, if you're having trouble with a joint that has previously been injured or operated on, remember that such a joint is not "normal." Even if your discomfort is mild, you should see a doctor immediately. Self-help is for "normal" bodies.

In the battle against inflammation the only real difference between what you can do for yourself and what your doctor can do for you is a matter of degree. Doctors have access to special equipment and powerful drugs, as well as having the exclusive right to perform surgery. Generally, however, self-help and doctor help are quite similar.

Self-help falls into three general categories: mechanical, thermal, and chemical.

Mechanical

Rest

The simplest method of combating inflammation is to rest. You must give the part of your body that hurts a brief opportunity to heal itself.

With an upper-extremity sportache, you may want to try a sling or splint. Your pharmacy or surgical supply store has a variety of styles. Simple bandaging, typically with an elastic bandage, also may help. If you're moving around a lot, you may have to adjust your bandage frequently to ensure adequate immobilization.

For lower-extremity sportaches try crutches or a cane. (Use a cane on the side opposite your aching limb.) Rigid splints, though effective, are difficult to apply yourself. However, some flexible splints and braces are available and practical. Simple bandaging also may help, though constant readjustment may again be required.

Be sure you don't "overdose" when it comes to rest. Though you should definitely minimize stress for a few days, rest can quickly become counterproductive. Remember, your joints are mobilized and stabilized by muscles. Prolonged rest can produce muscle atrophy, a decrease in muscle strength and bulk. Atrophy doesn't take long to begin. Since muscle atrophy increases your susceptibility to aches, complete rest isn't a good idea for more than a short time, and then only in conjunction with other anti-inflammatory measures. After a few days you should try to do at least a minimum of exercise daily, carefully staying within the limits of pain.

When you begin an exercise program after a short period of rest, your initial goal should be to achieve a full range of motion in the joint or joints that have been bothering you. You may need someone to help you in the beginning, but your objective should be to achieve a full range of motion on your own, without pain. Then, gradually, you'll want to move the limb in question through its range of motion against resistance. This can be done with a partner applying progressive nondisabling resistance or by exercising with weights. Never exercise in the presence of pain, but try constantly to increase the challenge to the bone-joint-muscle system.

Compression

If you can gently squeeze or compress the site of your ache, you can help your body absorb excess fluid. Your swelling should go down. Compression may even prevent further swelling. If the pressure of fluid is causing your pain, compression — not too tight — may also bring pain relief.

The best way to apply compression is with an elastic bandage, readjusting it as needed. What you want is broad and complete compression. If the bandage you use is too narrow, it can cause pinching, with resultant swelling at the edges. Discoloration and a pins-and-needles or altered sensation can also be caused if your bandage is too tight. Obviously, that should be avoided. Also, remember that a moderate increase in swelling is to be expected at the end of the day, so it may be necessary to loosen your bandage after several hours of wear.

Elevation

Elevation is always recommended for swelling. The idea is to let gravity help your body fight inflammation by draining excess fluid. Your recovery should be faster if you can find a way to raise your inflamed joint higher than the next nearest joint.

If your wrist is swollen, put your arm in a sling so that your wrist is higher than your elbow. If your elbow is swollen, lie down or sit with your elbow higher than your shoulder. If your ankle is swollen, it should be higher than your knee, and if your knee is swollen, it should be higher than your hip.

Thermal

Cold

First-aid practitioners frequently talk about RICE. It's not their choice for dinner. RICE is a mnemonic, composed of the first letters of its four ingredients: rest, ice, compression, and elevation — four steps in the treatment of acute injury. RICE works for acute or chronic sportaches too. In fact, for sportaches, RICE is the key to self-help, not just a stopgap while waiting for the doctor. Rest, compression, and elevation are the basic mechanical responses to inflammation; ice is the most important thermal weapon.

Medical people have long used ice on fresh injuries. Recently, however, an increasing number of authorties have begun to recommend the ongoing use of ice (instead of heat), even after the first few days.

Heat is the second basic thermal option. My experience, both

as a doctor and an athlete, has been that cold (ice) is clearly superior to heat, both as first aid and as an important part of most rehabilitation efforts.

Why ice for sportaches? First, ice reduces swelling. Cold produces immediate vasoconstriction, a decrease in the size of blood vessels. When your blood vessels constrict the resultant decrease in blood flow tends to cause your swelling to decrease. Since a primary effect of heat is vasodilatation — which increases both blood flow and the potential for swelling — heat doesn't tend to be nearly as effective in minimizing swelling. Remember, you have to reduce swelling early in your treatment of an inflamed joint.

Once you've controlled swelling, I believe you should still stick with ice. After RICE has begun to reduce your other symptoms, you'll want to start exercising your injured limb. Moderate exercise is necessary to preserve muscle tone and bulk, as well as to minimize your susceptibility to reinflammation. At this stage, try to find the time to apply cold for ten to fifteen minutes before and after regular, gentle movement. Ice is a mild, temporary anesthetic. It allows you to exercise without excessive pain. Ice thus promotes deep circulation, at least if you exercise a limb after icing it.

Take that occasional tennis elbow pain that has been bothering you for years. Imagine that it suddenly flares up. There hasn't been any sudden, dramatic injury. Your ache has simply become an -itis. What do you do? Probably, you'll decide to quit playing tennis for a while. You may not have a choice. It will hurt just to hold a racket, much less swing it.

Since you've never had an elbow injury or operation, and since your symptoms are bearable, let's assume that you decide to try self-help. To rest your elbow, you may choose to put your arm in a sling during the day and wear a splint on your wrist at night. To reduce swelling, you may wrap an Ace bandage loosely around your forearm and elbow. In addition, for at least a couple of days, you should ice your elbow as often as possible, taking care not to injure your skin by applying the ice directly or by going more than fifteen minutes without letting your elbow gradually return to normal temperature.

After two or three days, let's assume that self-help seems to be bringing perceptible relief. You should then continue with ice

therapy. For the next few days ice your elbow, do some gentle range-of-motion exercises (perhaps hitting a tennis ball lightly), and after exercising, reapply cold. This technique is known as cryotherapy.

Cold can be applied in a variety of ways. Remember, however, to be careful. Ice, like fire, can "burn." For elbows, wrists, ankles, and feet, ice immersion is a good technique for application of cold, although a quantity of ice is required. Fill a bowl or bucket with ice cubes and cold water. Grit your teeth and dunk your aching joint a few times. Then hold it in the ice bath for eight or ten minutes.

Ice massage is another possibility. I recommend freezing water in a Styrofoam cup. The cup protects your hand and can be peeled away as needed when the ice begins to melt. Keep the ice moving over and around your sore joint. Be careful not to "burn" your skin.

Perhaps the simplest ice application method involves wrapping some ice cubes in a washcloth and taping or holding it against your limb. An extra advantage: As the ice melts, the cloth will gradually conform to the shape of your joint. When you're done the first time, you can simply put the wrap into a freezer for a perfect fit the next time.

Never use ice more than twelve to fifteen minutes at a time. As soon as you notice redness, stop your ice therapy for a few minutes while you rest or exercise.

Heat

Though cold is a must for swelling and is increasingly preferred during rehabilitative exercise, a number of experts still recommend heat once your swelling has subsided.

Unlike ice, heat feels good. Without a doubt, that's important. You may also find that your ache responds better to heat before exercise and ice afterward instead of cold both before and after. By all means experiment, keeping two important things in mind. Though heat feels good, it's definitely more effective if you try to move your aching limb a bit after each application. However, heat doesn't provide the mild anesthetic effect of ice. Also, prolonged use of heat can increase swelling. So, be careful. Resist the temptation to leave that soothing heat source on your aching limb for more than twenty to thirty minutes.

Heat can be applied in several ways. For moist heat, use hot towels over or around your aching limb, perhaps covering them with plastic wrap to retain heat and retard natural cooling. Or you may want to try soaking in a hot tub or shower. For dry heat, many people prefer hot-water bottles or heating pads. Moist or dry? It's up to you. Remember, however, that dry heat tends to provide a more constant source of soothing warmth.

One final note. There's considerable controversy over how much heat can be driven through your skin to your deeper tissues, which is where most sportaches develop. One thing is certain. Just by leaving a heating pad or hot-water bottle on longer or by making it hotter, you won't necessarily increase the benefits of heat therapy.

In fact, the more heat you employ, the greater the danger of burning yourself. Your skin's natural resistance to constant heat can be reduced if you aren't careful. If you use a heating pad, for instance, set it on medium for a short time, then turn it down to low.

Contrast Baths

A third type of thermal therapy can be to use heat and cold alternately. Contrast baths are usually done in buckets or basins. Hold your aching limb in one bucket or basin for five minutes, then quickly move it to the other. Continue this routine for half an hour. The theory is that quick changes from hot to cold will stimulate your body to marshal its healing powers. By all means try contrast baths, especially if your inflammation doesn't seem to be responding to either ice or heat alone.

Chemical Though over-the-counter anti-inflammatory drugs are relatively mild, they are by no means ineffective. The best, most readily available, least expensive, and least harmful nonprescription anti-inflammatory drug is acetylsalicylic acid — aspirin. Aspirin can produce an immediate anti-inflammatory effect. Heavy doses — up to eight or ten tablets a day — may relieve the symptoms of an acute or chronic sportache, especially if you also follow the four steps of RICE.

Your ache may eventually require a stronger drug, perhaps something that your doctor will either prescribe or inject locally. While you're still at the self-help stage, however, the best chemical weapon is aspirin.

Aspirin isn't without its drawbacks. It can interfere with normal blood clotting, cause internal bleeding (disastrous for gastric or duodenal ulcer sufferers), and, in some sensitive people, produce nausea and other gastrointestinal reactions, especially in the relatively large dosages required when you are treating inflammation.

Coated or buffered aspirin may help. The coating prevents a chemical reaction from taking place in the sensitive part of your stomach and small intestine. The drug passes to a less sensitive area before being absorbed into your blood stream.

Caveat emptor: The "harmless" aspirin alternatives — Tylenol, Datril, and so on — that have flooded the market recently cannot fight inflammation. Buy real aspirin if you're trying to manage an acute or chronic ache.

•

Self-help is not always advisable when you're faced with an acute or chronic ache. Sometimes, delay in seeking expert medical help can prove disastrous. How do you know when to do it yourself and when to see a doctor? Unfortunately, there are no hard-and-fast rules. You'll have to let common sense — and careful self-examination — guide you. There are, however, some classic situations that you should avoid. If any of the following stories sounds like yours, you probably should not treat yourself, even for a few days.

For a number of years, Dick was my neighbor in Concord, Massachusetts. We ran our first marathon together in Boston several years ago. Dick was half my age and had been a good college athlete. Though he ran that first marathon in worn tennis sneakers, he has since become a serious runner: several marathons, many races, the best equipment. Dick has always considered himself an athlete. Nevertheless, like so many of us, he has sometimes taken his body for granted.

One Sunday night, a few weeks before the 1979 Boston Marathon, my phone rang at home. It was Dick. "Rob," he said, "I'm in trouble. My right leg is red, swollen, and painful. I think it's too late for rest, ice, and aspirin. I can't run. I can't even walk without pain. Boston is only five weeks away. Help!"

When I got to my office the next morning, Dick was already there. His suspicions and my fears were confirmed. He'd developed gross swelling and inflammation in the muscles in the front of his leg — a condition I diagnosed as anterior compartment syndrome. Rather than plunging ahead with self-treatment for an undiagnosed problem, Dick had done the right thing to call.

Together we reviewed his history. It gradually became clear that Dick had carelessly ignored several important warnings from his body. As we talked, I learned that Dick had recently completed a race in New York's Central Park during which he remembered experiencing unusual leg pain. Just before the race — for which, he confessed, he hadn't adequately warmed up — Dick had repaired his running shoes, rebuilding a worn-out portion at the outside of his heel. We decided that he had apparently added too much new material. As a result, the heel and sole of his shoe had started to roll to the inside. To maintain his foot in its most stable position, Dick had overworked the muscles in the front of his right leg. During and after the race his right leg had bothered him, but he had ignored the pain. Dick refused to interrupt his training for Boston, despite increasingly persistent discomfort.

By the time Dick came to see me it really was too late for self-help. In my office in March Dick presented all four classic symptoms of inflammation: his pain was acute, and in addition he had serious swelling and visible redness, as well as a constant sensation of heat.

Case History 1: Dick Hudson

Dick and I decided to employ aggressive, anti-inflammatory therapy. I prescribed a strong anti-inflammatory drug. In addition, Dick switched to alternate training methods (biking and swimming) to maintain his fitness while staying off his feet. With luck and hard work he managed to run — and finish — the 1979 marathon. Of course, he had to go a lot more slowly than he liked.

The moral of Dick's story is simple. If your symptoms include all four cardinal signs of inflammation — especially swelling — don't risk self-help. See a doctor immediately. Your problem is serious, and you should take the precaution of getting expert diagnosis and treatment.

If your problem developed slowly, like Dick's, you've had your opportunity to try self-help and blown it. If your pain, swelling, redness, and heat developed overnight, you probably have an injury instead of a sportache. Either way, you're *not* a candidate for self-help.

Case History 2: George Jenkins

I tell patients like George to telephone before coming to see me. George, in his mid-fifties, is semiretired, but he's anxious to stay fit. He lives four hours from Boston. We've worked together to manage a variety of problems George has encountered with his feet during the past few years. Often he treats his own aches without even checking with me. Sometimes, however, he panics.

Recently, George telephoned me late one evening. "Rob," he said over the phone, "I think it's that damned bursitis again. It's my right foot. It hurts even though I've stopped running. I tried aspirin, even those pills you gave me for acute bursitis last year. No good, I still have pain."

"George," I asked, "have you changed anything recently in your running routine?"

"Nope, been running two or three miles three or four times a week, just like always this past year."

"I'm not sure it's bursitis," I responded. "Take off your shoe. Press the bones on the top, not the bottom, of your foot, just ahead of where they join your toes. Does one hurt more than another?"

"My God, yes! The second one hurts like hell. And it's swollen right where it hurts. What is it, Rob?"

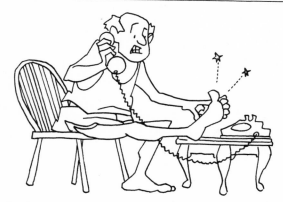

"Sounds like a stress fracture. Don't horse around. Get here as soon as possible."

As I would do with any patient in a similar situation, when George arrived in my office the next day I ordered a fresh set of X-rays of his foot. Comparison with previous X-rays indicated a hazy change right around the painful spot. Additional views, taken during the next twelve weeks, showed the classic pattern of bone reaction and repair.

There was one point of departure, however. Views taken three weeks after George's initial visit showed a slight crack on both sides of the bone. Given too much stress at that point, George could have suffered a complete fracture.

While he was waiting for the stress fracture in his foot to heal, George continued his fitness program with bicycling and swimming. Within two months, he was running again.

The moral of George's story: Be suspicious of bone pain, especially if it's combined with swelling. See a doctor. Have X-rays taken. Don't try self-help, at least until you're sure you don't have a stress fracture.

Case History 3: Mary McKenna

Mary had forgotten all about the time she had twisted her left knee on the ski slopes during her senior year at college. She had stayed off her feet for a couple of weeks after the accident, using crutches. The ugly swelling around her knee had eventually subsided and the joint had never bothered her again. Like many people who have made a seemingly complete recovery after joint injury or surgery, Mary never gave her "damaged" knee a second thought as an adult.

Of course, for about twenty years after college, Mary had never skied again or participated seriously in any other sports. She had become a wife and mother immediately. Nevertheless, when I first saw Mary, she was approaching forty and had become very anxious to get fit. In fact, she was in training at the time for a Bonne Bell ten-kilometer road race, having accepted a challenge from her eldest daughter, a high school track star.

Jogging, Mary had decided, was an excellent way to get into shape. She especially liked the idea that running had started to help her lose some of the thirty excess pounds she'd collected over the years. The fact that she was locked into a deadline — three months until race day — seemed particularly attractive. Like many other busy men and women, Mary had tended to procrastinate in the past when it came to her own health. She told me the typical saga of repeated diet attempts, half-fulfilled health-club memberships, and broken New Year's resolutions. But now, finally, she had found an activity she enjoyed. And it was working!

Mary had purchased several books about running. She had obtained proper footwear and was following a sensible training schedule. Nevertheless, about three weeks into her training, her left knee had begun to hurt during her daily run. The pattern of pain persisted and increased. By the fifth week nothing Mary tried seemed to help. She tried new shoes, running on a cinder track, aspirin, and other variations. Zero. In fact, every time she got out of a chair, her knee seemed to lock. Eventually, Mary noticed perceptible swelling. Even though she had stopped running, her knee pain persisted night and day. That's when she finally decided to come to my office.

Mary and I decided that her previously injured knee should be checked by an orthopedist. His subsequent examination revealed a torn cartilage of long standing, a by-product of Mary's long-forgotten ski accident. The stress of running had awakened the quiescent knee. If Mary had persisted in running she could have caused irreversible bone damage. In her stubborn effort to "run through" her initial knee pain, Mary had already risked permanent damage to the joint.

Swift, judicious surgery eliminated the cause of Mary's knee pain and bone damage. She is now biking, swimming, and playing tennis — still avoiding the exceptional stress of running. In-

cidentally, she has lost weight and recently told me she is content to go through life beating her husband at tennis.

The moral of Mary's story: Previous, often forgotten, injury or surgery can render a joint pain-free, but not normal. Under stress, especially constant stress, such a joint can flare up, causing irreversible damage. Are your joints "normal"? Not if they've been injured or operated upon surgically in the past. Only an ache in a normal joint should be treated without medical advice.

•

How long is it safe to be your own doctor? If your acute or chronic symptoms begin to subside after a few days, you should continue to do what you're doing until your pain and other symptoms are completely gone. You know your body better than anyone else, including your doctor. If self-help seems to be working, don't let anyone tell you that you need pills, shots, or surgery.

Remember that once your inflammation passes, you'll still

have to address your underlying problem. If you go right back onto the tennis court, golf course, or running track, you'll probably find that your ache returns almost immediately. You need to make adjustments in your equipment, environment, velocity, technique, or conditioning. Don't forget EEVeTeC, just because the crisis of inflammation has passed. Otherwise, you'll be back on the sidelines again before you know it.

If self-help doesn't produce perceptible results within a week to ten days, or if your symptoms worsen, call a doctor. You've done the best you can on your own: now you need an expert.

11
OK, Doctor, It's Your Turn

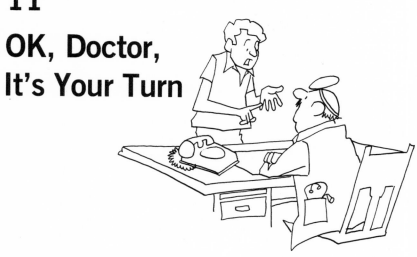

WHEN SHOULD YOU SEE a doctor for your sportaches? By now you should be able to answer that question without a moment's hesitation. If your ache is only occasional, you don't have a medical problem. You probably don't need medical treatment. Instead, you need to make appropriate adjustments within the context of your sport. EEVeTeC is your answer.

There is really only one exception to the rule that you don't need a doctor for your occasional aches: If the joint now bothering you has ever been injured or operated upon, or if you think you may have arthritis, you should see your doctor at the first sign of pain. You probably should have checked with a doctor before taking up your sport. Abnormal bodies require exceptional care. In most instances, however, you'll be wasting both your time and your money to go to a doctor for treatment of a simple sportache. Doctors generally can't help unless you've developed symptoms of inflammation.

Certain acute or chronic aches do require expert medical help. Remember, however, if you consult a doctor about an acute or chronic sportache, you should expect treatment *only* for your inflammation. You'll still have to apply the McGregor Solution to your ache once your inflammation has subsided.

If you've developed symptoms of inflammation and you've

decided that you need to see a doctor, your first question will probably be the same question that most people would ask in your situation: "Where do I go?" Acute or chronic inflammation is a common medical problem. All licensed practitioners are familiar with it. Nevertheless, the symptoms of inflammation can be difficult to control and eliminate.

You'll want to take your inflamed limb to a doctor who is familiar with the management of inflammation in otherwise healthy and active people, a doctor with a long-term interest in your health, as well as a real commitment to your continued participation in sports. Finding such a doctor, however, may be difficult.

•

The medical community has developed an elaborate referral system, based on the assumption that treatment for illness and injury is best performed by specialists. When it comes to managing the pains of fitness, however, the traditional medical referral system doesn't work as well as it should. Unfortunately, most doctors with the specialized knowledge to cope with sportaches are already very busy taking care of injuries, emergencies, bone disease, and a heavy operating schedule.

Doctors respond best to the challenge of disease or injury. However, acute or chronic sportaches require management, in contrast to traditional medical treatment. That's why the traditional medical referral system begins to break down when you have a sportache.

If you have developed an acute or chronic sportache and you have a family doctor or a doctor friend, by all means call and ask for a referral. If your own doctor asks to see you first, make an appointment, especially if he or she is involved in sports and likely to know what you're going through.

If you are referred to a specialist, phone ahead. Ask if the doctor treats sports-related problems. Regardless, you should probably make an appointment. At this stage, you need to be certain that what you have is an ache, not an injury or disease. Like it or not, you are going to have to spend some time and money in a doctor's office.

What if you don't know a doctor you can turn to for advice or help? In that case, one excellent way of joining an informal "referral" network is to ask around at your local club, park, or

playground. Talk to people involved in your sport — coaches, equipment experts, other athletes. Sportaches, after all, are very common. Lots of people in your community will have gone through exactly what you are going through now. In no time, you'll probably have the names of at least one or two local doctors with a reputation for dealing effectively with the pains of fitness.

This informal system isn't infallible, but it generally works so well that you might consider using it even if you have a family doctor or physician friend who can also plug you into the traditional medical referral system.

What about a sportsmedicine clinic? It's safe to assume that the doctors at a sportsmedicine clinic will have at least a passing interest in sports, as well as a degree of familiarity with athletic ailments. Remember, however, that sportsmedicine clinics deal primarily with injuries, not aches. Also, at least a few doctors have gone into sportsmedicine because it's fashionable and they think it's lucrative and not because of any particular interest in the dilemma of the recreational athlete.

Sportsmedicine is just beginning to attract doctors who are totally committed to increasing their understanding of the physiology and biomechanics of sport, doctors as dedicated to working with joggers, hackers, or duffers as they are to treating pro teams and celebrity athletes. However, there's still no guarantee that you'll receive any better treatment for your inflammation at a sportsmedicine clinic than from any other knowledgeable, interested practitioner.

If you're determined to try a sportsmedicine doctor, there are a couple of things you ought to know, in addition to the fact that recreational athletes don't always get as much attention as the pros. Within the national orthopedic, podiatric, osteopathic, and chiropractic societies there are official sportsmedicine groups or "colleges" many members join. A "nondenominational" group is the American College of Sports Medicine. All the various sportsmedicine groups or colleges provide educational information in the form of journals and meetings to their members. The designation "fellow" after his or her name means that the member has met and maintained special qualifications.

By all means, try your local sportsmedicine specialist. He or she may prove a highly satisfactory partner in the management of your acute or chronic sportaches. However, the only sure thing is that you'll see fewer wheelchairs and more running shoes in the waiting room at a sportsmedicine clinic than you would in the average orthopedist's office.

•

Do you have to go to an M.D.? Absolutely not. If you're suffering from an acute or chronic sportache, any licensed practitioner may be able to help. Recreational athletes regularly report excellent long-term results after taking their problems to acupuncturists, osteopaths, chiropractors, and other non-M.D. doctors. In addition, I know that many of my fellow podiatrists are contributing greatly to the management of lower-extremity sportaches.

Nevertheless, the majority of recreational athletes who seek medical help end up in the hands of an orthopedic surgeon. Don't be surprised if it happens to you. Remember, you have a joint problem, and orthopedists are joint specialists. When you plug into the medical referral system (traditional or informal), the input "joint problem" produces the output "orthopedist." It's almost automatic.

An orthopedist's waiting room is quite a place. You'll find the elderly, the obese, the lame, and the obviously injured. Your fellow patients will have crutches, canes, even wheelchairs. No doubt you'll feel out of place. You should. You're suffering from the pains of fitness; the people around you are sick or injured. You want to run; many of them would be delighted to walk.

Check your orthopedist's weekly schedule. If he or she has an active surgical practice, office hours are probably sandwiched between shifts of surgery and hospital rounds. When it's

An orthopedist's waiting room is quite a place.

time for your appointment, your doctor may just have come from surgery or from seeing a patient who will never have a normally functioning body. Your primary concern right now is running, tennis, or golf. Do you really think this doctor is going to share your sense of urgency about your ache? Be realistic.

Margo's story is a good example of how the medical referral system can frustrate the recreational athlete. What happened to this forty-year-old tennis enthusiast is also a sad commentary on what can happen if you take your sportache to a doctor, even if all you want is treatment for your inflammation — which, after all, the medical community should be able to provide — and not advice about how to use EEVeTeC to deal with your underlying problem.

At the start of the 1979 tennis season, Margo was bothered by some pain in her left knee. Since her husband is himself a prominent surgeon, she was able to obtain an emergency appointment with one of the world's authorities on sports-related knee injuries. With only a few days' notice — this doctor, like many others who are well known, is normally impossible to see without an appointment made months in advance — she saw a New York orthopedist who is a living legend in the sportsmedicine community.

Here's how Margo described the visit: "He examined my knee briefly, checked my X-rays, and quickly described some strengthening exercises he said I should do every day. 'Stay off your knee for two months,' he ordered, before heading for the door. 'But it's the beginning of summer,' I exclaimed. 'What about tennis?' Already in the hall, the doctor paused, looked back, and barked, 'Make it three months.' ''

Obviously, you should research your medical options in advance, before your symptoms become acute or chronic. Even better, try to heed your body's warnings of impending trouble. Use EEVeTeC. Adjust your equipment, environment, velocity, technique, and conditioning at the first sign of a sportache. If you can prevent your ache from becoming acute or chronic, you'll avoid the need to spend time and money with a doctor.

Let's assume, however, that you've decided you do need a doctor. Moreover, let's say you've determined where to go. Next, you need to be prepared to evaluate the treatment you're going to receive. After all, the first doctor you see may not be the best doctor *for you*.

You should expect two things from any doctor:

1. A *diagnosis* — his or her opinion, in terms you can understand, as to what is causing your pain and other symptoms.
2. A *prescription* — your doctor's suggested course of action. This may or may not include a piece of paper authorizing a pharmacy to sell you certain drugs. Without exception, however, your doctor's prescription should be accompanied by expert advice on what you can do to rehabilitate your aching limb, in addition to controlling your inflammation.

If you are not satisfied with the treatment you receive at the hands of a doctor, don't be shy. Ask questions. It's your body — your ache — and you have every right to insist that any doctor you see be thorough and precise about his or her diagnosis and prescription.

Diagnosis is a two-step process. First, your doctor will need to take a detailed history of your complaint. Then there should be at least a brief examination.

The history your doctor will take should include many of the same questions you would ask yourself if you were compiling your own medical history. To be certain that you and your doctor waste as little time as possible, you should prepare your answers to obvious background questions in advance. Be as thorough as possible. Remember, your doctor needs medical information, not a sports history. Your sports history will be key later, when you are trying to use the McGregor Solution to avoid a relapse. At present, however, you have medical symptoms that must be resolved before you can use EEVeTeC to eliminate your problem once and for all.

Most doctors will begin their examination of you with an X-ray of your aching joint. Although there's justifiable public concern about unnecessary X-rays, an X-ray of an acutely or chronically inflamed joint is an essential diagnostic step. In this instance the benefits of X-ray far outweigh the risks. No doctor can be certain you don't have an injury or disease without first seeing an X-ray. If your ache were causing only occasional discomfort, you might argue that an X-ray would be unnecessary. But when you have acute pain, an X-ray is absolutely required. In fact, you shouldn't balk if your doctor also wants to X-ray the opposite, uninvolved joint. What may appear "abnormal" in one of the joints of an arm or leg may be the same in the other limb and, therefore, "normal" for *you*.

Next, you should expect a hands-on examination. Your doctor will touch and move your painful limb. You must cooperate. Try to answer fully and thoughtfully when your doctor asks what you feel as he or she palpates your painful joint and tests its range of motion. Remember, if you're not willing to participate in the diagnosis and treatment of your condition, you're wasting time and money at the doctor's office.

Worse than the uncooperative patient is the disinterested doc-

tor. Your symptoms may be common and your problem may appear easy to diagnose, but no responsible physician should ever jump to conclusions. Unfortunately, it happens more than it should.

Let's say your doctor asks a couple of cursory questions, glances at your X-rays, tugs at your aching limb once or twice, scribbles a prescription, and then heads for the door. By all means, speak up. You're not some crackpot in off the street feigning illness or injury. You're in pain. You've either tried self-help or your problem is acute. You want and deserve answers. You have every right to expect a well-formulated diagnosis from your doctor, in addition to detailed advice about treatment. If he or she doesn't have the time to ask and answer relevant questions, find another doctor immediately.

You should certainly expect your doctor to present the diagnosis of your problem in terms you can understand. Since your symptoms are the symptoms of inflammation, don't be surprised to hear a medical term ending in -itis, meaning that the part in question is inflamed. But your doctor shouldn't just throw an "-itis" at you. He or she should take time to explain, in lay terms, what exactly is meant by the diagnosis.

When your elbow was bothering you only on the tennis court, there was no need for technical mumbo jumbo. You had elbow pain. That's all. You may have been heading toward tennis elbow or epicondylitis, as the doctors call it. But you weren't there yet, and there was no reason for you or anyone else to use medical terminology.

Now that your elbow pain has become acute or chronic, however, it is appropriate for your doctor to use terms like lateral epicondylitis or medial epicondylitis. Such diagnostic terms pinpoint your problem. You don't have a fracture or a dislocation. Nor do you have bursitis or tendinitis. If your condition is diagnosed as epicondylitis, you have inflammation of the area immediately around the epicondyle (bump in your elbow bone) either on the outside (lateral side) or on the inside (medial side) of the joint.

When you are treating a simple sportache on your own, it doesn't matter whether your occasional twinges are the result of stress to a tendon, bursa, muscle, ligament, or other tissue. The McGregor Solution is the only way to eliminate your ache, and EEVeTeC doesn't require that you pinpoint your potential medical problem to relieve your present symptoms. Even if you have some acute or chronic pain, if you've decided to try treating your inflammation on your own first, you don't need to consult a medical dictionary. However, if your discomfort is severe enough to prompt you to go to a doctor — or if self-help hasn't worked or doesn't seem appropriate — a medical diagnosis is something you should welcome and not resist. Your problem must be precisely identified before your doctor can select the appropriate anti-inflammatory treatment. Make certain you understand what the diagnosis means, but don't be put off by your doctor's effort to label your problem medically. The label is an important part of what you're paying for in a doctor's office.

Your doctor's *prescription,* his or her plan of action, should accompany the diagnosis of your problem. Most doctors will recommend conservative treatment first. However, your particular needs can make a difference. Let's say you've already tried self-help — RICE plus aspirin. Or perhaps you can convince your doctor that you urgently need to eliminate your inflammation (because of work, travel, a competition, or whatever). He or she may then prescribe relatively aggressive anti-inflammatory measures from the outset. Usually, however, doctors will suggest RICE first — all the more reason for you to employ self-help *before* seeing a doctor.

Doctors treat acute or chronic sportaches the same way you do, with a few extra weapons in their arsenal. The doctor's options fall into five categories: mechanical, thermal, chemical, electrical, and surgical. Let's look at each.

Mechanical

In addition to the slings, splints, bandages, crutches, and canes you yourself can use to ease stress and alleviate inflammation, your doctor has an additional method of immobilization: a plaster cast. One of my podiatric colleagues automatically casts any runner with Achilles' tendinitis. "Otherwise, they don't rest," he says. "Despite my warning, they're out of my office and into their running shoes. Then, when they pop the tendon, they're in deep trouble."

If your doctor prescribes rest, ask, in detail, what you're allowed to do. Find out how long your limb should be immobilized. The trend today is toward shorter and shorter periods of absolute rest, so you may want to be wary of any doctor who simply prescribes indefinite rest. Nevertheless, a few days of inactivity are almost always advisable in the presence of acute or chronic pain.

If your doctor expects you to act intelligently, he or she must give you the intelligence. It is important for you to understand exactly what your doctor wants you to do or *not* do. If your doctor's instructions are not clear to you, ask whatever questions you must to be informed. As my doctor friend Joe might say, "It's your problem."

Thermal

Your doctor may want to use relatively sophisticated techniques for applying heat or cold. Plain ice remains by far the most effective means of generating and applying cold. But heat may be applied through diathermy (electrical deep heat) or with a hydrocollator (moist heat).

Chemical

Here's where your doctor has a number of options unavailable to you over the counter. The matter of drugs can be confusing. But don't be afraid to ask questions. When your doctor prescribes a certain drug, ask why that particular substance is best for you, what the risks are (if any), and whether you should anticipate any side effects.

It's impossible to explain all the available chemical options here, but a few basics may help you evaluate your doctor's choice. Remember, anti-inflammatory drugs act primarily to reduce inflammation. However, such chemicals often relieve pain as a secondary effect of decreasing inflammation.

Anti-inflammatories range in strength from mild to very potent. All drugs have the potential of unpleasant or dangerous side effects. Generally, however, the stronger the drug, the higher the risk. Therefore, relatively dangerous drugs should be used only when milder drugs have failed or are contraindicated. (Note: Never take two or more drugs simultaneously without a doctor's specific permission. If you're taking some eye medication, and something else for a digestive problem, and then you toss in your favorite cold remedy, plus an anti-inflammatory drug, don't be surprised if the lid blows off. It's best to let your personal physician know *everything* you propose to take — before you start.)

Some injectable drugs, like cortisone and the other so-called steroids, work exclusively at the site of your inflammation. In contrast, oral drugs go everywhere, via your blood stream. As a result, injectables can be administered in smaller dosages. Nevertheless, a growing number of doctors question the advisability of injecting athletes for either acute or chronic inflammation.

More and more, steroids are believed to weaken or damage tendons and other tissue into which they were routinely injected in past years. Therefore, you should not expect your doctor to suggest a cortisone shot without attempting to treat your inflammation more conservatively first. In fact, if he or she readies a syringe after a cursory history and exam, you probably should decline the injection, at least until you get a persuasive explanation and/or a second opinion. Ten years ago cortisone shots were common. Now it's rare that steroids are used as a first line of attack against inflammation.

No drug, oral or injected, cures sportaches. With luck, the chemical your doctor prescribes for you will help eliminate your symptoms — but only your symptoms. Chemical treatment must be accompanied by gradual rehabilitation of your affected limb, as well as by appropriate changes in your EEVeTeC. Otherwise, before long, you'll need more pills or another shot. The cycle will continue until you finally have to quit your favorite sport permanently.

Electrical

Electrotherapy has been around for quite a while. However, not all of its indications and contraindications are well documented. Your doctor may propose one of three electrical treatment methods. If, after careful consideration, you decide that whatever rationale has been given makes sense for you, there should be little harm in trying electrotherapy. It can help. On the other hand, it may do nothing for you at all. And it's generally quite expensive.

1. In ultrasound, high-speed sound waves sometimes help fight inflammation. I've used ultrasound successfully. But it's expensive, requires a trained operator, and works better on some parts of the body than others.
2. Electrical nerve stimulation can be used to make muscles contract. It's sometimes difficult or impossible for a muscle or group to be exercised voluntarily. An electrode, placed at an appropriate site, causes the use of certain muscles, thus relieving swelling and pain.
3. Transcutaneous electrical nerve stimulation can also relieve pain by forcing regular muscle contractions. The net result is inhibition of certain sensations, most notably pain.

Surgical

There's a common misconception that surgery can cure sportaches. It's true that an operation can relieve acute or chronic inflammation. If you have a particular inflammatory response called compartment syndrome, for example, surgery can be quite effective in eliminating your symptoms. However, surgery won't cure a sportache any more than rest, ice, cortisone, or ultrasound. Only EEVeTeC can eliminate sportaches. More important, surgery is a serious proposition. All surgery involves risk.

Since life and limb aren't at stake, any surgery performed to alleviate inflammation must be considered elective. As always, before submitting to elective surgery, you should understand exactly what other options you have. Be certain that you and your doctor have considered or tried virtually every other potential remedy for your acute or chronic inflammation.

Surgery can be quite final in its unique way. Therefore, be sure to resolve any doubts before agreeing to an operation. You should certainly ask your surgeon the following questions: How common is this procedure for this problem? What kind of results can I expect? Will I be able to return to my sport? What limitations can I expect? What do we do during the postoperative period? Don't hesitate to get a second opinion about surgery, even a third. It's that important.

On the positive side, surgery can completely relieve the symptoms of an acute or chronic ache. It works best if you follow your doctor's orders closely during rehabilitation. At some point, however, you'll be back on your own, probably well before you are able to plunge back into your sport. Just because your joint has been repaired surgically, you're by no means immune to sportaches. In fact, now that you no longer have a "normal" body, you may be more susceptible than ever to the pains of fitness. Of course, you'll probably be fine after surgery as long as you never want to play sports again. But that option is presumably unacceptable. Use EEVeTeC for steady, careful progress toward pain-free sports participation.

•

In addition to diagnosis and prescription, your doctor owes you one more thing: prompt, courteous, and reasonable service. Unfortunately, it doesn't always work that way. Many doctors don't have the time or the inclination to manage the pains of fitness. Management requires discussion and cooperation. Doctors don't want to explain or teach: they want to heal. In addition, the management of simple sportaches requires a working knowledge of sports and biomechanics, neither of which is included in medical school curricula.

Remember Steve Devereux's sore right elbow? During his sixth months of chronic pain Steve took his aching limb to an orthopedist in New York, supposedly one of the top tennis elbow specialists in the world. Steve's experience was maddening. I remember my own frustration as he recounted it to me.

"First I had to wait for three months as the doctor's office repeatedly rescheduled appointments," recounted Steve. "I persisted. I guess I should have hesitated when I was required to pay the $150 consultation fee before my appointment. But I was really hoping for worthwhile advice or help.

"I saw the doctor for all of eighteen minutes. He asked me a few questions, examined my arm, looked at my X-rays, and then quickly described a series of arm and upper-body exercises that he said he thought I should do.

"I asked if he had an explanation of his exercises on paper. He talked so fast, there was no way I could remember everything he'd said. He shook his head and looked at me rather strangely.

"I asked about tennis. He said, 'Sure, just start playing and see how it goes.'

"Before I could pose another question, he and his aide — another doctor who had sat in silently throughout my brief consultation — were on their way. 'Let us know how you do,' he said. Then he was gone.

"I dressed slowly. When I opened the door, the nurse was waiting with another patient. I left dazed."

I wish Steve's experience were exceptional. It was not. I've heard from dozens of recreational athletes who've had similar encounters — often with doctors whom I know and respect.

If only doctors were honest enough to confess that they sometimes have no answers and that they can't perform miracles. There'd be less frustration and disappointment all around. The medical community might actually receive credit for convincing the public that sportaches can be avoided or managed only by the individual — with EEVeTeC, and not with pills, shots, or surgery. However, for the time being, it's up to you to determine when you've got a problem that requires medical attention. Obviously, if you don't have to see a doctor for an acute or chronic sportache, you shouldn't. The medical profession doesn't need or want your business, and you don't need the hassle and expense.

One final note. Remember, anti-inflammatory treatments, whether self-administered or prescribed by a doctor, are designed primarily to reduce or eliminate inflammation. Don't confuse symptomatic relief with the management of your underlying problem. If your ache becomes an -itis, you or your doctor will have to treat the symptoms of your inflammation. But symptomatic relief alone is just the beginning.

When a painfully inflamed joint is driving you crazy, relief from your inflammation will seem like a lifesaver — temporarily. But don't forget that every episode has a cause. If you merely rest your aching joint and relieve the symptoms of your inflammation, you'll feel better. However, as soon as you resume playing your favorite sport, twinges of pain will be back. Eventually, your ache will return — with a vengeance.

Lots of eyebrows were raised recently when my colleagues and friends read in a local newspaper that Bill Lee, who was then a pitcher for the Boston Red Sox, had said that Dr. Rob Roy McGregor had cured his pitching troubles. Since I'm a podiatrist, everyone naturally assumes that I restrict my medical practice to feet. Bill Lee had been suffering from an aching shoulder — or so the public thought. However, Bill was accurately quoted. Together we had eliminated a nagging ache that had threatened his career as a pitcher and had kept coming back whenever Bill started pitching again, despite previous treatment by other doctors.

When I saw him as a patient, Bill actually had two problems. His forward foot bothered him when he pitched. That was his first problem. As a result, however, Bill had also developed chronic shoulder pain.

Bill had discovered that he could eliminate his shoulder pain by resting. However, as soon as he started pitching again, his shoulder always started to hurt. My diagnosis? Because of the recurrent pain in his foot, Bill had altered his pitching style. This change had eventually triggered the pain in his shoulder. Whenever Bill rested, his foot pain would go away. He would then use his regular delivery until his foot pain started to come back. At that point, he would alter his delivery again, trading foot pain for an aching shoulder.

Bill and I solved his problem — and eliminated both his foot pain and his shoulder pain — by making an appropriate adjustment in his equipment. We designed an orthotic that redistributed his weight so that Bill could have confidence in his pitching motion. He was able to return to his former pain-free form. We had found a way to correct his problem, which as it happens was in his feet, rather than merely treating his shoulder pain, as several other doctors had tried to do. Bill's answer, of course, was EEVeTeC.

Remember, if you play sports, you're likely to develop occasional aches. Simple sportaches will become acute or chronic if you let them. If you fail to make appropriate adjustments in your sports equipment, environment, velocity, technique, or conditioning, knee pain can become runner's knee, elbow pain may develop into tennis elbow, hip pain can become golfer's hip, and so on.

Once you have acute or chronic symptoms, you'll be forced to suspend or cut back participation in your favorite sport while you deal with your inflammation. If self-help is not successful, or if your pain and other symptoms make self-help inadvisable, you'll need a doctor. However, your simple sportaches do *not* have to become acute or chronic. In most instances, you can avoid letting the pains of fitness become medical problems. That's what the McGregor Solution is all about.

Afterword: It Hurts but You Don't Want to Quit

AMERICA'S MARATHON LAST SEPTEMBER was as difficult a race as I have ever run. At the classic point — around twenty miles — I "hit the wall," running out of energy and will power almost simultaneously. It was an experience I hope I never have to repeat. When I finally crossed the finish line in Chicago, I was mentally and physically exhausted. But I did finish — thanks to EEVeTeC. When I didn't think I could go a step farther, I adjusted my laces to make my right foot more secure, stretched for a couple of minutes, shortened my stride length, found a stretch of grass by the side of the course in Lincoln Park that was easier on my feet than the pavement, and somehow made it across the line. I didn't want to quit, and EEVeTeC allowed me to keep going.

We've said it before, but I'll say it one last time. No matter who you are — whether you're an athlete who is anxious to prevent an occasional twinge from developing into nonstop pain or someone who is rehabilitating a limb and fearful of a relapse — EEVeTeC works.

EEVeTeC is also an important tool if you're someone who takes care of people with sportaches. The day after America's Marathon last September, I went to Louisville, Kentucky, where I participated in week-long series of clinics given before a big race that took place on the following Saturday. Tuesday night I stood in the amphitheater of Iroquois Park, giving my talk to the assembled runners. It was virtually the same "Sportaches" presentation I had given three days earlier in Chicago.

The next day I visited a new sportsmedicine facility at St. Michael's Hospital in Louisville. There I met Russ Ostrum, a physical therapist, who was in charge of the new facility. Russ told me, "I can't thank you enough, Dr. McGregor, for your talk last night. I've already used it." I asked Russ what he meant. "Well, I got a call from a basketball player this morning, and he started telling me about his problem. He wanted to know if he could come in to see me. I told him that he'd better begin by working through EEVeTeC. I suggested some adjustments in his equipment and his conditioning. Frankly, it sounded like his problem might have a lot to do with his basketball shoes. We left it that he would get a new pair, try a few other adjustments in his EEVeTeC, and then come in to see me if nothing else seems to work."

We hope your doctor will soon be responding as Russ Ostrum did to the basketball player. Or maybe you won't even telephone for medical help or advice until you've already adjusted your *E*quipment, *E*nvironment, *V*elocity, *T*echnique, and *C*onditioning. EEVeTeC is the answer, as I hope we've persuaded you. When it hurts but you don't want to quit, EEVeTeC is the only choice. You're on your own, but you're not alone.

ROB ROY MCGREGOR

April 1982
Concord, Massachusetts

ABOUT THE AUTHORS

DR. ROB ROY McGREGOR was the chief staff podiatrist at Sports Medicine Resource, Inc., Brookline, Massachusetts, from 1977 to 1982. He now maintains a general podiatric practice at Longwood Podiatry Group, Inc., in Brookline and serves as chief of podiatry and assistant professor of orthopedics at the University of Massachusetts Medical Center.

An avid runner and marathoner himself, Dr. McGregor opened the first runners' clinic in America at the New England Deaconess Hospital in 1976 and has helped to design the popular Etonic line of running, golf, and tennis shoes. He continues to serve as a shoe consultant to Etonic, Inc., and is also medical adviser to The Footwear Council, sportsmedicine consultant to the Bonne Bell Company, and a long-standing member of the Massachusetts Governor's Committee on Physical Fitness and Sports. He belongs to a number of medical and nonmedical sports-related groups and has lectured across the United States, Europe, and Japan.

During the late 1970s, Dr. McGregor made regular appearances as a health and fitness "tipster" on *Evening Magazine,* WBZ-TV, Boston. More recently, he has appeared regularly on *Five on Sports Magazine,* WCVB-TV, Boston, where he has been "speaking of sportaches."

He attended American University and is a graduate of the Temple University College of Podiatric Medicine (D.P.M.) and the Pennsylvania College of Podiatric Medicine (a postgraduate D.P.M.). Dr. McGregor resides in Concord, Massachusetts, with his wife and family.

•

STEPHEN E. DEVEREUX is presently serving as the executive director of Rob Roy McGregor Associates, Inc., Brookline, Massachusetts. A member of the Massachusetts Bar since 1977, Steve also acts as chief coach of the International Tennis Federation, London, England. During the past five years, he has spent approximately twelve weeks each year traveling on behalf of the I.T.F., mostly to Third World countries in Africa and Asia.

A graduate of Phillips Academy in Andover, Harvard College, and the Northeastern University School of Law, Steve played competitive tennis nationally and internationally from 1958 to 1970 and has been a teaching professional since 1966.